PIONEERS OF THE UNSEEN

FRONTIERS OF THE UNKNOWN

A Library of Psychic Knowledge

Edited by Dr. Paul Tabori

BEYOND THE SENSES: A REPORT ON PSYCHICAL RESEARCH
IN THE SIXTIES
by Paul Tabori and Phyllis Raphael

A GAZETTEER OF BRITISH GHOSTS
by Peter Underwood

CROOKES AND THE SPIRIT WORLD
by Sir William Crookes

PIONEERS OF THE UNSEEN
by Paul Tabori

ANATOMY OF WITCHCRAFT
by Peter Haining

CESARE LOMBROSO,

FRONTIERS OF THE UNKNOWN

PIONEERS
OF
THE UNSEEN

PAUL TABORI

SOUVENIR PRESS

© Copyright 1972 by
All rights reserved

First British edition pu
by Souvenir Press Ltd., 95 Mortimer Street
London, W.1., and simultaneously in Canada by
J. M. Dent & Sons (Canada) Ltd., Ontario, Canada

ISBN 0 285 62042 8

Printed in Great Britain by
Northumberland Press Ltd.,
Gateshead

PRE

CONTENTS

ILLUSTRATIONS

INTRODUCTION

Ideal and Reality

(1)

There are several encyclopaedias of occultism and psychical research, histories and who's whos have been published in a dozen languages; yet I do not think that anybody has made a close study of the men and women who have devoted their lives (or at least a substantial part of their time) to what Harry Price called "the search for truth". No statistics have been compiled indicating whether they have been more numerous, for instance, in Poland than in Spain, no break-down has been made of the average age, education, religious affiliation or main occupation. It would be, indeed, an immense labour and the results might very well be disappointing for anyone wishing to draw general, valid conclusions. For even a small sample would show such tremendous differences, such contrary trends in the composition of this large and motley company that it would be impossible to arrive at any clearcut and informative results.

Psychical researchers have included physicists and physiologists, psychiatrists and neurologists, journalists and lawyers, businessmen and civil servants, police officials and criminologists, educators and artists, actors and engineers—one could go through a whole classified telephone directory, picking out half the professions and occupations listed there and find a representative of each of them in the membership of the various societies, associations, ad-hoc groups, scientific bodies devoted to this vast field. And as their origins and qualifications differ, so does their attitude, their basic approach— ranging from total scepticism to almost child-like credulity, from the unswerving determination to prove everything either a fake or an illusion to the often pathetic desire to excuse even the clumsiest deception, the most obvious trickery. If there is any field where Heisenberg's famous law about the act of observation and the person of the observer affecting the object of observation applies fully, it is psychical research. There have been innumerable cases where three experts attended the same séance, observed the same phenomena and came to three completely different evaluations.

Certainly, there are few areas in which arguments are so violent and continuous. Charges and counter-charges can fly thicker than hail; feuds whose origins are as obscure as the ancient Sicilian vendettas, centring on what someone said or did in 1911 or between two trains in Bradford; accusations of lechery, theft, forgery, even murder—all these seem to be part and parcel of psychical research. Much of this remains hidden, festering, never reaches the pages of a newspaper or the courts—which, in a way, makes it even more alarming and long-enduring. I have yet to meet a truly dedicated worker in this particular vineyard who has anything really good to say about his colleagues, living or dead; at the most you find them being damned with faint praise. One of them whom I am proud to call my friend and who has spent over half a century in this discipline, reminds me of a shy forest creature darting forth and then rushing back into shelter— eulogizing a particular series of experiments or their protagonist, only to qualify the admiration with some devastating and utterly uncomplimentary afterthought.

I treasure a letter which one outstanding expert wrote to another. Both of them are dead but I still feel reluctant to identify them—nor is it really necessary for they represent archetypes. It says, in part:

> ... We are bound to meet next week at the lecture of X. I'll thank you not to address me as I shall refuse to recognize your presence or, indeed, your existence. By questioning my competence and my honesty, you have put yourself outside the pale. I have always suspected your sanity but now I have at last resolved the dilemma in my mind as to whether you are a knave or a lunatic. I am quite certain that you are both.

There have been, true enough, paragons of virtue, models of integrity whose achievements are admired and emulated. Until one day some little detail, some new fact is unearthed about them which immediately is supposed to deflate their reputations, negate their fame. I do not think that there is a single major researcher who has escaped this fate. Iconoclastic fury seems to be a fundamental feature in the occult; as someone put it, psychical researchers are ready to sue each other at the drop of a bit of ectoplasm.

(2)

Let us put aside for the moment these all-too-human foibles (after all, they are not entirely restricted to psychical research) to try and define the qualities of the ideal psychical researcher—the requirements for doing his job properly, regardless of the reactions of his fellow-workers or whether such a paragon ever existed.

If we apply the Heisenberg principle to our subject, it is obvious that the general character and personality who observes the phenomena—actual or alleged—is even more of a decisive factor than in most other fields. In addition, the ability of the observer to prepare clear and unbiased reports is an essential requirement. This does not only mean that he must be accurate but that he should commit himself as far as possible to a definite stand, whether positive or negative. The expert and adept will not only look at the account itself but balance carefully the personality of its author. Even if all reputable researchers are assumed to be trustworthy, to paraphrase Orwell, some are more trustworthy than others.

Though Price and many others have fought for it, there are very few universities that have admitted parapsychology into their curriculum and thus it is extremely difficult to obtain specialized training—yet this would seem essential if psychical researchers are not to be recruited haphazardly or enter this area by individual and random decision. Hereward Carrington who spent a lifetime in the service of "psychic science", summed it up concisely: *

* *The Story of Psychic Science*, Rider & Co., London.

...our ideal investigator must have a thorough knowledge of the literature of the subject; he must have a good grounding in normal and abnormal psychology; in physics, chemistry, biology, photography, and some laboratory experience; he must be a keen observer, a good judge of human nature and its motives; he must be well trained in magic and sleight-of-hand; he must be shrewd, quick of thought and action, ever on the alert, patient, resourceful, open-minded, tolerant, rapid in his observations and deductions, sympathetic, and have a sense of humour! He must be free from superstition, and at the same time unswayed by bigotry—theological or scientific. In short, an ideal psychic investigator is hard to find, and it is probable that such a man is born rather than made.

Carrington—whose life we will examine in detail in our first chapter—set the standards pretty high—but then, he was speaking of an ideal. His description reminded me of the natural scientists who created the idea of chlorophyllogen, a hypothetical substance that does not exist in Nature—but whose existence had to be predicated in order to explain the vital process of photosynthesis, the essential process of organic survival. Such an ideal would be difficult if not impossible of attainment; still, it was necessary to establish it so that reality could be measured against it. The flood of material that is published every year and has accumulated into a veritable ocean cannot be assessed without knowing something about the standing and standards of the investigator in each case; whether he is more or less cautious than necessary, willing to commit himself or refusing to stick his neck out; whether his background and his previous work invest him with the necessary authority or whether he is lacking in the necessary credentials. The relative value of all reports must vary accordingly.

There was a time, of course, when anybody could set himself up as a psychical researcher, claiming that his interest or dedication was sufficient to be heard or read. There have been just as many charlatans and mountebanks, lightweights and downright crooks among the self-styled discoverers and explorers of psychic phenomena as among the fake mediums and dishonest purveyors of "messages from the Great Beyond". But, on the other side of the medal, we must demand certain clear-cut qualifications from the critic and sceptic alike. It would be a strange trial, indeed, in which either the prosecutor or the counsel for the defence would be total laymen, ignorant of law and innocent of usage and precedent.

When Professor Henry Sidgwick, the eminent philosopher and first president of the British Society for Psychical Research, made his opening presidential address in 1882, he said:

"We must drive the objector into the position of being forced either to admit the phenomena as inexplicable, at least by him, or to accuse the investigators either of lying or cheating or of a blindness or forgetfulness incompatible with any intellectual condition except absolute idiocy ... We have done all that we can when the critic has nothing left to allege except that the investigator is in the trick. But when he has nothing else left to allege he will allege that ..."

It is exactly here that the psychical researcher's own standing and character become of paramount importance. True, eminence in one particular field does not necessarily make you of equal ability in a different one; a celebrated psychologist might still be like wax in the hands of a clever conjurer or an accomplished ventriloquist and a great engineer may be helpless when faced with a purely psychological or mental exploitation of otherwise normal, rational forces. And once again it must be emphasized that while the most experienced researcher may be tricked at certain occasions, it is most unlikely or practically impossible that he should be throughout a longer series of séances or a prolonged sequence of experiments.

Thus, a sense of proportion, a balanced judgment appear to be the first truly essential requirements. Even so, the dedicated researcher might find himself in the position which George Orwell described in a letter I received from him a few weeks before his death. "If they slap me from the right and kick me from the left, I know I am standing exactly in the proper place." The extreme sceptic or even the consistently

critical will be assailed by those to whom the truth of
spiritualism is an article of faith, as little subject to query as
papal infallibility to the devout Roman Catholic or the un-
changeable integrity of the atom to the pre-nuclear age. If he
is inclined to spiritualism (and, of course, there have been
many eminent psychical investigators who *were* spiritualists)
he will be similarly attacked by those to whom survival after
death is a myth and who ascribe all psychic phenomena either
to trickery or hallucination. Many outstanding scientists and
thinkers have kept back from this field because they were
afraid that their reputation would become tarnished, their
past achievements in entirely different areas would be forgotten because they did not stick to the ultra-scientific, scrupulously sceptical attitude which the anti-spiritualist organizations have adopted and preserved. Carrington recalls that even
William James, "one of the sanest and most balanced minds
who ever lived", suffered from criticism of this character,
being called too credulous and positive. Others, at the far
end of the scale, were denounced for being too critical and
negative.*

Thus, after the first requirement of striking a balance between the two extremes, intellectual honesty is the second,
immediate requirement—and one even harder to fulfil. Only
the strongest minds can resist being swayed or influenced by
the pressures of majority opinions—when, standing up for
what they consider the truth, even in the tiniest details, would
run counter to them. If it is not the fear of ridicule or abuse,
it may be the understandable weakness for approval, the
search for popularity that clouds one's judgment. Quite a few
men have suffered ostracism in their academic or social *milieu*
because they defied these conventions. Others have held views
which they did not express because they were afraid of sharing
the same fate.

The social and professional dangers of being involved in
psychical research could be best illustrated by the tragi-comic
case of the Talking Mongoose; a story spread over four years.
It involved the Isle of Man, the B.B.C., the British Film Insti-

* In *The Psychic World*, Methuen & Co., London, 1938.

tute, the London Law Courts, Harry Price's National Laboratory of Psychical Research and several other places, bodies and organizations. The cast of this real-life "spectacular" included a piano salesman turned farmer; his daughter, who for the first seventeen years of her life had never left their lonely mountain farm; his wife, a charming woman of strong character; a former editor of *The Listener*; an ex-chairman of the London County Council; eminent K.C.s, taxidermists, doctors, B.B.C. officials, film people and hosts of others. Price and R. S. Lambert (then editor of *The Listener*) published a well-documented book called *The Haunting of Cashen's Gap* —but the story went far beyond the book nor could it all be told at the time.

In February 1932 Harry Price received a letter from a Miss Florence Milburn of Peel, Isle of Man. Miss Milburn informed him that an animal "somewhat like a weasel" had attached itself to the family of a farmer named James T. Irving who lived at Doarlish Cashen, or Cashen's Gap, at the top of a mountain in the middle of the island, one of the loneliest spots in Britain. This strange animal, Miss Milburn added matter-of-factly, could talk in several languages, read thoughts, catch whispers from fifteen or twenty yards away, sing hymns and do a number of other, equally amazing things.

Three years later Harry Price visited the Isle of Man with R. S. Lambert, after having had a report from Captain M. H. Macdonald, a friend and associate, who had spent a night and two days with the Irvings. Macdonald, a businessman and well-known racing motorist, "heard" Gef, the Talking Mongoose several times—talking in a shrill, rather feminine voice —though he never heard him when all three members of the family were together in his presence. However, during Price's and Lambert's visit, the elusive mongoose did not turn up and all they could do was to investigate the scene, question Vorrey Irving, a girl of fourteen who was supposed to be the mysterious animal's particular friend and make copious notes. It was a most disappointing, inconclusive visit and the book which the two investigators wrote left many questions open.

However, the Talking Mongoose caused a different sensation. Mr. Lambert was a Governor of the British Film Institute where one of his colleagues was Lady Levita, wife of Sir Cecil Levita, chairman of the L.C.C. in 1928-29. (Harry Price was also connected with the Institute, having helped to start the National Film Library to which he contributed about 100,000 feet of old and historical films which he had accumulated over many years.)

Soon after his return from the Isle of Man, Mr. Lambert was invited to tea by the Levitas with whom he was on friendly terms. His host and hostess were anxious to discuss certain affairs of the British Film Institute; he was equally anxious to keep off the subject. In his rather difficult position he hit upon the idea of telling them about his recent adventure at Cashen's Gap. This account of a "physic adventure" apparently created a wrong impression in the mind of Sir Cecil. Some weeks after the tea party he invited Major Gladstone Murray, Lambert's superior at the B.B.C., to lunch with him at the Carlton Club and made a good many remarks about Mr. Lambert's work at the British Film Institute, the occult in general, Harry Price, the National Film Institute and the Talking Mongoose. Some of these remarks were of such a serious critical character that Mr. Gladstone Murray put them into a memorandum on the same afternoon.

The upshot of the tea party and the Carlton Club lunch was a libel action brought by Mr. Lambert against Sir Cecil Levita. His position at the B.B.C. and his livelihood were jeopardized; he *had* to take action. All this, of course, originated directly in his interest in psychical research, his association with Price. The case began on November 4, 1936, and lasted for several days. Mr. Justice Swift went into the whole story of Gef and thus the Talking Mongoose found itself the central, if invisible, figure of a libel case. The judge's summing up was in favour of the plaintiff, and after an hour's absence the jury returned with a verdict for him. "They found that Sir Cecil Levita spoke the words alleged, that they were not true, that he had no right or duty to speak them, that they were spoken maliciously, and that the damages were to be £7,500 . . ." a very considerable sum for those days.

The case caused a considerable sensation and led directly

to the institution of a Parliamentary Board of Inquiry into the relations between the B.B.C. and its staff. The trial had shown these to be most unsatisfactory—there had been considerable and almost dictatorial pressure on Lambert not to sue for fear of unfavourable publicity for the Corporation. The Board's report recommended a number of reforms, including a Staff Association, the equivalent of a trade union, which have been carried out in the last decades. Thus Gef has even managed to change things at Portland Place!

Mr. Lambert continued as editor of *The Listener* until, in 1939, he resigned and settled down in Canada, where he continued a distinguished career in radio, film and literature.

But there have been a good many others, less fortunate, who suffered considerable harm and loss because they engaged in research, committed themselves to investigation in fields which were (and in many places still are) considered disreputable and beneath the dignity of an academic or a public servant.

(3)

And yet the truly dedicated psychical researcher must ignore all these considerations. Unless he remains unswayed by the views and criticisms of others, unless he has the courage of his own convictions (however unpopular these may be) he will betray his vocation. He must be above financial interest. And truth must be his paramount concern—whether it means the exposure of a dishonest, fraudulent medium or the open admission that he *has* witnessed some occurrence which has no "normal" explanation and which, by the existing scientific standards, is beyond human reason. That such an occurrence can be of the smallest or the most trivial kind, must make no difference. If a matchbox is moved half an inch by some agency that cannot be identified as physical, if the most commonplace sound or sight have apparently a supernormal source, he must not hesitate to say so.

To err on the side of credulity can be just as wrong as to be hyper-critical. I have met a good many eminent people in this field who went out of their way to employ only negative arguments, to decry and deny all positive accounts. They made an absolute virtue out of their scepticism and extracted every ounce of *kudos* from attempting to make others look either "knaves or lunatics" like the writer of the letter I have quoted. There seems to be a natural tendency in nearly all psychical researchers to do so under certain conditions. It may well be that during a series of sittings ninety-five per cent of the phenomena are proved to be fraudulent—but five per cent still remain inexplicable. The temptation to ignore the five per cent, maintaining that if the ninety-five per cent is demonstrated fraud, the rest cannot possibly matter, is very strong. I have once compared the occult to a curtain stretching for hundreds of thousands of miles through which research and intuition have managed to put a few pinholes. We don't know what we see through these random holes. It may be the tip of the feather on a lady's hat; it may be an infinitesimal particle of the key to the universe—we cannot tell. But to deny that the pinholes exist and that there is *something* on the other side, would be to renounce the wisdom of the ages and to give up the eternal search for knowledge. And thus only the dishonest and the timid investigator will ignore, at his peril, that fascinating and exasperating five per cent which cannot be explained away or ascribed to fraud.

There is, of course, the other extreme. Anybody writing about the paranormal or supernatural without being a practising spiritualist is bound to run afoul the very vocal propagandists for what, in effect, is a religion and not a scientific or philosophical discipline. Now, most spiritualists have their favourite medium by whom they swear—and who, by extension, must be above all suspicion, spotless and perfect. If anyone questions this, he is immediately accused of groundless scepticism, of crass materialism. Once I wrote what I considered a balanced and fair assessment of an American medium about whom many millions of words were published —proving quite conclusively that for most of her career she had shamelessly fabricated her phenomena. She was dead and the evidence was so overwhelming that one would have thought it needed no particular elaboration. Yet there were some spiritualist papers who took up the cudgels on behalf of the remarkable lady—quite ignoring the facts. Obviously spiritualists are so bent on proving the continuity of life, the reality of survival after death, that they refuse any consideration or respect to anybody holding the opposite view; and, even worse, shut their ears to any definite, negative evidence that is opposed to their preconceived beliefs.

Not so long ago I visited a voice medium in a London suburb who was highly recommended by a number of people including one who had written her biography. She was a pleasant, no-nonsense woman, obviously certain of her own powers though she was careful not to promise anything. Yet she tried hard enough—and, as far as I was concerned, failed totally. She did not get a single thing right about my past, my family, its deceased or living members; and she got rather cross with me because I would not provide her with any indication whether she was doing well or badly. Yet she was far more successful when she turned to my wife—she produced at least two facts she could not possibly know . . . and when she received confirmation of them, proceeded very quickly and very skilfully to erect a whole edifice on these slender foundations. She had "messages" for both of us—and these were of the usual, monumental banality as if those who have passed over had suddenly lost all originality and wit. Yet I would not have dreamt of condemning her "mediumship" as useless or fraudulent—nor issue a certificate of authenticity. It may have been an "off-day" for her; but in any case, I felt —and this is the simple rule for the psychical researcher— that it was not my task to prove or disprove anything; that all one could do was to report fully and honestly about one's experiences. If the facts observed seem to indicate a positive conclusion, this should be presented frankly and fully. If not, it should be stated with equal lack of bias. As Dr. Richard Hodgson wrote in the *Proceedings* of the Society for Psychical Research:

There is no royal road to sound opinions on such matters generally; there is nothing for it save to examine each narrative on its own merits, and with close individual care; the mind meanwhile prepared for either fate—whether to prick some bubble of pretension into empty falsity, or to discover beneath some unpromising envelope a germ of inexplicable truth.

"The bubble of pretension" is often highly polished and attractive and it takes some doing to prick it. Nor is psychical research a scientific discipline in which final, rounded-off results are frequently possible. How often does it happen that a particular mediumship seems to be well established—and then, disconcertingly, fraud is discovered; or, alternately, that a dubious mediumship reaches a phase when it is subjected to the most severe controls and yet produces at least promising and even unassailable results! Carrington set up two general propositions as guide-lines. They were simple enough:

(1) All is possible.

(2) The strength of the evidence should be proportioned to the strangeness of the facts.

The first of these principles predicates an open mind—which all great psychical researchers have possessed to a greater or lesser extent. (No man is utterly without prejudices.) The second refers to the quantitative and qualitative features of whatever evidence is available. When Harry Price reported his experiences with the alleged spirit-child, Rosalie, Professor Joad told him that he would go very far with him, his old friend, but here they had to part company—though he did not doubt Price's word, he could not bring himself to share his belief. Certainly, the more extraordinary and apparently impossible the alleged phenomena, the stronger the evidence must be if it is to be accepted. This is a truism yet it must be stressed. If a certain reported fact differs only a little from the generally accepted facts of science, the mind finds it easier to assimilate it—and it appears *a priori* more credible. If, on the other hand, it totally violates—or seems to—some of the very fundamentals of modern science, the evidence must be proportionately stronger so that our inborn mental resistance should be overcome. Here the ideal psychical researcher will remember, however, that from the point of view of scientific achievement if a single tiny "supra-normal" fact would be established, this alone would provide a basis for a more open-minded approach.

As an example of the occult hard or impossible to swallow, Carrington cites lycanthropy, the age-old belief in the ability of certain people to turn themselves into wolves, hyenas or other beasts of prey. There is an immense amount of support-ing material, covering a dozen countries, going back many centuries—yet, in spite of the popularity of fangs and claws, of maiden victims and cobwebby Transylvanian castles in the Hammer Films' productions, no one seriously believes in were-wolves and vampires today. Why? Because whatever evidence, as contrasted with belief and legend, is available, is not strong enough to create belief. Yet there are many psychic pheno-mena which various people find comparatively incredible. Physicists and biologists cannot swallow telekinesis and materialization; psychologists gag at clairvoyance and spirit communication. The first group's experience denies the alleged facts; the second set of facts is opposed to the philo-sophy and experience of the latter. All this creates a mental barrier which is impossible to overcome.

Yet the religious believer, the mystically-inclined, find little difficulty in accepting the spiritualist theory; to them it is quite reasonable and rational. To the psychical researcher with a medical or psychological origin it is a paramount con-sideration that much of our mental life is linked with the functions of the brain, with consciousness. Speech, sight, taste, movement, memory—all these are traceable to definite areas and any injury to the one concerned will impair or destroy the ability of receiving sensory impressions and of reacting to them. Memory has been identified with personality (at least to a considerable extent); and, of course, it has an intimate connection with the activities of the physical brain. So the psychologist cannot conceive the human personality surviving *without* the physical brain. Many of the outstanding psychical researchers—some of whom we will meet in these pages—rejected the spiritualist hypothesis, the theory of survival after death, while they were willing to accept the supernormal and parapsychological. Richet, Schrenck-Notzing, René Sudre are outstanding examples of this dilemma and this only too understandable attitude. Yet, as Carrington pointed out, this argument is purely *a priori* and should facts ever prove survival, they must be accepted and the physiological theories must be adjusted accordingly. But, in the meantime, it is impossible for the psychologist to accept the idea of survival easily; that is why he demands absolute demonstrations before conceding it to be a fact. Those psychical researchers who came to it from the psychological discipline have an inborn, natural mental resistance to the idea which could only be overcome by an overwhelming mass of facts without any other "reasonable" explanation.

While objective students of occultism will agree that there is a good deal of untainted, respectable *evidence* in favour of survival, this is not the same thing as *proof*. The difference is not only semantic but essential; and the average scientist will always demand proof before accepting it. Clear-cut cases are rare; one only has to refer again to the innumerable cases of mixed mediumship when obvious fraud is often inextricably interwoven with apparently genuine phenomena. And the ideal psychical researcher will always remember that there is a good deal of seemingly spiritualistic material which has purely material, normal (often hysterical or hallucinatory) origins. Thus great caution is needed not to swallow everything offered by the champions of spiritualism. This is not to question or attack the validity of their theory nor the good faith and fair-mindedness of many outstanding men who have embraced it. Spiritualism is a workable, justifiable hypothesis —where the difficulty begins is in its acceptance as more than a theory. And here the psychical researcher needs more than ever a sense of proportion and a balanced judgment.

(4)

Other psychical researchers have approached their tasks and the guidelines of their work from different, sometimes, more specialized points of view. In 1936 I talked to Professor Charles Beth who held the chair of religious philosophy at

Vienna University and was considered one of the outstanding representatives of scientific occultism.

"I decided that my main life task would be to examine religion and faith in every manifestation," he told me. "Thus I came to the idea that these manifestations and their forms must never be examined independently, separately; it is necessary to look upon them from a higher point of view, as parts of a single great idea. So we must never separate the history and the psychology of religion. Religious psychology has an extremely difficult but very lofty task—to investigate the extreme limits of psychical possibilities. My special interest has been telepathy and clairvoyance and one of the things I found necessary to evaluate in my long-term experiments was the study of the latest achievements of physics and other natural sciences. Certainly the ideas of time, space, even of causality have been badly shaken in the world-image of modern physics; and in the same way, I felt we had to re-examine the ideas of space and time in modern philosophy. And for me the essential thing in psychical research is to remember constantly that phenomena have always existed before their explanation and interpretation were found . . . I do not want to quote the tag from *Hamlet*—yet it is one which every true scientist must keep in mind all the time ..."

Thomas Mann also gave considerable thought and time to psychical research; in the early twenties he delivered several lectures about it though he looked upon the occult sciences as "more interesting than important". In a long interview he gave in 1923, he explained his attitude to psychical research:

"The world is full of spiritual and mental problems, of exciting questions which men have tried to answer with the most miraculous hypotheses, with confused and intangible theories. Spiritualism which might find its first hesitant ancestors in the *Odyssey* where the spirits of the Greek heroes pass in front of Ulysses—spiritualism which invokes with childish ease Aristotle or Napoleon to put senseless and illogical words into their mouths—this spiritualism cannot be the basis upon which occult phenomena can be understood or settled in a satisfactory manner. Human dignity and reason protest against this. But the problem remains a problem and urges us to find a solution if lost in the reaches of meta-physics. When metaphysics becomes empirical, experimental, we find ourselves faced with the occult phenomena. Natural science cannot refuse contact with metaphysics; after all, Einstein's theory also reaches beyond mathematical physics, into the regions of metaphysical conceptions. I feel the seriousness; I did not choose deliberately to seek it; but I think that occultism is a burning question which more or less demanded my attention. Of course, I am a writer and not a scientist; but I have every sympathy with those psychical researchers who refuse a rigid rejection of all the experienced phenomena of which reliable reports are given in good faith and with proper accuracy. After the last great war people no longer sneered at these researches nor belittled them; but this, un-fortunately, did not mean that they had found a peaceful and balanced view. It was more like fatalism, a quiet *laisser faire-laisser aller*. However, it could not mean a final attitude. Be-tween the extreme explanations one had to follow the golden mean. German science which had represented until now the stiffest orthodoxy was filled to a certain extent by a liberal spirit; the English and the French went even further. Richet and Flammarion in Paris examined thoroughly the pheno-mena which they viewed with severe criticism. And it was a French scientist who said: 'I do not maintain categorically that there was no trickery only that the possibility of trickery was excluded.' This is the right approach, the proper spirit. We must first and foremost realize the truth that true science had never lost touch with the occult phenomena—whatever other, fancy names it may have invented for them...."

On the other hand, Anatole France, speaking in the same year, claimed that the only legitimate task of psychical re-search was to prove that there *was* no life beyond the grave, that death ended it all. He quoted Cicero's *De Senectute* and added:

"Cicero's true and reassuring conception of death filled me with admiration. If there is no survival after death, then we are worrying unnecessarily. And if there is a God, it is certain that the bitterness of our earthly pilgrimage will be followed by endless bliss."

France was not at all willing to believe in the Other World; but he liked to talk about events connected with it. The author of *Penguin Island* did a certain amount of research himself:

"I neglected nothing to penetrate to the depths of this question," he explained. "I attended numerous spiritualist gatherings, formed acquaintances with famous mediums and watched them during their work. But I did not experience even once anything interesting, anything that would have deserved serious thought or anything that passed beyond the frontiers of the mind . . . Remember, how unimportant and commonplace the alleged utterances of the most famous 'spirits' are! If in the other world we lose our peculiarities, our individual qualities, is there any sense in talking about survival at all? After all, we consider the continuity of our egos the most important and the most beautiful forms of immortality awaiting us up above would have no meaning for us if we were deprived of our individuality and if our characteristics, our weaknesses, loves and hates, desires and joys would not survive with us. The problem of immortality is nothing but the continuation of our egos, the maintenance of our individuality—which are, in truth, infinitely insignificant. I think all psychical researchers should devote themselves to the unmasking of the crooks and tricksters proliferating in this field . . ."

"And if they find something that they consider genuine?" Anatole France was asked.

"Then they should be investigated themselves . . .", laughed the great writer.

France spoke scathingly of Henri Bergson, the famous philosopher who was more inclined to a non-materialistic conception. And Bergson himself summed up eloquently *his* ideal of a psychical researcher:

"There is the superstition of the ignorant and the unlettered," he said. "This might hurt them and their immediate setting and it is, I believe, curable though not easily. There is also the superstition of the learned and educated— what has been called the 'stupidity' of doubt. And this, to me, is far more dangerous and pernicious for it can bar the way to important discoveries, stultify questing minds, deny new approaches. The explorers of the unknown, the pioneers of the unseen must fight on two fronts if we are to open new vistas, find new means to answer the age-old questions. Doubt can be just as deadly as gullibility."

And Dr. R. J. Tillyard, the well-known New Zealand biologist, closely associated with Harry Price, added what must be the final word when he pleaded for the scientists to enter psychical research:

"Many years ago," Tillyard wrote in a long review of Conan Doyle's *History of Spiritualism*, "when the question of psychical research was brought to his notice, Huxley replied: 'Supposing these phenomena to be genuine, they do not interest me.' We are sorry to be obliged to have to record so unscientific a remark from so great a man, and even sorrier to have to admit that Huxley's attitude is still that of the great majority of biologists at the present day . . . It is a sad commentary on human nature that, even at the present day, when the reality of some at least of these phenomena has surely been put beyond the shadow of a doubt by the work of such men as Lodge and Richet, no scientific man can take up the study of psychical research without 'losing caste' and undergoing either secret or more or less open persecution from his fellows."

Tillyard was writing almost forty years ago. Today we can begin to evaluate whether the work of the pioneers has borne fruit, whether the prejudice and hostility have lessened or disappeared? There was a great upsurge of interest in the occult after the first world war—as there seems to be after each great conflict or holocaust, to follow each immense bloodletting of mankind. This did not seem to happen immediately after the second world war—but, as if by some delayed action bomb, the explosion came in the late fifties and early sixties. Today, especially in the United States, the esoteric and the supernatural have become fashionable—a very undignified adjective to use but the only fitting one. (Some writers have even called it "chic" or "part of the scene".) More and more psychical research organizations are springing up and though these are often of dubious value and motivation, at least they provide a meeting ground and a forum of discussion for those genuinely interested. The Society for Psychical Research in Britain is continuing on its sedate, circumspect and highly respectable way; the Ghost Club, well over a hundred years old, a neutral catalyst for sceptics and believers, shows no sign of flagging and its meetings are always well-attended, attracting celebrities and the ordinary membership alike. Progressive universities in America and elsewhere are beginning to show open-minded sympathy to the establishment of laboratories for E.S.P. and other paranormal phenomena. As for "ghost hunters", Harry Price would be both surprised and dismayed at their proliferation. Cambridge University has offered a scholarship in psychical studies; the current President of the American Society for Psychical Research is a most distinguished psychologist at the Menninger Clinic. In the spring of 1970, for the first time in its history, the University of California offered an extension course in parapsychology: *Old Myths and New Science, an Overview of Psychic Phenomena.* Dr. Margaret Mead, the brilliant American anthropologist whose *Growing Up in New Guinea* and *The American Character* are classics, has even persuaded the highly respectable and selective American Association for the Advancement of Science to recognize parapsychology as an accredited science and acceptable for affiliation.

A convenient and convincing test of the much wider acceptance by scientists, psychologists and (an important addition) by clergymen of the significance and validity of the occult sciences is to examine the contributors to the series of conferences organized by the Parapsychology Foundation of New York which the late Eileen T. Garrett, a most remarkable medium herself, inspired and guided for almost twenty years. The first of these took place in Utrecht, in July-August 1953. Its four working groups dealt, respectively, with quantitative studies, with the psychotherapeutic and psychoanalytical approach, with spontaneous phenomena and qualitative research and finally with the personality of the sensitive (the accepted term for "medium".) The participants came from Britain, the United States, France, Germany, Sweden, Argentina, Austria, Holland, Switzerland, Finland, Italy, Denmark and Holland; apart from the foreign visitors, there were also an additional number of prominent Dutch scholars, university professors, psychiatrists, analysts and officials of the Netherlands Ministries of Education and of Public Health. The speakers included Professor Hans Bender of Germany, Dr. E. J. Dingwall of Great Britain, Dr. Jule Eisenbud of the United States, M. Gabriel Marcel of France, William H. Salter of Great Britain, Dr. Gertrude Schmeidler of the U.S.A., René Sudre of France, Professor Emilio Servadio of Italy—to mention only some of the most outstanding. This was followed by four other similar conferences in 1954, 1955 and 1956: an International Philosophic Symposium was held at Saint-Paul de Vence, followed by a meeting of an International Study Group on Unorthodox Healing at the same place, covering the period of April 20-May 1, 1954. The following year there was a conference on Spontaneous Phenomena at Cambridge, England; and in April-May 1956 there was a symposium on Psychology and Parapsychology at the Abbey of Royaumont, France. At the first of these Austria, Canada, France, Germany, Great Britain, Holland, Switzerland and the United States were represented; some twenty philosophers, psychologists, physicists and experienced investigators of paranormal phenomena were invited, apart from a few specially qualified observers and special guests. The main lectures and reports were delivered by such eminent specialists as Professor Pascual Jordan and Professor Denis Saurat, by Gabriel Marcel and Professor H. H. Price, by Aldous Huxley and Robert Amadou. Professor Aloys Wenzl of Germany, Dr. Jule Eisenbud and Professor C. J. Ducasse were among the other speakers. It is hardly necessary to add the long list of equally distinguished people who contributed to the remaining three meetings which were equally international in character.

A conference on Parapsychology and Psychedelics took place in New York late in 1958; in 1959 a more comprehensive conference was held in France in order to bring together scholars, who (in Eileen Garrett's words) "on research and writing might seek to strengthen the bridge that links modern parapsychological studies with the latest efforts to probe man's mind as it is influenced by the chemistry of the body". Of the impressive list of both conferences Dr. J. R. Smythies, of the Worcester Foundation for Experimental Biology, Shrewsbury, Massachusetts, Dr. Leon Katz, of the Department of Physics, University of Saskatchewan, Dr. Alain Assaily, a French specialist in neuro-endocrinology, Francis Huxley, Dr. Ernest Rothlin, professor of the University of Basle might be chosen as typical representatives of a wide variety of approaches.

In 1966 I attended such a conference myself at Le Piol, the beautiful inn on the outskirts of Saint-Paul de Vence which Mrs. Garrett made her headquarters for many years. The topic was *Survival after Death*. The participants included physicists, philosophers, psychical researchers, several clergymen, writers and biologists. There were provocative, well-reasoned papers, a great deal of discussion—formal and informal—and certainly I left with the impression that the whole vast field has become far more accessible to open and frank argument, that whatever extreme views were aired, they received sympathetic hearing and that the pioneers who had fought so hard and suffered so much to make psychical research "respectable" did not toil and struggle in vain.

(5)

To illustrate this struggle, its heartbreaks and triumphs, its setbacks and achievements, I have chosen six of these pioneers of six different countries. The choice was not an easy one for in this long and motley parade there are hundreds of possible candidates, some more attractive or interesting than the others—but all of them clamouring for attention. Many of them have been the subjects of biographies or have written their own life stories; others have scattered a great deal of autobiographical material in their different books. All of them belong to our own century though in some cases their work began before the nineteen-hundreds.

The first of them, Hereward Carrington, I was fortunate enough to meet in person near the end of his long life. He is now largely forgotten, his books out of print, his various exploits rarely mentioned. American by adoption though British by birth he was a lonely, ascetic figure of high principles and a complex psychology—a man of many interests besides psychical research which, however, was the centre of his life.

Sir Oliver Lodge, of course, is equally famous in the history of physics as in the occult disciplines. In almost nine decades of his long career he investigated lightning and electromagnetic waves, radio and the influence of moving matter on ether; he developed and named the coherer, an integral part of wireless telegraphy. He was one of the first to try to reconcile science and religion—and succeeded to his own satisfaction if not to that of many of his colleagues. He was also a most accomplished and articulate popularizer of science and of his ideas on personal immortality.

Baron von Schrenck-Notzing was a neurologist and alienist who came to psychical research through his experiments in hypnotism and his investigations into the mechanics of the subconscious. His huge book *Materializations Phenomena* became a classic and his work with the mediums Eva C., the Schneider Brothers and others has set the pattern in many countries for the approach to physical mediumship.

Charles Richet, the French physiologist, devoted much of his scientific activity to researches in serum therapy and was the discoverer of anaphylaxis, the specific supersensitivity of the smooth or involuntary muscles of the human body to a protein previously introduced into it. He was awarded the 1913 Nobel Prize for physiology and medicine. But Richet was also deeply interested in psychical phenomena and while he shared Schrenck-Notzing's concept of them, he was equally opposed to Pavlovian materialism and excessive credulity. Certainly, among all the distinguished Frenchmen involved in this area, he has done most to enlarge and open up the occult to Cartesian logic and pure metaphysics compatible with natural sciences.

With Cesare Lombroso, the Italian physician and criminologist, we reach an unusual type of investigator. Lombroso, as we know, had an obsessional theory: he believed that a criminal represents a distinct anthropological type with definite physical and metal characteristics, that he is the product of heredity, atavism and degeneracy. This theory has long been disproved and discarded (though now and then it still crops up in racial connotations) but Lombroso turned to psychical research partly to find some relief from his own excessive preoccupation with criminology and the "Lombroso types". His work, especially with Eusapia Paladino, was nonetheless interesting and valuable.

The last in this selective portrait gallery is not a psychical researcher in the ordinary sense of the word. Raphael Schermann, the "psychographologist" was an extraordinary human being whose full story has never been told. He was certainly a pioneer for he linked precognition, psychology and the more or less accepted scientific discipline of graphology in his own person. His life and his traumatic end ought to provide enough material for a whole television series or a long feature film.

These six studies are not intended to be full biographies of their subjects; they only present the highlights, the most striking features in their careers in psychical research. But I hope they will serve to attract the reader to a fuller exploration both of the whole subject and of the pioneers.

I would like to thank the Harry Price Library at the University of London for invaluable help in collecting and checking the material for this book.

London, April 1972   Paul Tabori

HEREWARD CARRINGTON

When I met Hereward Carrington, he was almost seventy, a tall spare man whose face, though marked by illness and old age, still showed the traces of almost classical beauty. I was taken to his laboratory (which was also his home) in the very heart of Hollywood, at 1145 Vine Street. We had already corresponded for a couple of years and he greeted me as an old friend. Though it was the hot, searing early autumn of California, he wore a pullover and a coat and he seemed to be afraid of catching cold. We talked for several hours and I found that he had a surprisingly youthful mind, reacting with quick brilliance to every topic, fishing from his copious memory nuggets of experience, recollections of meetings and people, quoting verbatim opinions and descriptions that covered over fifty years. He offered us fruit and soft drinks, explaining that he was a vegetarian and neither drank nor smoked though he had no objection to his friends doing either. Our visit ended when a young, pretty lady arrived and more or less shooed us off. She was his secretary and guardian angel who, not much later, became his second wife.

I spent some twenty months in Los Angeles and we met four or five times. I was planning a television series based on the material of the late Harry Price and his investigations. A famous star and his wife were to appear in it and we did a good deal of preparatory work, including a pilot script. Carrington helped generously; as I did not bring my files and archives with me, he allowed me to consult his fine library, read the teleplay and made some highly useful and perceptive comments. Like so many Hollywood projects, this one also went down the drain—at one stage nine lawyers were involved, all trying desperately to earn their fees by complicating matters—and a few months later I returned to England. But we kept on corresponding and I was delighted to return his kindness by putting some of the resources of the Harry Price Library at his disposal for illustrating one of his later books. His final work, his fine *Essays in the Occult* reached me just before Christmas 1958. Then, about a week later, I heard that Carrington had died on Boxing Day, just over seventy-eight years of age.

Carrington never wrote an autobiography—or rather, he told his life story in numberless fragments scattered over his books which total well over a hundred. He was born at St. Helier, Jersey and educated in London and Kent; and he was eight when his mother took him on a visit to America. Mrs. Carrington, her younger son and her daughter, crossed on the Norddeutscher Lloyd boat, the *Elbe*; among their fellow passengers there were three huge Falstaffian gentlemen who said that they had made several crossings, one after the other, because they liked the food on board so much better than that served in German restaurants or Continental hotels. What fascinated Hereward, however, was not their appetites but the interest they showed in psychic phenomena. They discussed the recently published book, *Phantasms of the Living*, with Mrs. Carrington, especially the evidence for telepathy, the coincidence of apparitions with the death of the person they represented and various similar subjects. The young boy absorbed it all, with rapt interest. It wasn't the "ghostly horrors" that attracted him but the scientific side, the inexplicable yet apparently well-observed and recorded marvels.

His parents were agnostics who had lived in the East for many years and had conceived a strong dislike of missionaries; if anything, they were inclined to Buddhism. Their children grew up with little or no religion, were encouraged to have open minds, given a chance to study all religions from the purely historical or anthropological point of view. Carrington became an amateur conjurer early in his life which led him to the history of the technique of magic; he gave his first "performance" when he was thirteen. Six years later he came across a few books dealing with the sort of pseudo-spiritualistic tricks the Davenport Brothers popularized; and this increased his general scepticism as to survival after death or paranormal phenomena. Then, one particular book, which took the opposite view though not the extreme spiritualist one, made him decide to join the Society for Psychical Research, read their publications and experiment himself. By the time he arrived in the United States (he was just nineteen) he had decided to devote himself to psychical research as far as it was possible and as his main occupation.

Carrington's older brother, Fitzroy, had preceded him by some thirteen years. His interests were almost entirely centred on art; he was twenty-three when, in 1892, he joined the famous art dealers, Frederick Keppel & Co. in New York, staying with them until he became curator of the department of prints at the Boston Museum of Fine Arts, editing *The Print Collectors' Quarterly* and publishing a whole series of books on engravings and etchings on which he was a widely accepted authority. The younger Carrington settled first in Boston where his brother was already installed. Here he soon became associated with the American Society for Psychical Research which at that time was a branch of the British one and was under the leadership of Dr. Richard Hodgson. (The American Society had been founded three years after the pioneer British organization, in 1885, but was turned into a branch in 1889.) Dr. Hodgson died, suddenly, in 1905 and two years later the American Society was reformed as an independent body, this time under Dr. James H. Hyslop. Carrington became Hyslop's assistant and worked with him for almost two years. Later he was Research Officer of the A.S.P.R. and represented it at a number of international congresses. Though during his early American years he worked as an editor, he soon devoted himself entirely to psychical research, writing and lecturing about it for the next half-century—while at the same time he also produced books on such diverse subjects as contract bridge, yoga, magic and nutrition.

There were two mediums with whom Carrington was specially associated and whose work, in some way or other, influenced his life and career. One was the Italian Eusapia

Paladino and the other the American woman known simply as Margery. It is a striking fact that while Carrington has written a great deal about Eusapia there are very few references to Margery in his works, especially during the last thirty years of his life. And yet, personally, he was closer to the American woman than to the Italian medium.

Eusapia Paladino was a fat, middle-aged, semi-literate Neapolitan woman, with pretty hands and small feet but rather coarse features. She was about forty when the first detailed reports of her mediumship were published in the *Bulletin of the Psychological Section of the Medico-Legal Society of New York*. These were based on a series of seventeen séances, held in Milan at the home of Dr. Giorgio Finzi, the physicist. The participants included some of the most famous scientists of the late nineteenth century: Giovanni Schiaparelli, director of the Milan Astronomical Observatory who had discovered what were later called the "canals" of Mars; Carl du Prel, the German philosopher, author of four or five basic works on spiritualism, mysticism and the secret sciences; Angelo Brofferio, Professor of Physics at the Royal School of Agriculture, Portici; Dr. G. B. Ermacora and the host, Dr. Finzi. Some of the sittings were also attended by Richet and Lombroso. The final report, signed by Schiaparelli, Du Prel, Brofferio, Ermacora and Finzi stated:

"... in the circumstances given, none of the manifestations obtained in a more or less intense light could have been produced by any artifice whatever.
... the same conviction can be affirmed in regard to the greater number of the phenomena taking place in darkness.
... that which we have seen and verified is sufficient in our eyes to prove that these phenomena are most worthy of scientific attention."

This was a truly glowing testimonial though Richet was more cautious in his conclusions. Following the Milan sittings, Eusapia was invited to various capitals and centres for séances, starting with a series at Naples under the direction of Professor Wagner of the University of St. Petersburg. The

Russian zoologist seemed to have been completely convinced of Eusapia's genuine powers—though his critics pointed out, a little unkindly, that he was both extremely short-sighted and also hard of hearing. It was he who arranged Eusapia's visit to Russia some time later.

In 1893-94 another series of sittings was held in Rome, directed by the Polish investigators, Dr. Julien Ochorowicz and M. Siemiradski. Later séances at the Italian capital were attended by Richet, Schrenck-Notzing, Lombroso, Professor Danilewski of the University of St. Petersburg and Dr. Dobrzycki, director of the Warsaw *Medical Gazette*. Dr. Ochorowicz initiated Eusapia's Warsaw stay where forty séances were held. These were hailed as highly satisfactory by their organizers. In the same year four séances were held in Professor Richet's home on the Ile Roubaud in which, for the first time, two eminent British researchers, Sir Oliver Lodge and F. W. H. Myers took part. Professor Sidgwick, the first president of the British S.P.R. also attended some of them with his wife. Both Myers and Sir Oliver reported to the Society with Sidgwick offering corroborative testimony. But the record of the Roubaud sittings had come under fire from Dr. Richard Hodgson with whom Carrington had worked in Boston. Though he had not been present at the Richet home, Hodgson developed a theory as to the different ways Eusapia *could* have cheated and he harshly criticized the inadequate control methods. The participants in the Roubaud séances disputed this theory and invited Dr. Hodgson to the next series of sittings which Myers arranged at his own home in Cambridge for August and September 1895. These were a complete disaster. Apart from a few and uninteresting phenomena, the lady from Naples was found again and again cheating quite brazenly. Dr. Hodgson purposely allowed her a free hand—in order to see if she would cheat. And of course, she did. For Eusapia, with commendable though disconcerting frankness, had already told Lombroso: "Watch me! You must watch me all the time—or I'll cheat."

No wonder that Professor Sidgwick declared: "Inasmuch as Eusapia Paladino has systematically practised trickery for years . . . I propose to ignore her performance in the future as those of other persons engaged in the same mischievous trade has to be ignored..."

Still, the Cambridge fiasco did not put an end to the Paladino mediumship. It was balanced by a series of séances held at the home of Colonel De Rochas at l'Agnelas which at least established Eusapia's "mixed" mediumship—she would cheat when given the chance; but she could produce phenomena under strict control that could not be explained by fraudulent or mechanical sources. She and her "control" whom she called "John King" continued to tour Europe and there were repeated French and Italian reports sufficiently impressive for the British Society for Psychical Research to send a commission to Naples—to determine "once and for all" whether Eusapia was genuine or not. It consisted of Carrington, W. W. Baggally and the Hon. Everard Feilding. It was to be the first important and prolonged investigation in which he participated. He was only twenty-eight but his much more experienced colleagues accepted him as their full equal.

The sittings were held in the rooms the three researchers hired at the Hotel Victoria, Naples, and covered November and December, 1908. Carrington (who had already published two books, *The Physical Phenomena of Spiritualism* in 1907 and *The Coming Science* in 1908) gave a full and carefully balanced report in *Eusapia Paladino and Her Phenomena*, published less than a year after the séances. Dedicated to the memory of his father "as a token of my respect and esteem for his unrecognized genius", it was obviously intended as his first *magnum opus*. Elaborately documented, it provided a biographical sketch of the extraordinary lady, attempted to establish the place she had earned in the history of modern spiritualism, gave a historical résumé of her career from 1891 to 1908 and then offered a detailed report of the eleven sittings Carrington and his colleagues had with her from November 21 to December 19, 1908. The young researcher summed up the theories advanced to explain the phenomena, gave his own hypothesis and ended with biological and psychological considerations. In his appendix he also answered a particularly violent attack on the Paladino mediumship by Mrs. L. I. Finch which she had published in the *Annals of Psychical Science.* Though he had no illusions about the medium's character, Carrington based his own evaluation of her upon the assumption that her phenomena were genuine and the result neither of fraud nor of hallucination. He came to some interesting conclusions as to the cause and origin of her powers:

> "Spirit" being supposedly pure mind, or closely related to it, it cannot act upon the material world directly, or effect changes in it. In order for this to take place there must be some intermediary, as I have before insisted upon; but I now think we are in a position to see in what this intermediary consists. *It is the nervous, vital force of the medium, externalized by her beyond her body and utilized by the manifesting spirit for the purposes of its manifestation* . . . We might conceive that this vital energy is utilized by the manifesting intelligence, who imbibes and clothes himself with it, as it were—creating a sort of temporary fluidic body through which it can manifest—can come in contact with the material world, move material objects, be seen, felt, and even photographed. Normally, such an intelligence would be separated from our world by the veil of sense; but now a link is supplied enabling the phantom to become more "material" in a way, for the time being— sufficiently so, at least, to cause the various manifestations . . . and to produce the various manifestations so frequently attested to in Eusapia's séances.

He also faced quite squarely the vexing and discouraging problem of the Neapolitan lady's mixed mediumship. Carrington made no secret of it that Eusapia had made repeated attempts to fake phenomena and, in some cases, succeeded in doing so—though without fooling the trio of Anglo-American investigators. Yet at the same time there were many occasions when inexplicable things happened under perfect and complete control. If Signora Paladino could produce genuine phenomena, why did she ever cheat at all and leave herself open to attack from sceptical critics because of this? Carrington himself felt that the majority of people would prefer to believe, she invariably cheated and that all phenomena occurring in her presence were necessarily fraudulent. But his views changed after the series of sittings. Before, he found it hard to accept that the same medium could be both fraudulent and genuine, preferring the first alternative. But the sittings removed this *a priori* objection which he came to regard as worthless and conclusively disproved by the facts.

Still—why *did* Eusapia cheat? Carrington had a simple explanation:

I believe that she does this sometimes simply and solely because of her love of mischief. She delights in seeing onlookers mystified at the phenomena produced through her mediumship, and when she is in a trance state she remembers very little of what takes place, and, as it were, misses all the fun! But when she is in a normal state and can observe what is going on, she will try fraudulently to produce phenomena simply and solely for the love of the thing. Still, I admit that this is but a small part of the reason. Some of it is doubtless premeditated fraud—intended to deceive her sitters, and which she would pass off as genuine phenomena if she could. But I am convinced that the great majority of her fraudulent phenomena are produced in a semi trance condition, and that she is unaware of her movements . . . There is a strong impulse to produce phenomena, and, if she is not restrained, she will endeavour to produce them in a perfectly normal manner. But if she *is* restrained genuine phenomena will result—as we have repeatedly ascertained.

Whatever his views, Carrington thought the Paladino mediumship sufficiently important to arrange another series of séances with her. After the official report of the Feilding-Baggally-Carrington committee was published in the *Proceedings* of the Society for Psychical Research, a most detailed account of 260 pages, he made careful preparations for her visit to the U.S. Eusapia landed in America on November 10, 1909, and left on June 28, 1910. She even gave a séance on board ship in one of the officers' cabins at which "materializations" and the usual phenomena occurred—a most impressive affair at which knocks, raps, touches, fall in temperature, a "ghastly appearing hand and fingers" followed each other, not to mention a floating "hideous, black, mask-like thing". Not only were all the participants convinced, some even had hysterics while others remained long under the "shattering impression" of the experience.

Twenty-seven séances were held under Carrington's direction and four at Columbia University. The phenomena seen were of the usual character—levitations of the table opened the proceedings, followed by raps and scratches upon the table, in response to raps and scratches made with Eusapia's fingers above it. The curtains of the cabinet blew out and about this time usually she demanded less light. Then movements of objects took place in the cabinet; a bell was rung, the tambourine played. These objects were then moved out of the cabinet and deposited on the séance table; and, finally, the small table itself, within the cabinet, dragged along the floor and was thrown out or lifted on to the larger séance table. Following these phenomena "touchings" ensued and occasionally visible hands and faces were seen. Eusapia sat *outside* the cabinet, the curtains of which were behind her and her hands and feet were held or "controlled" by those seated on either side of her.

Though even during the twenty-seven séances—the first of which was a sort of "press conference", attended almost solely by journalists—there were some attempts by Eusapia to cheat which were firmly foiled by Carrington and his fellow-researchers, there were a number of impressive phenomena. But the Columbia séances ended in complete disaster. Carrington deliberately absented himself from the sittings at the Physical Laboratory which were attended by Professor Hallock and E. B. Wilson of Columbia, Professor R. W. Wood of Johns Hopkins, Professor August Trowbridge of Princeton, Doctors Charles L. Dana and Frederick Peterson, two of New York's most eminent neurologists and psychiatrists, Professors Miller, Montague and Pitkin, also of Columbia, represented the faculty of philosophy while the others were physicists and biologists. Professor Bigiongari acted as interpreter; there were stenographers and a trained nurse who searched Eusapia before the séances started.

The reports of these four sittings, held on January 17, 19, 22 and 24, 1910, were rather contradictory. Carrington simply said that the results were negative, that Eusapia was exhausted, that no new experiments of any kind were tried when they should have been—but of course, not being present at them, his judgment could only be second hand, based on his own previous sittings with Eusapia. But some of the press reports spoke of the total discrediting of the Italian medium. The American correspondent of the London *Sunday Chronicle* reported:

EUSAPIA EXPOSED: UNMASKING A FAMOUS MEDIUM.
'TECS UNDER THE TABLE.

Eusapia Paladino is the most talked-of spirit medium in the world today (the article began). Great professors have believed in her and she has been hailed in Europe and America as the greatest spiritualistic phenomenon of the last decade. But she has refused the challenge of some American university professors who suggest that she shall be placed in a canvas sack with an opening at the neck only. The opening shall be laced up the back, they say, and the lacing done in such a way that it can be opened only by cutting. They further suggest that the sack shall be fastened to the floor, and at the close of the séance shall show no signs of having been tampered with. Another condition is that she shall submit to an examination by women to prove that she has no apparatus concealed. Signor [sic!] Eusapia does not, however, like the idea and has refused to submit to a trial in this form. She says she tried it once in Venice and nearly died. She offers to perform her spiritualist feats with her feet and hands tied.

The article went on describing Eusapia as a "coarse-looking woman of the Latin type" who, when anyone doubts her genuineness, "shrieks and gets very excited".

Carrington does not speak of any actual "unmasking" though he says that the fourth Columbia séance was "of such a nature as to leave on the mind of Professor Wilson 'the strongest possible impression of fraud'. In other words, they were typically 'bad séances', and would never have served to

convince anyone of the supernormal character of the phenomena. They certainly would not have convinced me; and
would probably have served to confirm me in the belief that
nothing but fraud had been employed throughout!"

This was a little disingenuous—for it did not mention the
rest of the *Sunday Chronicle* report which was more than
explicit. It seems that two detectives, dressed in "tight-fitting
black suits and black stockings" were secretly introduced into
the darkened séance-room and wriggled their way along the
floor till they had reached their assigned positions on either
side of the séance table, under the chairs of the sitters. There
they were in a position to observe Eusapia closely—while she
evidently hadn't noticed their entry at all. They saw her for
a few minutes tapping the feet of the controls with her own
feet.

> Then she placed her right foot cross-wise, so that the heel
> rested on the foot of one control and the toe on the foot of
> the other. To these men it would seem that she had both
> feet on theirs. Presently a foot came from beneath her dress,
> and it was placed under the leg of the table which was
> gently chucked into the air. Then the foot withdrew and
> the table descended to the floor. It was repeatedly lifted
> after this and every time, whether in a partial or complete
> levitation, the medium's foot was used as the compelling
> force. At different times throughout the séance the medium
> caused rappings upon the table by striking the free foot on
> the left leg of the table about three inches from the floor...

The "psychic breeze" (another of Eusapia's "specialities"),
one of the detectives said, was produced by "blowing upwards
with the bottom lip protruding, just as a woman does when
she desires to blow a stray hair from her eyes..."

Other details of the trickery were given; and the article
ended by the proud boast that "it has remained for a party of
American investigators to expose the trickery which had impressed learned men of many countries . . . to believe in the
genuineness of her mediumistic phenomena..."

Yet Eusapia remained in the States for another six months.
Carrington himself had three more séances with her. One of

them, held in a private house, included Professor Nicholas Murray Butler, President of Columbia and took place only three days after the "unmasking". It was not a good one, according to Carrington and certainly not "evidential" because of the inexperience of the controllers and the conditions under which it was held. But ten days later, on February 7, the results were "very good . . . on the whole", with a number of remarkable levitations, touches and other phenomena. There was a final one on the evening of May 9, 1910, after both the *New York Times* and *Collier's Weekly* had published exposés of Paladino's trick methods. It was arranged so that Carrington could test the explanations proposed in the papers and the various reports—"so far as I was enabled to".

It was the first time Carrington controlled Eusapia throughout a sitting during her whole American trip. It was a typically "bad séance". He caught her several times in trickery or attempts and had no difficulty in doing so.

That was the end of it as far as Carrington was concerned. He never sat with Eusapia again; she returned to Europe; she died less than eight years after her American trip, in 1918. But Carrington maintained throughout the next fifty years what he had written in his first, 1909, book about her: ". . . it is to be hoped that Eusapia Paladino will be ranked, not as a vulgar impostor, but as a rarely gifted individual, possessing powers worthy of the deepest study and respect; as a delicate and sensitive piece of organic machinery, which should be guarded and cared for with the utmost kindness and consideration."

In the long account devoted to her American visit, he argued that poor séances proved nothing while good ones proved the apparently supernormal character of the facts. Until someone had seen both good and bad séances, he was not entitled to express any opinion about the *whole* case, to dogmatize one way or another. The European investigators who studied Eusapia, were not influenced by the exposure in their attitude of belief. They contended—as Carrington did —that had Eusapia been studied long and carefully enough, genuine phenomena would have been observed—as well as the fraudulent ones to which she resorted, in an attempt to reproduce genuine manifestations when they failed to appear.

Perhaps Carrington was overstating her case; but Paladino's reputation has grown rather than dimmed since her death. Many of her séances were held under rigorous control; many of her phenomena had never been duplicated. But she was, as one Italian professor put it, "half-angel, half-cheat—and are not most women the same?"

In the first bulletin of the American Psychical Institute which Hereward Carrington founded, he explained the reason for setting up this new organization:

> ...Owing to the American Society for Psychical Research's change of policy and their almost exclusive concentration upon one case of mediumship, many psychic students in America felt that another organization was greatly needed, which would approach a wider range of psychic subjects, from a different standpoint, and if possible concentrate its activities upon scientific research, largely by laboratory methods.

The "one case of mediumship" was that of the medium known as Margery, in real life Mrs. Le Roy Goddard Crandon, the second wife of a distinguished Boston surgeon, author of standard works upon his chosen subject and formerly connected with Harvard University. She was considerably younger than her elderly husband, a good-looking woman with a strong, impressive personality. The Crandons dominated psychical research for nearly twenty years in the United States, almost wrecked the American Society and set scores of famous scientists, psychologists, magicians, journalists and others at loggerheads.

Her mediumship was characterized by an amazing variety of phenomena. She produced (or didn't produce, according to the view you took) apports, telekinesis, direct voice, clairvoyance, she could do automatic writing in several languages, she materialized "hands" and teleplasmic forms, she did cross-correspondence tests—you named it and she would deliver it. She was a veritable da Vinci of the occult, the most versatile lady in all psychical history.

Her mediumship began in 1923 when she was forty. Dr. Crandon, a voracious reader, had become interested in psychical research when he read a couple of books on the subject, then went on to study a wide selection of the available literature—and "the subject came to occupy a major place in his extra-professional mental life". As a result, but more as a joke, Mrs. Crandon and her friend Mrs. Katherine Brown, went to a medium who informed them that a "male spirit" was present who gave the name of Walter and claimed to be Margery's brother. (Walter was killed by a railway-engine in 1911 when he was twenty-eight; he was five years Margery's senior.) A few days later Dr. Crandon visited the same clairvoyant and obtained from him "evidential messages from his brother-in-law". Margery had been told that she was herself "a potential medium of great power".

It was between May and November 1923 that most of Margery's simpler phenomena were developed.

Six months earlier, in December 1922, the *Scientific American* had offered $2,500 to any medium producing "a visible psychic manifestation" under its test conditions. The committee investigating the claims of those who were to submit to the tests consisted of Dr. William McDougall, the eminent psychologist, Dr. D. F. Comstock, a retired professor of the Massachusetts Institute of Technology, Dr. W. F. Prince, then research officer of the American Society for Psychical Research, Henry Houdini (Erich Weiss), the famous magician and escapologist, and Carrington. J. Malcolm Bird, the editor of the *Scientific American*, acted as secretary and as he put it "stage manager" to the group—though, according to W. F. Prince "not by action of the committee". He was chiefly responsible for procedure—"the strict function of committee members being to act as judges".

Bird became one of Margery's most enthusiastic supporters. He later succeeded Dr. Prince as research officer of the A.S.P.R. and inevitably carried this enthusiasm to his new post. The book he wrote about Margery runs to over 500 pages; about two-fifths of it is devoted to the 133 sittings which she held from May 1923 to April 1924. The materials had been furnished by Dr. Crandon. At the first 63 sittings no record was made of the arrangement of the sitters or the degree of control and even in the subsequent 70 séances this information was provided only "incidentally or otherwise". Certainly, nothing like Schrenck-Notzing's or Harry Price's scrupulous, methodical procedure was followed and Bird himself calls it "the informal stage of the mediumship". Yet both he and Dr. Crandon claimed that an immense variety of psychic phenomena took place.

In December 1923 Dr. Crandon and Margery visited Paris and London. According to Dr. Crandon: "Margery enters a laboratory in Paris or London for the first time, and, under conditions laid down by the most experienced men in the world, the phenomena begin within a few minutes." Theodore Besterman, who devoted a chapter in his *Some Modern Mediums* to Margery, gave a rather different account. "Nothing especially notable occurred during the five sittings then given" ("then" refers here to the European visit). Margery herself had some "psychic photographs" taken by the notorious Mrs. Ada Emma Deane whose crude "spirit pictures" produced on Armistice Days around the London Cenotaph were found to be impudent frauds—the photographs of very much alive footballers. Bird actually printed some of her crude fakes in his book, with two "spirits" hovering in a cotton wool cloud to the left above Margery's head; the caption declared: "The one nearer Margery is the one recognized as Walter."

All this was the preliminary to the decision of Dr. Crandon to enter his wife in April 1924 as a contestant for the *Scientific American* prize which none of the previous competitors had managed to earn. The séances took place between April and August. What *really* happened during them became a matter of the fiercest controversy—nor could the full truth be told for a long time.

Carrington devoted quite a lot of space to Margery Crandon in his *The Story of Psychic Science*, published in 1930. He listed her as first of the important new mediums that had come forward during recent years, in the company of Eva C., Willi and Rudi Schneider, Stella C., and Eleonore Zugun. He spoke of the psychic lights which he said, were observed "on numerous occasions" at the Margery sittings. He described, in detail, how he experienced the phenomenon called "independent voice" with her:

> ...Certainly the most striking evidence which has been obtained, of late years, is that occurring in the séances of "Margery", the celebrated Boston medium. Here, an "independent voice" has been heard from almost the very beginning of the mediumship, and occasionally under excellent conditions of control. Thus, at a sitting held May 19, 1924, a voice was distinctly heard in one corner of the séance room, by all those present, when Bird had his hand tightly clasped over the mouth of the medium, and every sitter's mouth was held by a covering hand of his neighbour. On this occasion, I myself was controlling the medium, and heard the voice distinctly, as did others.

He explained why ventriloquism could not possibly explain the striking phenomenon—though he gave no details as to what the voice said or did—and added: "The 'independence' of the voice thus seemed to be proved, and was held to be so proved by the investigators of the Margery mediumship at the time..." However, he added a note of caution:

> ...All of which, of course, does not prove that the independent voices produced at Margery's séances are genuine. I am not at present discussing that point. All that I have endeavoured to do is to examine the theoretical possibility that such voices might have been produced by means of ventriloquism, and I think we may confidently conclude that such an explanation in no wise serves to elucidate or explain them.

He summed up the whole mediumship in a rather curious way:

> ...The manifestations themselves are varied, complex, and subject to various interpretations. Many investigators have come to a wholly negative conclusion with regard to these facts; others, equally competent, have arrived at a more or less positive conclusion; while others are content to hold

their judgment in suspense. It is certainly one of the most baffling and extraordinary cases in history—and this is true, no matter how we may choose to regard it. For my own part, I occupy the same position as I did when rendering my formal Report in the *Scientific American*, which is that, despite the difficulties involved in arriving at any just estimate of this case, and despite the uncertainty of many of the phenomena and the complicated social, ethical, personal, physical and psychological factors involved, a number of seemingly genuine, supernormal manifestations yet remain, which are of the profoundest interest to psychical, as well as to ethico-sociological science.

There are some unusually interesting adjectives in this paragraph. Few psychical researchers refer to "ethical" or "personal" elements or repeat the "ethico-sociological" connotations in such a marked manner. Carrington, writing some six years after the sittings, was not being entirely frank. He couldn't be—both because he was a gentleman and because Margery was still alive.

Henry N. Gilroy has been associated with Carrington a long time; it was he, actually, who introduced me to the veteran psychical researcher in Los Angeles. At my request he put his recollections on tape. He was certainly close enough to Carrington to be the recipient of quite personal and intimate confidences. These were made some time after the actual events. Gilroy had this to tell about Margery:

Of course, most people don't know this—but he (Carrington) had a love affair with Margery—on the q.t. They had an understanding that it would not affect in any way the report of the *Scientific American* magazine as to whether her mediumship was genuine or not. Their little love affair went on for several months and he told me how difficult it was to have their little trysts and get-togethers.

Certainly these facts must have been in Carrington's mind when he referred to those "ethical and psychological factors". Nor was he the only investigator who became Margery's lover. The lady was of an ardent temperament and with a more than elderly husband needed virile consolation. That she combined the fulfilment of her very natural needs with what might be called *captatio benevolentias*, "the capture of the good will" of her controllers was more than likely. Would it have been possible for Carrington to denounce his mistress as a fake? If her mediumship was a mixed one, wouldn't he have subconsciously stressed the positive features rather than the negative ones?

Bird and Carrington were almost unreservedly partisans of Margery's genuineness. Dr. Crandon, in the symposium "The Case For and Against Psychical Belief" (edited by Charles Murchison and published by Clark University, Worcester, Mass. in 1927), emphasized this. He wrote:

> ... One member, the most experienced student of this subject in the world (i.e., Carrington) declared the phenomena to be of first quality and supernormal. The Secretary of the Committee (J. Malcolm Bird) reached the same conclusion.

But the four other members were either incapable or unwilling to accept the mediumship of Margery. This, her husband insisted, was their fault. An ancient and familiar argument; to discredit the critics, it has been always convenient to cast doubt upon their good faith or ability. But the Boston surgeon would hardly be anything but a vigorous and persistent advocate of Mrs. Crandon.

The *Scientific American* Committee report was adverse by a majority of four to one. Even Carrington who voted for Margery, had his reservations by then. "Many of the observed manifestations might well have been produced fraudulently— and possibly were so produced." He added, however: "But I am convinced that genuine phenomena have occurred here" —plumping therefore for a "mixed mediumship" with which he was only too familiar through his experiences with Paladino.

Dr. Crandon naturally did not like this result; Margery did not get the $2,500 prize. In addition there was a confused and unpleasant incident involving a carpenter's rule. Houdini had devised a strong cabinet to immobilize the medium. Then

came a séance at which "Walter" declared that the magician
had placed a wooden two-foot rule in the cabinet so that he
—Houdini—could accuse the medium of trickery. Houdini
replied that it was Margery who took the rule into the
cabinet so that *she* could accuse *him* of framing *her*. A little
melodramatically, he swore by the grave of his dead mother
that he had no knowledge of the rule.

By December 24, the controversy had exploded upon the
front pages. It became a glorious free-for-all, a farrago of
personalities, of challenges and counter-challenges, in many
ways startlingly childish. Dr. Crandon, apparently despair-
ing of getting sufficient scientific acknowledgment of his
wife's powers, decided to try and obtain it from a foreign
source. He invited Dr. Eric Dingwall, then Research Officer
of the British S.P.R. who spent January and February 1925
with the Crandons. His conclusions were—inconclusive:

> I did not succeed in achieving my primary purpose (he
> wrote in his report which was published in the Journal
> of the London S.P.R. in June 1926) of coming to a definite
> conclusion as to the genuineness or otherwise of the
> phenomena. During the course of the (twenty-nine) sittings
> the evidence seemed to me at one time for, and another
> time against, their supernormal nature, but never to
> incline decisively either way.

Dr. Dingwall came under fire both from the supporters
and the critics of Margery. In May and June there was
another series of séances with some Harvard instructors, a
graduate student and several professors and physicians. Mr.
Hudson Hoagland, the spokesman of the group, published a
report in November 1925 in the *Atlantic Monthly*, presenting more than twenty items of evidence, direct and collateral,
leading to a verdict of "normal production" of the "ectoplasmic limb" that was the "great phenomenon" of these
séances. Once again the published report of the group was
adverse to the mediumship. And all members of the Harvard
group signed a statement that "the group is in absolute agree-
ment that the only conclusion possible to them is that
trickery accounted for all the phenomena; that the only

possible difference of opinion in the group is to what extent the trickery was unconscious".

The argument over Margery split the American Society for Psychical Research from top to bottom. Many of its officials resigned and the "Margery faction" remained in control. Her sympathizers became convinced of the genuineness of the phenomena and in their *Journal* kept up a "heroic defence" of the medium. Between September 1925 and January 1926 there were more private sittings in the Crandon circle. In January 1926 Dr. Crandon made yet one more attempt to obtain some official or scientific endorsement. A committee of the American S.P.R., consisting of two psychologists and one physicist, sat on the case but after the fourth séance Dr. Crandon terminated the experiments. He had good reason to—the professor of physics declared himself "firmly convinced of fraud" while the other two did not report and the American S.P.R. was silent on the whole matter.

In July 1926 Margery—or "Walter"—developed a new and striking phenomenon—spirit fingerprints. These were produced by a complex process—for "Walter" objected strongly to getting printer's ink or lampblack on his "teleplasmic terminal". He must have been a very finicky spirit. At "his" suggestion they tried a bucket of hot wax and a sheet of plate glass. "Walter" dipped his "terminal" in the wax, then pressed it on the glass. This did not work very well so the resourceful "entity" proposed that the glass should be covered with soft wax and that he should press his fingers upon it. Again, the results were not too good. Then Dr. Kerwin, Margery's dentist and friend, thought of "Kerr", a proprietary brand of dental wax which became plastic when warmed. This technique was successful—and for the first time in occult history a spirit obligingly and permanently recorded his three-dimensional thumb-prints (*only* his thumb-prints) as requested.

Or did he?

Late in 1931 it occurred to Mr. E. E. Dudley, a former officer of the A.S.P.R. to ask every person who had ever sat with Margery to supply him with inked prints of his or her right and left thumbs. This was quite a chore for there had been scores of them—in J. Malcolm Bird's book which covers only about eighteen months, the list of the participants runs to fifteen pages though, of course, many were "regulars"— but Dudley persisted and obtained most of them. Collating carefully this mass of material with the "Walter" prints, he was amazed to discover that the "spirit's" thumb-prints, left and right, were *identical in every respect* with those of Dr. Kerwin, Margery's friend and dentist, *who was still living.* He published his findings in the bulletin of Price's National Laboratory of Psychical Research, London, in 1932; he explained that there was not one chance in billions that Kerwin's prints and "Walter's" did not belong to the same person.

Many a murderer has been hanged because of fewer than *ten* correspondences between his own finger-prints and those found at the scene of the crime. In this case almost ninety were found in the right thumb-print and about seventy in the left one. The evidence was overwhelmingly, decisively damning.

This was a bombshell indeed. Margery's dentist was completely exonerated in the whole affair. No one really solved the question as to how "Walter" palmed off the thumb-prints of a living dentist as the impressions of his own dead ones. A finger-print expert, Professor Harold Cummins stated: "There seems just ground for suspecting the use of artificial dies."

But can you forge finger-prints? The pro-Margery faction —which composed the sadly truncated but still active American S.P.R.—denied this. But Mr. Dudley's discovery prompted a number of people to experiment with the aim of ascertaining whether three-dimensional fingerprints in the form of moulds or dies, could or could not be produced from two-dimensional inked prints on paper. It was Professor Cummins of Tylane University who succeeded in actually producing three-dimensional dies in hard wax and other substances from ordinary thumb-prints on paper, proving that fingerprints *could* be forged, copied and transferred (complete with sweat-gland markings) to any object which the original fingers never touched. He published his findings in *Police Science* in 1934.

Though Dr. Crandon and his friends protested violently and brought forward the most esoteric arguments to account for the identity of "the Walter" and "Dr. Kerwin" finger-prints, Dudley's findings almost killed the Margery medium-ship.

In *The Psychic World*, a book published in 1937, Carring-ton does not mention Margery at all though he has many references to D. D. Home, Eusapia Paladino and other mediums. But in *Psychic Oddities*, published fifteen years later, he was obviously no longer bound by any personal con-siderations. Dr. Crandon had died and Margery herself had passed away in November 1941. Carrington was still in favour of the "mixed mediumship" theory:

> ...I attended more than fifty séances with Margery (he wrote) during the summer of 1924, and became thoroughly familiar with her phenomena at that time—though many others were added after I had ceased to sit. Among these were the famous "thumb-prints"...Six different commit-tees sat with this medium—two from Harvard, one from Johns Hopkins, Dr. Eric J. Dingwall (for the S.P.R.) and two others, as well as our "Scientific American" Committee. The verdict in all these cases was negative. While all this is true, I am strongly of the opinion that some genuine phenomena occurred during the early years of Margery's mediumship. At least certain things occurred which were extremely puzzling, and which were never really explained ...Nevertheless, there was, of course, much fraud during the later sittings (especially), while the preposterous "thumb-prints" were conclusively shown to be such. I am inclined to regard this as a "pigeon-hole" case which must simply be filed, under the general heading of "non-proven". It was, however, a most interesting case to investigate.

Perhaps some nostalgia lingered, some memory of this strange woman who had had a most genteel upbringing, was conditioned by staunch New England traditions, held only a single job before she married (in a congregational church)—

but whose subconscious must have revolted against all the restrictions and limitations which her ordinary life entailed. We do not know how many other lovers she had though we can guess at the identity of some of them. Carrington appears to have kept his head with remarkable detachment and was able to disengage himself from Margery's spell quickly enough.

Carrington sat with many mediums and divided them, by and large, into two main categories—those whose powers he considered doubtful or not proven and those whom he believed to be possessed of genuine supernormal powers. Apart from Margery, he included a large group of seventeen who gathered at Lilydale, a famous "occultist camp" about sixty miles south of Buffalo which he visited in the summer of 1907 on behalf of the American S.P.R. and Dr. Hyslop. He spent two whole weeks in this strange place, run by the National Spiritualist Association—and came to the conclusion that all seventeen were completely fraudulent. They included a spirit photographer, some trumpet and materialization mediums, a gentleman specializing in slate writing who was particularly clever—but whose methods Carrington had no difficulty in detecting. Lilydale must have been quite a place, visited by hundreds of spiritualists every year; the large hotel in the grounds was filled the greater part of the year and the many cottages were rented by mediums of all descriptions, offering everything the true believer's heart could desire—with astrologers, palmists and fortune-tellers also plying their trade.

Carrington admitted that the investigations of the *Scientific American* Committee in connection with the $2,500 prize were hardly more satisfactory than his experiences in Lilydale sixteen years earlier. Apart from Margery the Committee examined the claims of a Mrs. Stewart (who maintained that she could produce coloured writing on cards), of Nino Pecararo who offered "general physical phenomena", Valiantine whose speciality was trumpet voices and several others. Without exception these all failed to produce any phenomena—or produced fake ones. Carrington, by the way, never came across a single case during his long career as an investigator of a "genuine independent voice", that is a spirit voice that was produced without the medium's vocal chords being involved. However, here again Carrington encountered some examples of mixed mediumship. It happened at one of Mrs. Stewart's séances that a "strong smell of incense manifested itself" which all noticed—though there was no incense in the house. Once Carrington demanded that the trumpet should move and touch him in one particular spot—and this happened sometimes, without fumbling, within a very few seconds. On other occasions "supernormal information" was seemingly given by the "voice" which the medium could not have known—although the voice itself was undoubtedly fraudulently produced! Thus again and again he came across the same baffling and exasperating trickery mixed with unexplained and often inexplicable happenings.

He had a brilliant and penetrating ability to discover fraud —and also the method of the swindler. Thus it took him only a few minutes to see through the trick of Armagasilla, the Spanish medium who claimed to read cards clairvoyantly after they had been locked in metal boxes. Only—Armagasilla provided the box himself, refused to use any other nor would he agree to have two padlocks on it instead of one. It was a rather transparent bit of legerdemain with which he held the box securely in his right hand and used his left thumb to force up the long lid at the far end until a small slit was made—an opening between the lid and the box proper. This was quite enough to read the card, especially as he always took the box to the window, with a bright light behind him.

Carrington also sat with the famous Bangs sisters of Chicago in 1909. May and Lizzie practised slate-writing—which he found blatantly fraudulent—and he also analysed their way of producing "spirit paintings" or "portraits". The ladies simply substituted one canvas for another, under cover of their voluminous dress, the table or window-curtains. Yet they had their firm partisans who remained their champions long after their trickery had been exposed; one irate Admiral accused Carrington of never having visited the Bangs house —and then had to retract his charges when the psychical investigator gave a detailed description of the interior and incontrovertible proof of his séance with the two clever and unscrupulous ladies.

Mixed mediumship, too, was Carrington's verdict as to the celebrated Maria Silbert with whom he sat at the British Psychic College in London under the auspices of Hewat McKenzie. He was impressed by the "curious manifestations" which included brilliant flashes of light and a series of touches on one of the controllers while the medium was clearly visible, in fair light, securely held hand and foot. The controller was Dr. Eric Dingwall and Carrington sat on his right. While the distinguished British researcher experienced the touches, Carrington leaned over and scrutinized his left side but saw nothing visible touching his colleague—though he continued to feel the touches throughout this period. The lightning-like flashes appeared to come from the *top* of the cabinet, about three feet above the medium's head. Carrington was not quite happy about Maria Silbert's claims but he did not deny that she might have had some genuine power.

Among the genuine mediums there were only three whom Carrington considered both authentic and remarkable—though there were quite a few others whom he acknowledged as non-fraudulent if not particularly interesting. We have already spoken of Eusapia Paladino. To Carrington she remained the greatest physical medium of all time; the one who convinced him of the reality of the so-called physical phenomena. Of course, as we have seen, he was aware of her mixed mediumship, of her often mischievous or deliberate frauds—but there was more than enough left, in his views, to balance these.

The other medium was Mrs. Leonore E. Piper whose mediumship began in the 1880's when William James saw her and drew the attention of Dr. Hodgson, of the American S.P.R., to her remarkable abilities. During a long career she sat with Sir Oliver Lodge, Dr. Hyslop, Professors Walter Leaf and Henry Sidgwick, F. W. H. Myers and many others. Carrington himself had two sittings with her in January 1908 in Boston. He was introduced to her by G. B. Door and as he was the guest of William James during his stay, he had a chance of discussing the sittings with the eminent psychologist and philosopher every evening. Much of his experiences with her impressed him greatly though he had his doubts. One particular incident, however, he considered especially remarkable:

> The medium was in trance, with her eyes closed; her head was turned to the left and resting upon the pile of cushions, upon the table. While the writing was proceeding. (Mrs. Piper communicated mostly by automatic writing, or rather, her "guides" did.) I extracted a small pair of nail-scissors which had belonged to my mother, and very quietly laid them upon the table (baize-covered) without saying a word. Immediately an attempt was made to draw the scissors, and a little later a clearer attempt, coupled with the words, "Those were mine; I used to use them." (My mother supposedly communicating.) I repeat: had Mrs. Piper been perfectly normal, and had her eyes been open at the time, she could not possibly have seen the scissors in her position, nor could she have heard me place them on the table.

Carrington considered the case of Mrs. Piper one of the most remarkable in the whole history of science. He found it particularly interesting that the messages she delivered were often "intimately connected" in some mysterious manner with those received through other "automatists", mediums using automatic writing. Carrington thought that very detailed analysis was needed to determine whether "the intelligences communicating through these various psychics" were merely portions of their subconscious minds or whether they were really the individuals they claimed to be. He took great pains to marshal all the objections and criticisms of the second possibility. He acknowledged that there was often great similarity between the artificial personalities created by hypnotism etc. and these mediumistic personifications; that many of the "communications" were often wrong or downright lies; that many of them were most uncharacteristic; that their form was often ignorant, pedantic or ungrammatical. There was proof, too, that a large number of these messages had been elaborated by the medium's own sub-conscious mind or that it was obtained by telepathy. There was an *a priori* improbability of these communications as they were so rare; many of them had been obtained by fraudulent means. He dealt with the point of view that physiology and psychology were identical; that the mind depended on the brain which made any talk of spiritistic "communications" nonsense. And finally he put forward the argument that in view of our ignorance of the powers hidden within human beings, it was too early to postulate any "spiritual world"— when the history of science has shown that what was taken for "supernatural" in the past became so often explicable by natural causes and processes.

But, based on his séances with Mrs. Piper and many other voice and automatist mediums, he also elaborated all the positive arguments for the genuineness of these communications—or at least of a significant part of them. Such a process, he explained, must be unavoidably selective with no analogy to experimental thought-transference. It was a peculiar fact that only memories of the dead were tapped in this manner. Nor was there any evidence that such a form of universal telepathy existed; to apply it to all mediums was quite wrong. If these had an easy access to all living memories, why did they make so many mistakes, often show so much confusion? This was inconsistent with "omniscient telepathy". Again, there was a great difference in the clearness of communicators —that is, the alleged entities who spoke through the mediums. Many of these communications were inconsistent and the communicators often changed, yielded to another, either voluntarily or because they seemed "tired" by the ex-hausting process. There was much inconsistency in the assumptions of the telepathic theory; for while some of the messages were disconnected and fragmentary others were relatively easy and flowed smoothly. If selective telepathy was true, why did it not obtain many facts apart from those given? In order to account for many of the "communica-tions" it was necessary to assume clairvoyant, premonitory and other powers in the subconscious mind of the medium— which seemed unsupported by the facts.

Carrington was therefore, on balance, inclined to the non-telepathic, supernormal theory to account for the mediumship of Mrs. Piper and of others. In 1932 and 1933 he conducted two series of instrumental tests of the independence of what is generally known as a "spirit control", both with the distinguished medium, Eileen Garrett. The first took place in March 1932, under the auspices of the New York Section of the American S.P.R. At that time Carrington was still on good terms with the Society, the Margery partisans had not yet gained control of the American Society. By the time the second series was held, in May 1933, Carrington had established his own American Psychical Institute and he used this organization for his experiments. Both sets of tests were, however, conducted under his supervision. Eileen Garrett knew that she was to undergo some tests but was quite unaware as to *what* these tests were to be. The primary object of the experiments was not to secure supernormal information but to study the trance personality alleged to speak through the medium—to ascertain whether the trance control was an independent mental entity, as it claimed to be, or merely a subconscious personification. Eileen Garrett was *not* a physical but a mental medium and this made the task both simpler and less likely to be attacked by anti-spiritualists.

What Carrington did was highly original and ingenious. He used a galvanometer and a list of one hundred so-called "stimulus words" (much as the word-association tests of psychiatry and psychoanalysis). The medium's reactions were tested twice—first when she was in trance and her "control", an Arab called "Uvani" was supposed to take over and again, when she was in her normal condition. The reaction times, reaction words and galvanometer deflections were carefully and systematically noted. More than one list of stimulus words was used, crystal balls, automatic writing, skinspace sensibility, reactions to sound, the effects of a hypnotic mirror and a metronome were all involved in the tests; during the second series Mrs. Garrett's second "control", someone she called "Abdulatif" was also tested—and so were some of the sitters with the same standard list of words and galvanometers.

In an exemplary report, illustrated with graphs,

meticulously worked out mathematical and other tables, Carrington summed up the results—which, to him, were highly interesting—if not entirely conclusive:

> ...The differences between the reactions of the normal Mrs. Garrett and the trance personality "Uvani" will at once be evident. The types of words given as responses, the length of the reaction times and the galvanic deflections were all extraordinarily different. Correlation of the figures thus obtained showed that they differed fundamentally. Generally, when one personality revealed a strong emotional reflex, the other showed little or none, and vice versa. At first sight this would seem to show the complete independence of the two personalities, without further argument being necessary—and it would do so, were it not for one complicating factor! This is, the great differences also shown to exist between the same personality on one occasion and on another, i.e. the differences shown between Mrs. Garrett in one sitting and Mrs. Garrett in a subsequent sitting; and between "Uvani" at one time and "Uvani" at another.

Yet even so, Carrington concluded, the differences in reactions in "Uvani" and Mrs. Garrett were, in most of these tests, far greater than the usual differences between two normal individuals. The tests undertaken were fraud-proof, rendering simulation impossible. The genuineness of the trance was proved. Carrington was not sure, however, whether "Uvani" represented a mere fragment of her subconscious mind or a separate mental entity of some sort, having no seeming connection with any portion of her subconsciousness. Carrington thought that a much longer series of experiments was needed to settle this question. But he was confident that his approach marked a new line of investigation and a novel method of attack upon a most important problem. The results he obtained, he felt, justified the conclusion that no "ordinary subterranean mental bond" existed between Mrs. Garrett's subconsciousness and the "Uvani" personality; for if they had existed, the experiments would have brought them to light. The experiments indicated, *for the first time,* by laboratory methods and by instrumental tests, the mental independence of a so-called "spirit control" separate and apart from the conscious or subconscious mind of the medium.

We have seen the immediate inspiration of the establishment of the American Psychical Institute—the impossibility of working within the framework of the American Society for Psychical Research which, for over ten years, was dominated by Margery and her partisans.

But there was another, equally strong reason for Carrington's move. Ever since he began to work with Dr. Hyslop, he felt the need for some organization that would carry out scientifically orientated, open-minded and objective researches in the vast field. He had helped Dr. Hyslop to establish the American S.P.R. and worked with him, as his assistant, for the first eighteen months of the society's existence. In 1920 Carrington set up his own organization which was (with the single exception of Fritz Grünewald's Berlin institute) the only psychical laboratory at that time. (Harry Price's followed several years later.) This continued for about two years when Carrington had to abandon it, mostly for lack of funds. Two years earlier he had earned his doctorate of philosophy at Penn College, Iowa.

It was early in 1932 that Carrington met his future wife, Marie Sweet Smith to whom he paid such glowing tribute in many of his books and writings and who became one of the secretaries of the Institute. It was she who helped him to lay out the plans of procedure for the creation of the institute and laboratory and start an active campaign. Many American and European scientists were recruited for the Institute's Scientific Council, including such eminent researchers as Professor Max Dessoir, Professor Hans Driesch, Count von Klinckowstroem and Dr. Rudolf Tischner of Germany; the Hon. Everard Feilding, Lord Charles Hope, Dr. L. P. Jacks, Sir Oliver Lodge, Harry Price, Professor F. C. S. Schiller of England, Dr. Pierre Janet, Dr. Eugène Osty, Professor Charles Richet of France, John Hays Hammond jr., Dr. Frederick Peterson, Dr. Walter F. Prince and Dr. R. A. Watters of the United States—not to mention Dutch, Swiss, Czech, Italian, Greek, Austrian, Norwegian and Russian *savants*. Headquarters were established at 20 West 58th Street, New York City where visitors were welcomed. A valuable reference library was donated by Carrington himself, a large number of photographs and articles for a Psychic Museum had been accumulated and the Laboratory was fully equipped. Funds were solicited from patrons, life, founder, sustaining, active and associate members.

An ambitious programme was laid out to investigate such varied problems as magnetometers, apparatus for direct communication, eye machines, human radiations and life, the law of coincidence, psychic lights and various other phenomena. In his book *Laboratory Investigations into Psychic Phenomena* Carrington gave a summary of the work of his Institute from 1932 to 1938, six years of intense activity. Because there was an almost complete lack of physical mediums, Carrington and his associates had to turn their efforts in other directions—largely the investigation of instrumental tests which had been devised in the past—in order to ascertain their validity and authenticity. Their experiments with magnetometers, both exposed and enclosed, showed no evidence to support the theory that these instruments are normally operated by other than natural causes, based on definite physical laws or that there was anything "psychic" associated with the deflection of these needles. Their deflection was due to normal causes, aside from possible cases of genuine telekinetic action.

Carrington also experimented with the so-called "cylinders of Matla", a Dutch spiritualist who conducted a long series of séances over several years and published his findings in five volumes in Dutch, condensed later in a one-volume French edition. Matla and his colleagues constructed a number of pieces of ingenious apparatus to prove instrumental communication between this world and the next. These included large cardboard cylinders, hermetically sealed, but connected by a piece of rubber tubing to a manometer that would show the amount of air displaced in the cylinder. The "communicating entity" was asked to enter the cylinder, thereby displacing a certain amount of contained air whose amount could be measured. The other Matla-apparatus was the dynamistograph, an elaborate piece of apparatus, essentially a delicate balance or key upon which the "Man Force" (as Matla called the alleged spirits) was asked to exercise pressure. Letters of the alphabet appeared in turn at the opening of a circular dial (much as today's Dymo printers) and if the key were depressed at the moment the letter in question appeared, it would be imprinted upon a sort of ticker-tape.

Carrington conducted a great many experiments at the Institute over the period of a whole year. The séance conditions and the instrumental technique varied; the results were interesting for they did obtain "phenomena", some at request, some spontaneously. But when they were carefully checked, it was shown that delicate temperature changes plus coincidence could also account for them, their value was totally negated.

As for the "dynamistograph", Carrington did not attempt to duplicate Matla's instrument exactly but constructed others on the same general principle, only more sensitive. Here, again, the results were inconclusive; the dynamistograph phenomena were due to vibrations, tremors, coincidence—though Carrington did not exclude the possibility of telekinesis when mediums were present. However, he found no evidence whatsoever to support the theory of "instrumental communication". Nor were the thorough tests with the "Will Board of Alrutz" any more successive; Carrington and his associates deduced that any device which can (and will) under normal working conditions give both positive and negative results, during the same observation, is unreliable and unfit for the study of supernormal phenomena—and this fully applied to the "Will Board" which did not register the effects of normal will. The experiments at the Institute disproved the existence of Dr. Russ's "eye-rays"; when there was an apparent needle swing, this was due to optical illusions or after-image effects. It was the same with Rutot's triangles and with research into the behaviour of galvanometers. What Carrington and his team had painstakingly done was to examine a number of claims and disprove them—which did

not mean that he considered this work a waste of time. For as
he summed it up in his *Laboratory Investigations*:

> ...If genuine supernormal phenomena *exist*—as they most
> certainly *do*—then the discovery of their nature and causa-
> tion presents an extraordinarily interesting field for
> intrepid, open-minded investigators of the next generation
> ...It is my belief that the great discoveries of the present
> century will be made in the field of psychical research; and
> in this belief I am by no means alone. With adequate sup-
> port and co-operation such discoveries can be made!

Carrington's long life was crowded with incident and
adventure in the realm of the occult. He recorded some of his
personal experiences in his *Psychic Oddities* which was a
rather light-hearted and informal account of the fantastic and
the bizarre. They ranged from the strange behaviour of an
aluminium plate which acquired mysterious scratchings—as
if made with an etching needle—for which no normal
explanation could be found—to mysterious disappearances of
objects (something that the Germans have dubbed *die Tücke
des Objektes*, the waywardness or wickedness of the object);
from lights, electricity and psychic phenomena to haunted
houses and poltergeists. It was Carrington who unmasked the
Nova Scotia poltergeist in 1907—which turned out to be a
whole small town's conspiracy against an old man who was a
spiritualist and whom they wanted to make ridiculous.
Strangely enough, when Carrington produced incontrovertible proof, old Judge X., the victim of the plot, refused to
accept it.

The Carringtons shared a good many strange, even
ridiculous experiences—though some of them were grim
enough. The eminent researcher recorded the extraordinary
behaviour of a "bewitched potato" whose skin (a small piece,
about half an inch long and a quarter of an inch wide)
acquired an inexplicable life of its own, moving up and down,
curling and uncurling for no possible "natural" reason at all
...not just for minutes but for thirty-six hours—and observed
by several outsiders.

Once, during a lecture, Carrington had to stop suddenly

for he was seized by an extraordinary dizziness—which stopped as soon as he moved to the other side of the table. His wife, who was in the audience, told him later that she distinctly saw a greyish "aura" like a shadow, surrounding him at his original place; it remained there when he moved and it was several seconds before it disintegrated. Was it an "obsessing entity" trying to get possession of him? He had other, strangely occult experiences—as at the time when with a friend he went on a walking tour across the South of England and both were simultaneously filled with the same sensation: that, without any effort, they could leave the ground and float in the air. Nothing of the sort actually happened—but the feeling of physical ecstasy was extraordinary, an experience Carrington never forgot. He himself turned "psychic" at least once when, during a series of E.S.P. experiences, he had a fantastic score of "hits"—having never achieved anything like it either before or after.

We have seen the unusually wide interests of Carrington, ranging from bridge to yoga, from diet to magic. But his main preoccupation always remained psychical research and parapsychology. Within these wide disciplines he joined an apparently never-quenched curiosity to healthy and practical scepticism. Unlike many psychical researchers who love jargon and obfuscation, he wrote always clearly and with conviction. He was a firm believer in the reality of psychic phenomena—though almost at the end of his life he was still seeking a general and acceptable explanation for them and remained a true agnostic.

The last two decades of his life were spent mainly in California. It was here that he revived and expanded his Institute. Henry Gilroy knew him well during these years and has painted an affectionate but balanced picture of his friend:

"I had been an admirer of Hereward Carrington for many years. His book, *The Phenomena for Astral Projection*, which he wrote with S. J. Muldoon, has been most important in the shaping of my own thought. I met him first at a Rosicrucian lecture (it must have been about 1942) and we struck up a conversation, made an appointment to meet the next day and this developed into a friendship, which lasted almost sixteen years. I was executive director of his American Psychical Institute for a period of five years. Being so closely associated with him, made me almost like a son of his—for at that time he had no permanent female companion. He was interested primarily in getting the Institute started in California. As a matter of fact, at that time we did not have the money to hire an expensive attorney to draft the non-profit corporation papers so I got some books and typed out one and fortunately it went through. This was how we got our Foundation going under the laws of the state of California. Many a night I sat with him in his very large office plus apartment, above some stores on North Vine, where he had all his books and paraphernalia. I usually went up there after dinner and we discussed the problems of psychical research throughout the years and spent a good deal of time on Paladino and on Margery, his friendship with Houdini and his long correspondence with Oliver Lodge . . . One thing that is an interesting sidelight on his life and character is the fact (probably known to very few people) that Dr. Carrington was tubercular. He was very self-conscious of his thinness and even in summertime he wore a heavy set of woollen underwear and two vests under his shirt; then he would put on a sweater and a coat. This would make him appear much heavier than he was. He had trouble with tuberculosis all his life. He had a very good appetite yet because of his wasting disease he couldn't put on any weight no matter how much he ate, how hard he tried . . ."

Gilroy confirmed the earlier reports about Paladino—the extraordinary Neapolitan lady's addiction to cheating whenever she could.

"But if you wouldn't permit her to cheat," he added, "then the phenomena would be absolutely fantastic. You know that there would be always a curtain across one corner of the séance room in which Paladino sat, with her on a chair about four or five feet in front of the cabinet and a little table near her. Now they would tie her hands and feet to the chair; each of the investigators would have her under observation all the time. In spite of this, once she had gone into trance, from underneath the table would appear an exquisitely shaped hand, perfect in every detail, ending at the wrist where there would be beautiful lace, Paladino was a very heavy, coarse person. One time Carrington got permission from her to hold this hand; he could feel the bone structure, the firmness of the skin, the warmth of the flesh—it felt just like a human hand. Then he made up his mind that he wouldn't let it go. And suddenly, it was gone, it just wasn't there. Carrington said he'd seen many times these arms that would develop and recede again into the medium's chest area. (Not on this particular occasion when he held on to the hand.) But many times when she would ring bells or perform other tasks, they would see a visible arm and hand emanating from her chest area and, after the phenomena had ended, retract again. And all the time her hands would be tied to the chair ..."

No man in the world, Gilroy added, could tell a story better than Carrington. "And he did not know what it was to lie— he was the most truthful person I have ever met. Together we sat with many mediums, we went to many 'haunted' houses. We sat with Cartheuser whom I thought the biggest fake in the world—but Carrington said that when he sat with him in New York, he did get some really good phenomena which can't be explained. However, every time we had séances with him here in California, ten or twelve times, we never found anything startling or convincing about him. In fact, we caught him cheating, leaving his chair in the dark. He knew I had his number so he didn't particularly care for me. He's dead now. Carrington was more tolerant than I and he just looked the other way and winked, pretending he was taken in. But all the time he was a pretty hard-boiled character whom, I would say, it was almost impossible to deceive for any length of time ..."

One night, Gilroy remembered, he, Carrington, a mutual friend, Hal Styles (now the pastor of the Church of the Good Neighbour in Reseda, near Los Angeles) went down together to Long Beach where a one-armed medium gave sittings. "There were ten or twelve people in the circle—most of them little old widows, living on pensions. I was on one side of the medium and Carrington sat next to me. This fellow was real good; because of the fact that he had no left arm, he was the more impressive. The damned trumpet was going up in the air and coming round the people, touching them—until suddenly I got the medium confused, asking him a question when the spirit was supposed to be talking through the trumpet and the voice came through, proving that it was the medium and not any supernormal entity. Carrington whispered to me to ask the spirit to tell me my mother's name —which I did when the trumpet came round to me. And the voice said: 'I know but I won't tell you!' Carrington was amused and of course, did not endorse the one-armed faker..."

Gilroy also remembered that Carrington was a "half-assed amateur magician"—a pretty bad one but most persistent. "One night we threw a spook-show to raise money for the American Psychical Institute and it was really pathetic . . . He was a great psychical researcher but a godawful magician, fumbling almost every trick he tried. I told him so, too—and he didn't mind. But though he couldn't do the tricks himself, he was very good at teaching others and, of course, detecting when a trick was being employed by a medium."

When I asked Carrington's long-time associate and friend to sum him up, Henry Gilroy said:

"He was a great man. He knew his business far better than most people ever will. What little knowledge I have of psychical research I gained from him—as did thousands of people from his books, his lectures, his painstaking work. In California he did not discover a medium nor did he find a genuine case of haunting—but he went on to the end of his life as a true pioneer and an indefatigable searcher for truth. I was proud to be his friend."

Carrington's reputation has grown rather than diminished in the years since his death. He is still being quoted in new publications, his methods are being copied, his heritage lovingly maintained. He has a secure place in the select band of the explorers of the unknown and occult.

SIR OLIVER LODGE

For those who firmly deny that psychical research and science are compatible, who claim that even the most tentative belief in the supernatural is a disqualifying black mark against any serious scholar, the late Sir Oliver Lodge always represented an uncomfortable and difficult problem. Here was a great scientist, a brilliant expositor of scientific theory and discoveries who had been a pioneer in the development of electricity and radio; the man who had found the method of detecting electric waves by means of the coherer, who pointed the way of creating dust-free spaces, who, by his ignition plug, made the modern motor car viable—and at the same time a spiritualist, a firm believer in survival after death, a deeply religious man who saw no difficulty in reconciling his personal faith with the laws of the physical world he did so much to elucidate. The sceptics believed themselves charitable when they politely ignored this side of the great discoverer; the spiritualists, on the other hand, made the most of such a distinguished supporter—sometimes even too much for Lodge was by no means an uncritical partisan of all spiritualist claims nor a blind dupe of the fake mediums who tried to get his endorsement.

One of the arguments used, although with some hesitation, by the extreme materialists to belittle if not to discredit Sir Oliver's beliefs was to pretend that he did not really become a convert to the acceptance of the supernatural until the death of his beloved son, Raymond, early in the First World War. But this won't hold water—Lodge's interest in psychical research, in occult phenomena goes back much further though certainly his great personal loss must have made his commitment to the spiritualist cause far more profound and enduring. In a way his whole long life was a twin search for tangible truth and intangible verities—and, at least to his own satisfaction, he was convinced that he had achieved a measure of success in both these quests.

Born on June 12th, 1851, near Stoke-on-Trent, Oliver Joseph Lodge came from a long line of clergymen and school-masters. His paternal grandfather was Irish and a parson; he must have been also something of a prodigy for he begat twenty-five children of whom the twenty-third, Oliver's father, married the headmistress of Lucton School. Oliver was the oldest of seven sons of this marriage. Soon after his birth, his father set himself up in business as an agent for the sale of blue clay in the Potteries. With his devoted wife as his book-keeper and with his own great energy and thoroughness he prospered in his business and gradually added to it agencies for other materials used in the district. He hoped that his son would become, in due course, his partner.

Oliver's early schooldays at the Newport Grammar School in Shropshire, an old-fashioned boarding school, were most unhappy. He had no aptitude or interest in the classics; nor did he fare much better at the country rectory in Suffolk where one of his uncles, a former schoolmaster, was the incumbent. His schooling came to an end at fourteen when his father called him home to ease his burdens—and before long Oliver was helping his mother in the office work when he wasn't acting as a traveller for the paternal firm. For seven whole years he laboured dutifully at this, to him totally un-congenial, task. But in the meantime his interest in astronomy and geography developed into a passion for physics and, though his father disapproved strongly, he devoted every moment he could snatch from his daily work to study. It needed extraordinary willpower and concentration to continue. He passed the examinations of the Science and Art Department of South Kensington's Burslem branch with first class honours, studied biology under Huxley and chemistry under Frankland, attended evening classes in mathematics, mechanics and physics at King's College and finally defied his father's insistent plans for him by matriculating at London

University. He was twenty-five when he won his D.Sc. in his chosen subject, electricity.

Sir Oliver's subsequent career, his great scientific achievements, the honours his own country and others bestowed upon him do not concern us directly. But his training, his constantly enquiring mind (he was far more interested in discovering ever-new subjects for research than spending long years on following one particular path to its end), his clarity of logical expression, his ability to apply scientific methods to the apparently paranormal are all essential to evaluate his work in psychical research, his attitude to the problems of occult. You might disagree with him, deny the validity of his claims but you cannot deny his scrupulous honesty, his tolerance and broadmindedness.

His early experiences in psychical research dated back to the middle seventies when he was lecturing on mechanics at the University College, London. There he met Edmund Gurney who had spent several years collecting material for a book called *Phantasms of the Living*. Lodge was not particularly impressed with this "meaningless collection of ghost stories" and considered Gurney's activity a "futile occupation for a cultured man" nor did he accept his new friend's theories, inclined to turn the whole thing down as "a baseless superstition". However, Gurney's energy and seriousness were undeniable and it was through him that he met F. W. H. Myers, who was to become the founder, with Henry Sidgwick, of the Society for Psychical Research. From them Lodge also heard about the experiments which they had initiated with Professor Barrett of Dublin on telepathy. Barrett was much impressed with the results—so much so that he even tried to read a paper before a section of the British Association in Glasgow. It was received with contempt and remained unrecorded in the annual report.

In 1881 Lodge was appointed the first Professor of Physics at Liverpool's newly-established University College—a chair he was to occupy for nineteen years, until he became the first Principal of the University of Birmingham. It was on the Merseyside that the young professor (he was only twenty-nine) became first involved with some experiments in thought-transference (it was Myers who called it telepathy) when, following the visit of a music-hall performer, Irving Bishop, some employees of the drapery store of George Henry Lee & Co. tried to duplicate what appeared to be just a sensational case of "muscle-reading". Two girls in the drapery shop were found to be specially successful; their employer notified the S.P.R. (founded in 1882) who advised him how to conduct them on a more scientific basis. Malcolm Guthrie, the head of the drapery establishment, thought the results so remarkable that he wanted them to be confirmed by a scientific authority. He turned to the new University College; Lodge and his colleague, Dr. Herdman, a biologist, agreed to see the experiments. They took all possible precautions and many varieties of the tests were tried over several weeks. "The result," as Lodge reported some fifty years later in his autobiography, "was gradually to convince me that the faculty of thought-transference . . . was really a faculty possessed by certain people, and that the impression gained was independent of any sense indication." He sent a report to *Nature* and, somewhat to his surprise, saw it actually published. "We, or at least I, gradually came to the conclusion that it was possible for one mind to act on another directly without any physical intermediary of a known or customary kind..."

As a result of these experiments, his acquaintance with Myers and Gurney became more intimate; he paid several visits to the former at Cambridge, attended meetings of the barely established S.P.R. and, in January 1884, became a member. His interest was still largely concentrated on telepathy, as he explained in *Past Years*:

It should be noted that the S.P.R. was not, as most people seem to think, founded in order to establish survival; nor, indeed, had its programme anything specific to do with survival. Its object was to investigate obscure human faculties; and telepathy was the one faculty which it had, so to speak, experimentally established. Myers, indeed, went further, and held that, if mind could act on mind without the use of the bodily organs, the possibility of human survival, likewise without those organs, became increasingly probable. If mind could act without the use of the body, it might be able to survive without the use of the body too.

Lodge himself was not prepared to go that far. In 1884 he published a short paper in the *Proceedings* of the S.P.R., dealing with his Liverpool experiments; the form of these was to ask the "percipients" to reproduce simple diagrams which were completely shielded from them. Lodge recognized from the beginning the importance of statistics in experimental psychical research and the same issue of the *Proceedings* contained a letter of his addressed to Gurney in which he referred to

the valuable suggestion of M. Richet that feeble thought-reading powers or slight mental reverberations may be possibly detected in some persons by applying the laws of probability to a great number of guesses made by them on a limited series of objects.

He added various mathematical formulae which, he suggested, could be conveniently used for this purpose.

Some five years after he joined the S.P.R., Lodge was given the first opportunity to sit with a physical medium—the famous Mrs. Piper. She had been discovered by William James, the Harvard professor of psychology and brother of Henry James, and it was he who wrote to the S.P.R. about her strange powers. Lodge was particularly intrigued by James's account of the Boston sittings. In her trance state, James reported, she appeared to have access to information about the private affairs of people present—but, even more intriguing, she was also in touch with the deceased relatives or friends of her sitters. The first group of phenomena, Lodge thought, might perhaps be accounted for by a "far-stretched kind of telepathy" or by the fact that in the trance state Mrs. Piper "was temporarily dissociated from her body". Though no one, not even James, was prepared to go so far as to endorse the *certainty* of spirit communication. Lodge did consider the possibility that telepathy, which to him had been proved to exist between living people might also have to be stretched "so as to apply to dead people, too. A dead person—that is, one who had lost his material body—need not be debarred from communicating with a sufficiently sensitive living person on that account, if his mind still existed, and if it could act independently, or apart from his old instruments, upon receiving organs belonging to someone else."

The S.P.R. decided to invite Mrs. Piper to England for a series of thorough investigations. She and her two small daughters arrived in November 1889 and as they docked in Liverpool, Lodge was on hand to meet her, putting her up at a hotel until she could travel on to Cambridge where the first series of sittings was to be held. Having received a favourable report from Myers, Lodge himself went to Cambridge and had his first sitting with a trance medium.

> The result was quite astonishing (Lodge recalled in his autobiography) Messages were received from many subordinate people, but the special feature was that my aunt Anne . . . ostensibly took possession of the medium; and in her own energetic manner reminded me of her promise to come back if she could, and spoke a few sentences in her own well-remembered voice. This was an unusual thing to happen, but was very characteristic of her energy and determination. The sitting continued till midnight, a great deal more was said, and Myers and I were both exhausted when it was over.

The problem, as both Myers and Lodge saw it, was to eliminate the possibility of mind-reading—to obtain results through Mrs. Piper which were unknown to anyone present but could be verified afterwards. Lodge decided to invite the medium to his own house in Liverpool. There he had twenty-two sittings with her. These were far more successful than the previous Cambridge or the later London ones—perhaps because Lodge had a superb talent of treating mediums with courtesy and sympathy while never relaxing his rigorous vigilance. In his formal report which he contributed to the *Proceedings* of the S.P.R. he gave an eminently fair summary:

> By introducing anonymous strangers and by catechizing

her myself in various ways, I have satisfied myself that much of the information she possesses in the trance state is not acquired by ordinary commonplace methods, but that she has some unusual means of acquiring information. The facts which she discloses are usually within the knowledge of some person present, though they are often entirely out of his conscious thought at the time. Occasionally facts have been narrated which have only been verified afterwards, and which are in good faith asserted never to have been known . . . Concerning the particular means by which she acquired the different kinds of information, there is no sufficient evidence to make it safe to draw any conclusion. I can only say with certainty that it is by none of the ordinary methods known to Physical Science.

It is interesting to compare this judgment of the remarkable Mrs. Piper with the one Lodge recorded forty years later in *Past Years*:

I got into ostensible touch with old deceased relatives of whose early youth I knew nothing whatever, and was told of incidents which were subsequently verified by their surviving elderly contemporaries. I also investigated many other faculties that she possessed, such as the reading of an unopened letter applied to the top of her head, a phenomenon which had already been testified to by Kant, and Hegel, though by them it was called "reading with the pit of the stomach". At any rate, it was reading without the use of the sense organs, and therefore represented another obscure human faculty commonly called "clairvoyance".

. . . I took every precaution that I could think of; and on the whole the result of the Piper enquiry was conclusive . . . Directly after her visit I went with my wife to Alassio in Italy, at length thoroughly convinced not only of human survival, but of the power to communicate, under certain conditions, with those left behind on the earth.

Thus the Piper séances represented a decisive turning point in Lodge's beliefs and in his attitude to the occult. For him, at least, there was no turning back. Therefore the general argument that he only became convinced and committed after his son's death, cannot hold water.

Naturally, Lodge's report and his endorsement of Mrs. Piper's mediumship caused a great deal of discussion. It was the establishment of a *prima-facie* case for the genuineness of her powers that persuaded Richard Hodgson—whom we met in our previous chapter as Carrington's sponsor—to go to Boston and begin a serious investigation of her. Dr. Hodgson, a graduate of Cambridge, had decided to devote himself to psychical research and was instrumental in founding the American S.P.R. Hodgson employed Pinkertons to shadow Mrs. Piper during the day and report whether she went about making enquiries or did anything suspicious—or occupied herself in the way the sceptics thought she must. (It had been suggested that she got her information through libraries or tombstones and that she used agents for gathering material.) Gradually, Hodgson became satisfied that she did none of these things but led a perfectly normal life of a housewife and mother. He had many séances with her and in time established "friendly relations" with the "ostensible communicators of the other side" who appeared to control Mrs. Piper. He was promised that the conditions of her trances would be improved—for at that time when she went into or came out of her trance, she suffered convulsions that were sometimes extremely distressing to watch. Her chief "control" was supposed to be a dead French doctor or herbalist who called himself "Phinuit".

Hodgson, an extremely sceptical investigator, published a very long report on Mrs. Piper's mediumship in the 1898 *Proceedings* of the S.P.R. in which he supported, quite emphatically, the "spirit hypothesis". Inevitably this led to long and often acrimonious debate in which Lodge could not help taking part; though his interventions were always characterized by restraint and courtesy, markedly different from the violence and scurrilous personalities that marred so many similar discussions.

Richard Hodgson died in 1905. Next year Lodge invited Mrs. Piper for another visit to England. She arrived with her daughters, now grown up and stayed with Lodge and his family at Mariemont, Edgbaston. The character of the mediumship had changed; the new series of communications was now practically all in writing, in the medium's hand. This was, of course, long before tape-recorders and there had often been doubts as to what exactly the "communicators" had said. The written messages eliminated this uncertainty. Lodge prepared another report for the *Proceedings* in which he emphasized that all his previous conclusions were strengthened and verified; to him, the "body of evidence became overwhelming".

Lodge summed up in the *Apologia Pro Vita Mea* chapter of his autobiography what the Boston medium meant to his ideas and convictions about the supernatural:

> ... the revelation ... not only that the personality of certain people could survive, but that they could communicate under certain conditions with us. The proof that they retained their individuality, their memory, and their affection, forced itself upon me, as it had done already upon many others. So my eyes began to open to the fact that there really was a spiritual world, as well as the material world which hitherto had seemed all sufficient, that the things which appealed to the senses were by no means the whole of existence, that the reality of the universe was only dimly apprehended by us, and that our animal senses gave us no clue or indication to the wealth of existence operating in the intangible and the unseen.

According to Lodge's friends, Mrs. Piper was not the only one who made him declare his belief in survival. He also had a series of sittings with Mrs. Thompson, a very remarkable medium who particularly impressed both Myers and Lodge; though few records survive of her phenomena.

It was through Myers that Lodge met Charles Richet and they became close, life-long friends. Both had large families—Lodge, who had married in 1877 Mary Marshall, the only daughter of Captain Alexander Marshall and fathered six sons and six daughters of whom ten survived— and Richet proposed an "interchange of sons". During several years the young Lodges kept on going to Carqueiranne,

Richet's chateau in the South of France or to Paris while Richet's three sons Georges, Charles and Jacques, stayed at the Lodge home, each for the best part of the year. Sir Oliver and his wife also visited Carqueiranne in the summer.

In the summer of 1894 Myers and Lodge spent some weeks at the Isle of Roubaud (or Ribaud), one of the group off Hyères on an "occult holiday". The other guests included the Polish researcher Professor Ochorowicz—and Eusapia Paladino with whom four sittings were held. (We have already referred to them and their criticism by Dr. Hodgson in our previous chapter.) The island was leased by Richet for part of the year; accommodation was rather primitive. Lodge shared a bed with his friend, while Ochorowicz slept in a kind of outhouse and Eusapia was installed in a sort of tower; Myers had a room to himself which was infested with flies and turned into an oven by the evening. In his autobiography Lodge gave a remarkably vivid and amusing description of the idyllic but not entirely undisturbed life on Roubaud with grasshoppers, crickets, hornets, gnats, midges, sudden gusts of wind that could blow the soup in your face, long swims and even longer talks. It was also a miniature Babel; Lodge spoke French but had difficulty in understanding it when it was spoken rapidly; Ochorowicz's French was rather hesitant but at least intelligible; Eusapia, as we know, spoke nothing but a Neapolitan dialect. Still, they seemed to understand one another well enough.

The sittings were "very memorable" as Lodge put it and his first experience of physical phenomena. Like practically everybody who sat with Eusapia, he was quite conscious of the "mixed" character of her mediumship—though he was charitable enough to believe that she only resorted to trickery when her power was failing or was very weak. And she always had the alibi of warning her controllers to hold on tightly to her hands—otherwise some power she could not control would *make* her cheat. "I am willing to give her the benefit of the doubt," Lodge wrote, "so far as the morals of deception are concerned; for she was a kindly soul, with many of the instincts of a peasant and extraordinarily charitable . . . She needed, and indeed demanded, control; she claimed that she would do things normally in trance if she could; it was our business to prevent her—that is, to control her organism so that no normal part of it should be used."

Later, as we have explained in our chapter on Carrington, there was a sharp division of opinion as to the extraordinary Neapolitan lady. Lodge had only one more sitting with her—not a very satisfactory one; his friend Myers distrusted her and so did his wife—though later he seemed to have gradually regained his confidence as to her powers. Richet, while he had just as few illusions about the mixed mediumship, as Lodge, remained her staunch supporter while Richard Hodgson who had come over from America for the Cambridge sittings which Myers organized gave her no credit for any genuine phenomena at all. Lodge did not have a very high opinion of Carrington's American investigations of Paladino, commenting:

I did not take part in any rehabilitation of Eusapia. She went to America, where she was dealt with by novices and her career came to an end . . . Eusapia was not an altogether satisfactory medium, such as William Crookes had had to deal with. She did obtain abnormal effects, and she was willing to submit herself to control. But undoubtedly she would resort to normal means, or what we must necessarily call trickery, if the control was allowed to be ineffective; that is, if she was given an opportunity, she made use of it. But she never made preparations beforehand, nor do I believe that she wanted to deceive. Her power depended on the conditions, and when they were unsatisfactory it was liable to lapse.

This was characteristic judgment; always charitable, always willing to give the benefit of the doubt yet never blindly partisan.

Within the first year of the new century the Society for Psychical Research lost both its first President, Henry Sidgwick and another of his founders, Frederic Myers, who had been Lodge's introducer to occultism. This was an almost crippling blow and it was largely the selfless and prompt action of Lodge that saved the Society from collapse. It was quite a burden he had taken on for it was only a few months earlier that he had accepted the onerous position of Principal of the University of Birmingham—a post he was to fill with great distinction for almost twenty years. It was a striking proof of his deepening and almost overriding interest in psychical research that when he discussed the terms of his new office with Joseph Chamberlain, he made it one of his conditions that he should not be debarred from continuing his work in this field "although I knew it would be unpopular". Chamberlain evidently thought so highly of his chosen candidate for the important job that he accepted this, as well as Lodge's other, quite stringent demands.

Lodge was elected President of the S.P.R. to succeed Henry Sidgwick and was re-elected for the next two years, 1902 and 1903. As the anonymous author of his obituary in the Society's *Proceedings* put it:

> ... the fact that the reins of the Society were during these years in the hands of a man of outstanding distinction in science, combined with Lodge's own personal gifts of tact and geniality, prevailed to set the Society once again on a firm basis, and indeed to strengthen it by the attraction of a large number of members who became actively interested in its work.

Lodge himself set out his own approach and convictions unequivocally in his 1902 Presidential address:

> If any one cares to hear what sort of conviction has been borne in upon my own mind as a scientific man, in some twenty years familiarity with those questions which concern us, I am very willing to reply as frankly as I can. First, then, I am for all present purposes convinced of the persistence of human existence beyond bodily death; and though I am unable to justify that belief in a full and complete manner, yet it is a belief which has been produced by scientific evidence, that is, it is based upon facts and experience, though I might find it impossible to explain categorically how the facts have produced that conviction.

He remained closely linked with the S.P.R. for over forty

years. It was he who delivered the Inaugural Lecture of the Myers Memorial Lectureship in 1929 and three years later he was elected Joint President of Honour with Mrs. Sidgwick on the occasion of the Society's Jubilee. He remained a member of the Council until his death and also served on its Committee of Reference and Publication. Lord Balfour pointed out the important fact that he was the one eminent man of science who "wholeheartedly accepted the evidence for survival and the possibility of communication with the departed". His outstanding gift of exposition which he proved so often in his scientific work was also applied on behalf of his convictions. There is no doubt about it that in a sceptical and thoroughly materialistic age his scientific reputation did suffer because of it—that his scientific achievements were often belittled or ignored because he was stamped as a "rabid spiritualist". But this neither deterred him nor affected his achievements.

Shortly after the death of Myers, Lodge's friend "began to come through". It was in this period that the so-called "cross-correspondences" were developed and in this Lodge took an important part.

Given the acceptance of the genuineness of the mediums like Mrs. Piper or Mrs. Thompson, the opponents of the spiritualist theory, of the possibility of survival after death put forward the explanation that the medium, in a state of trance, must have access to the minds of living people. Lodge and his associates always made an allowance for the possibility of the medium reading the mind of the sitter; but when they obtained information which was unknown to those present, it was still usually *known to somebody* or was recorded somewhere—or it could not be later verified. "It was in order to stem this possible utilization of a hypothetical and unverified faculty of widespread telepathy or clairvoyance," Lodge explained, "that the efforts of the communicators were directed." (By the "communicators" he meant the spirits of the dead using the medium to make themselves heard or felt.) The theory of telepathy, Lodge felt, *had* to be pressed to the uttermost before the face value of the communications from the dead could be admitted as a real explanation—for, if it was once seriously established, a tremendous step would have been taken, the survival of man after death would have been scientifically demonstrated and the power of communication, without any bodily organisms, established with the deceased.

Lodge accepted quite naturally that there was a kind of Society for Psychical Research "on the other side" of which his late friends, Gurney, Myers, Sidgwick and others, were members. And he accepted with equal serenity that his friends were trying to invent devices that would put this over-stretched or extended telepathy out of court as a possible explanation. The first method "they" were using was afterwards called "cross-correspondence". These were communications referring to some theme in an obscure way, given through different mediums and in different forms about the same time so that no single medium should understand the meaning of what was being transmitted; yet the "spirit researchers" added some distinct sign or mark which later could be interpreted as indications that there was a connection between the fragments. When the messages were sent to a central office (the physical, mundane, S.P.R.) and compared, the connection between the different portions should be apparent, the meaning of the whole reference become clear. This elaborate system was used for many years through different and independent mediums who were widely separated geographically. One of them was Mrs. Piper in America, another Mrs. Verrall of England who had developed the power of automatic writing after Myers died; a third, the wife of an officer in India, who was known as "Mrs. Holland". In these "cross-correspondences" Lodge, like many other students of the occult, thought to establish a method offering a promising prospect of excluding the possibility of telepathy between living minds. He hoped it could be proved that one mind was acting on all these mediums; each separate portion of the message was so obscure that there could be no telepathy or any other means of communication between them. The evidence that was gathered was highly complicated and Lodge devoted himself to its study from the very beginning though he could not give it as much time as he would have liked.

J. Arthur Hill who, in 1932, published a volume of his

correspondence with Lodge, covering well over twenty years, patiently ploughed his way through the many volumes of the S.P.R. *Proceedings* which were devoted to these "cross-correspondences". He acknowledged the enormous amount of work and thought that had been put into the preparation of each case but sometimes "got rather impatient with this kind of evidence". He thought there seemed to be too many unknown factors—unknown to the general reader—and therefore the evidence could only be convincing to the investigators. Nor was more than a small part of the total material ever printed and such a selective evidence could be suspect. He wrote to Lodge about it and he replied in a characteristically fair and yet firm manner:

> ...the record of experience is instructive. I admit that this attitude postulates some faith—postulates perhaps a good deal of faith—in the competence of the investigator; but it is the usual attitude to take. I have often noticed that literary people are more sceptical than scientific people are; perhaps in connexion with psychical things quite rightly so; and of course it is entirely necessary that one or two scholars here and there shall take the trouble to go into the matter fully and work out both the strengths and the weaknesses.

> ...However it is extremely interesting to see the sort of impression made upon a perfectly fair-minded critic as to the cogency of these cross-correspondences. I have often said that people would imagine that anything could be made to mean anything, and that the interconnexions were after all only efforts of ingenuity. They are indeed the results of ingenuity; but, as we hold, not of *our* ingenuity; we consider that we are only deciphering what is already there to be deciphered.

Another method of proving the real identity of an alleged communicator which Lodge explored was to show scholarship or a knowledge of literature or of the classics far beyond the normal capacity of the medium through whom these communications came. This is beyond doubt one of the most difficult lines of research to follow. Yet Lodge and his associates often received messages in Greek and Latin. The late Dr. Verrall set his "friends in the flesh" puzzles which could only be solved by a very comprehensive knowledge or by reference to some of his (unpublished) manuscripts. Lord Balfour (formerly Mr. Gerald Balfour) spent a good deal of time working on these ingenious puzzles and he incorporated his findings in two important papers called *The Baptism of Statius* and *The Ear of Dyonysius*. Much of this material was also obtained through cross-correspondences, involving Mrs. Piper and an educated English lady who had no classical knowledge and who was known as "Mrs. Willett".

Lodge was well aware that some, perhaps a good deal of these communications may appear trite, pointless and even petty.

> ...but they are not at all beside the point (he wrote in *Past Years*). The object of the communicator was to establish his own personal identity against all manner of hypotheses that might be suggested as accounting for the communications. No better means could have been devised than those he actually made use of. Myers had devoted his life to the proof of survival, and was now able to clinch that proof in an unmistakable manner. I venture to say that anyone who takes the trouble really to study these things will have no doubt that the ostensible explanation is the true one, and that they demonstrated first the survival of the personality of F. W. H. Myers, and secondly his power of communication through the bodily organism of a living person endowed with the necessary faculty. With Edmund Gurney, also, I held at one time long conversations. The persistence of the mind and memory and character of the deceased individual from whom they purported to come was abundantly demonstrated.

This was as strong and unqualified an expression of a faith in survival as any man could expect; but it did not mean that Lodge had lost his scientific detachment or that he had made spiritualism his religion. To him psychical research was the most important (and perhaps the only possible) way to reconcile science and faith.

The central psychic experience of Lodge's long life came in 1915-1916. It concerned his youngest son—"his beloved Benjamin"—Raymond.

The bare facts of his all-too-short life were reported in *The Times*:

> Second Lieutenant Raymond Lodge . . . was by taste and training an engineer. He volunteered for service in September 1914 and was at once given a commission in the 3rd South Lancashires. After training near Liverpool and Edinburgh, he went to the Front in the early spring of 1915, attached to the 2nd South Lancashire Regiment of the Regular Army, and was soon in the trenches near Ypres and Hooge. His engineering skill was of service in details of trench construction, and later he was attached to a Machine-Gun Section for a time, and had various escapes from shell fire and shrapnel. His Captain having sprained an ankle, he was called back to Company work, and at the time of his death was in command of a Company engaged in some early episode of an attack or attempted advance which was then beginning. He was struck by a fragment of shell in the attack on Hooge Hill on the 14th September 1915, and died in a few hours.
>
> Raymond Lodge had been educated at Bedales School and Birmingham University. He had a great aptitude and love for mechanical engineering, and was soon to have become a partner with his elder brothers, who highly valued his services, and desired his return to assist in the Government work which now occupies their firm.

Sir Oliver claimed that he had been prepared for his son's death by a message which his friend Myers sent him through Mrs. Piper. This was "communicated" by "Richard Hodgson" at a time when a Miss Robbins was having a sitting at Mrs. Piper's house in Greenfield, New Hampshire, on August 8, 1915 and was sent to Lodge by Alta Piper, together with the original transcript.

The strange message began abruptly, as the alleged "Richard Hodgson entity" declared:

"Now Lodge, while we are not here as of old, i.e. not quite, we are here enough to take and give messages. Myers says you take the part of the poet and he will act as Faunus. *Faunus*."

Miss Rogers questioned the "communicator" about *Faunus* and was told, briskly:

"Yes, Myers. *Protect*. He will understand. What have you to say, Lodge? Good work. Ask Verrall, she will also undersand. Arthur says so."

"Arthur" was a reference to the late Dr. Arthur W. Verrall and the entity was obviously advising Lodge to consult his widow, Mrs. Verrall.

Miss Rogers who knew nothing about the Verralls, thought that "Arthur" was a reference to the mention of "poet" in the first part of the message and asked:

"Do you mean Arthur Tennyson?"

"No," the "communicator" replied firmly. "*Myers* knows... So does... You got mixed but Myers is straight about Poet and Faunus."

The "Faunus" episode has been described as one of the most striking single incidents in the whole of Psychical Research. As soon as he received the message from America, Lodge wrote to Mrs. Verrall, asking her whether "The Poet and Faunus" meant anything to her. She replied immediately —this was exactly a week before Raymond's death—saying:

The reference is to Horace's account of his narrow escape from death, from a falling tree, which he ascribes to the intervention of Faunus. Compare Horace's *Odes* II.XIII; II.XVII.27; III.IV.27; III.VIII.8. for references to the subject. The allusion to Faunus is in Ode II.XVIII.27-30:

> Me truncus illapsus cerebro
> Sustulerat, nisi *Faunus* ictum
> Dextra levasset, Mercurialium
> *Custos* virorum.

" 'Faunus, the guardian of poets' ('poets' being the usual interpretation of 'Mercury's men').

The passage is a very well-known one to all readers of Horace, and is perhaps specially familiar from its containing, in the sentence quoted, an unusual grammatical construction. It is likely to occur in a detailed work on Latin Grammar.

The passage has no special associations for me other than as I have described, though it has some interest as forming part of a chronological sequence among the *Odes*, not generally admitted by commentators, but accepted by me. The words quoted are, of course, strictly applicable to the Horatian passage, which they instantly recalled to me.

What Lodge was receiving then, was a kind of "ghostly shorthand". There was to be a heavy blow—but Myers promised to intervene to protect him from its consequences. Myers was "Faunus", Lodge "the poet" and the word "protect" was the operative one in the communication.

The War Office telegram reached the Lodges on September 17. It was not difficult to connect the Myers message and the tragedy—a fallen or falling tree, as Lodge pointed out, was a frequently used symbol of death. Later he consulted several other classical scholars about Faunus and they all referred him to Horace.

Eight days after the arrival of the telegram, Mrs. Lodge was having an anonymous sitting with Mrs. Osborne Leonard, the distinguished medium who was to become associated with Lodge not only throughout the "Raymond" sittings but for the rest of his life. (It was Lodge who introduced her to the S.P.R. for whom Mrs. Leonard provided one of the most rewarding subjects of research.)

At this sitting a message was spelt out by a tilting table, purporting to come from Raymond:

Tell father I have met some friends of his.

When Mrs. Lodge asked whether any name could be given, the "entity" replied: "Yes. Myers."

On September 27, 1915, Lodge had his first sitting with Mrs. Leonard—anonymously, at her house. She told him that her "control" was a young girl called Feda who was supposed to be speaking throughout the séance. "Raymond" told his father that Myers was the first person he saw when he "passed over" and that Myers had practically adopted him—"until, in due time, I too should come over" as Lodge put it in *Past Years*.

The sittings with Mrs. Leonard continued throughout the rest of 1915 and much of 1916. Before the year was out Lodge had published what was to become his most famous book about the occult—*Raymond or Life and Death, With Examples of the Evidence for Survival of Memory and Affection After Death*. He must have written it at extreme speed, under considerable tension—for its four hundred pages included a séance held at the end of March, 1916. Also, having finished the book, Lodge sent five or six copies of the text to various friends, asking for suggestions. As J. Arthur Hill recorded it in *Light*, a quarter-of-a-century later:

> When he received through a medium some statement which he could not immediately verify, he sent me a duplicate of that statement before verification. This would have proved, if necessary, that there had been no trimming of the evidence to fit the facts . . . I confess that my advice was to cut out some of the weaker evidence; and some of the others said the same. But Sir Oliver thought that would be dishonest. "It would make the case look stronger than it is," he said. This shows the downright integrity of the man.

It needed considerable courage to write and publish such a book in which he claimed to prove that Raymond's personality had survived death and that he could *and* did communicate with those he loved on earth. It was a painfully frank, revealing work and it inevitably provoked hostility and even ridicule. In later editions Lodge faced these unflinchingly and answered them to the best of his ability. According to Hill, Sir Oliver felt that it was his duty to write the book and his aim was mainly to comfort the millions who were similarly bereaved during those dark, terrible years.

In his correspondence with Hill, he demanded that when his friend read the proof of the book he should "take the gloves off" in his comments "and find fault as much as you can. Criticism beforehand is all useful." The press reactions, with a few exceptions, were more friendly than might have been expected—though a few were quite savage. The *Liverpool Post*, Lodge thought, was "quite intelligently and obstinately opinionated" and the *Birmingham Post*, "more illiterate than intelligently hostile". Perhaps it was his official connection with the educational system of both cities that caused this hostility. The Aberdeen Public Library banned it "with other books likely to corrupt the morals of the young", as Sir Oliver put it. (The ideas of Library Committees as to the morals and corruptibility of the young have certainly changed in the last half-century.) He was much heartened by a letter of Hill in March 1917 which related how a friend of his, Hill's, had been reading *Raymond* just before he went down with pneumonia. With the book still very much in his mind, he felt that if he died "it would only be promotion" and thus did not worry. He recovered and his doctor said that his tranquillity of mind had saved him. Thus the book was probably the deciding factor in his recovery.

The publication of *Raymond* brought great publicity and an even greater volume of correspondence to Mariemont, Lodge's capacious house. Nea Walker who became his secretary a few weeks after Raymond's death, recalled twenty-five years later the flood of letters that came from sympathizers, opponents and above all, from those who had suffered a similar grievous loss. To them Lodge said: "I am convinced of continued existence on the other side of death as I am of existence here." But while nothing would shake his conviction that he had acquired for himself direct knowledge of his son's survival, he was fully aware that his experience was an entirely personal one which many people could neither share nor believe. In a remarkable passage of *Raymond* he made it unequivocably plain:

Do I recommend all bereaved people to devote the time and attention which I have done to getting communications and recording them? Most certainly I do not. I am a student of the subject, and a student often undertakes detailed labour of a special kind. I recommend people in general to learn and realize that their loved ones are still active and useful and interested and happy—more alive than ever in one sense—and to make up their minds to live a useful life till they rejoin them.

While *Raymond* was a milestone in his spiritual and philosophical development, he did not depend on his own experience in psychical research to formulate and sustain his faith in a future life. His outlook on the universe was far wider. Inter-communication, he warned his readers, was not limited to messages from friends or relatives or to conversations with personalities of one's "own order of magnitude"; it must embrace, he claimed, "the highest of Revelations vouchsafed to humanity". He was both a believer in survival after death and in Christianity. Again, as he put it in *Raymond*:

> Christ was a planetary manifestation of Deity, a revelation to the human race, the highest and simplest it has yet had; a revelation in the only form accessible to man, a revelation in the full-bodied form of humanity.

Lord Rayleigh, the eminent physicist, certainly not a spiritualist, while he believed that Lodge had gone too far in his total endorsement of the supernormal, praised Sir Oliver's "great courage and candour . . . in saying what he thought about psychical matters". Obviously he had a reputation to lose and was prepared to risk losing it for the sake of what he so firmly believed to be the truth.

Raymond contained one particular passage which was much criticized—in which the hereafter was described in a way that was generally regarded as absurd. Others (Lord Rayleigh included) pointed out that many students of the occult agreed: trance utterances, showing supernatural knowledge, were almost always mixed with dreamlike material that came from the medium's mind and that the two were often difficult to tell apart. This seemed to be Lodge's own opinion—though, his critics said, he did not make it sufficiently clear.

The spiritualists, of course, saw no difficulty in all this. To them the *Raymond* case revolutionized their whole movement. Mrs. Leonard's mediumship was a very young one when she began her sittings with members of the Lodge family and then Sir Oliver himself. In August 1916 she was invited by Sir Oliver to stay at his home at Edgbaston and during the week she spent there she came into close contact with Lady Lodge and members of the large family. Raymond, of course was "very much present". According to Mrs. Leonard, he even gave a detailed description of the house Sir Oliver was to acquire in Wiltshire—long before his father had heard anything about it and told him that it was going to be his permanent and final home.

After Lodge's death, Mrs. Leonard wrote:

...Thousands of people must have read his works on the survival of the human mind after death, and especially the book which was inspired by his own personal loss, namely, the death of his son, Raymond...

Sir Oliver did not hug this sorrow to himself; neither did he keep the comfort he and his family derived from their communications with the Spirit World—and particularly with Raymond—to himself. He passed these messages on; he made the fullest use of them for the benefit of all those others who were at the time, and later, undergoing the tragedy of bereavement.

And it was obviously the death of Raymond and the subsequent sittings with Mrs. Leonard and other mediums that made him forsake, for the rest of his long life, the strictly detached, objective attitude of the purely scientific observer. Though some ten years later he was still advocating the continued search for the proofs of immortality by *scientific methods*, he himself had, as he put it, "soared above them in an atmosphere of faith". At least one of his critics (writing in the *Times Literary Supplement*) claimed that the book on Raymond was published against the advice of the S.P.R.— though without presenting proof for this. Certainly there were several of his friends and colleagues who had their reservations, apart from J. Arthur Hill. One, a professor at Birmingham University, was particularly upset by Raymond's revelations about alcohol and tobacco ("whisky and cigars") in the Beyond; others took exception to Raymond's explanation that in the afterlife, which was largely a world of the mind, cravings could be satisfied with the "mental illusion of the realities". Lodge was warned that this passage would certainly make him ridiculous. He replied: "But it is true." His non-spiritualist supporters interpreted this that he accepted the messages from his son as genuine without attempting to explain them.

Professor Cyril Joad, referring to this controversy in his long obituary article on *Lodge* (published in *The New Statesman and Nation* on August 31, 1940) presented a possible, balanced explanation:

> ...believers stress the difficulties of communication. These are so great that communicators are driven to make use of an intermediary on their side just as we have to employ an intermediary, the medium, on ours. Lodge suggested that this intermediary might be a *persona* of the original personality, extruded for the specific purpose of communication, while the spirit himself was attending to other-worldly business; alternatively, it might be an automatic personality such as is produced in hypnosis or under anaesthetics, or even a special class of intermediate creature which acts as a liaison officer between this world and the next. The subject of these spirit "guides" or "controls" is shrouded in confusion, but whatever view we take of the nature of the intervening agent, we may presume that it is of a lower order of intelligence than the mind of the communicating spirit. Now the distorting effect of the intervener on our own side is known to be great. Messages bear upon them all too plainly the imprint of the personality of the medium, his social status, economic position, culture, tastes, partialities, being clearly reflected. Thus spirits in the Summer-land described in Sir Oliver's book *Raymond* are depicted as drinking whiskeys and sodas and playing bridge. There was even a time, when the craze for midget golf was at its height, when ghosts relieved the burden of immortality by the propulsion of midget golf balls. So strong are these indications, that many have been inclined to ascribe the whole content of the messages to emanations

from the unconscious self of the medium. It is not necessary to go all the way with this hypothesis to recognize the
importance of the intervening "medium element" in the
message. Now if there are not one but two interveners, the
risk of distortion is obviously much greater...

Joad was willing to accept that at least some of the messages
from the Beyond could not be explained by the unconscious
self theory. At the same time he thought that Lodge was
"somewhat indiscriminate" in his receptiveness as a psychical
researcher; that he was apt to accept evidence which he certainly would not have admitted in his scientific work. According to Joad it was "surely wrong to encourage people to
believe that what they desire to think true is true, simply
because they desire to think it". But even he did not deny
that a good deal of *Raymond* would pass extremely rigorous
tests by any standards.

Others of the academic world preferred to excuse themselves as being unqualified to judge Lodge's work in psychical
research. Ambrose Fleming thought that Sir Oliver's commitment to survival of some part of the human personality after
death was not the outcome of mere scientific curiosity but a
firm belief in the value of human life and the eternal consequences of human conduct. Above all, Lodge refused to
consider the universe to be the outcome of an automatic
evolution but the creation of a Supreme Intelligence. Sir
William Bragg was even more evasive; while he agreed that
whatever Lodge had to say about life and death was listened
to widely and with rapt attention, he found this side of
Lodge's character something he was unable to discuss.

An anonymous book, published under the pseudonym of
"A Plain Citizen" some months after the first appearance of
Raymond and devoted entirely to an elaboration and critique
of the evidence, summed up the whole case in fifteen points.
The book was obviously written by a "believer" and someone
deeply sympathetic to Sir Oliver who claimed that "plain
men" were of the opinion, the great scientist had succeeded
in establishing certain conclusions:

(1) The existence in this world of invisible, intangible,

intelligent personalities who in some cases assert themselves to be the discarnate spirits of deceased human beings.

(2) The fact of intelligent communication taking place between such personalities and people who are still living.

(3) The probability of some of the personalities, being really what they profess to be, namely survivals after death.

(4) The probability that survival after death is not attended by a translation to any extra-mundane sphere.

(5) The probability that some of the personalities, whether discarnate spirits or other spirits inhabiting space in this world, haunt certain localities and also haunt certain living individuals.

(6) The certainty that human beings exist who are so constituted, physiologically and psychologically, as to be much more sensitive than is the average individual to the presence of spirits and also to be subject to control by spirits to some extent.

(7) The certainty that the Mariemont sittings were of a wholly genuine character and were really attended by some invisible spirits.

(8) The probability that one of the spirits attending the Mariemont sittings was the discarnate soul of Raymond Lodge, who died on September 14th, 1915.

(9) The probability that the release from a bodily environment was accompanied by the setting free of certain mental characteristics which had not made themselves observed during the lifetime of the young man.

(10) The certainty that the sittings with the professional mediums were not of a wholly genuine character, and that many of the communications received at such sittings were not derived from any supernormal source.

(11) The probability that the sittings with Mrs. Leonard, Mr. Peters, Mrs. Clegg and Mrs. Brittain were in part genuine, in the sense that they were attended by spirits, some of which were haunting the mediums while others, including the spirit of Raymond, were haunting the sitters.

(12) The certainty that many of the communications made by the several spirits, including Raymond himself, were untrue.

(13) The probability that the period of time during which the majority of spirits remain disembodied is comparatively short and that reincarnations take place.

(14) The probability that the number of individual souls in the world does not vary from time to time to any much greater extent than does the amount of matter or energy; though considerable differences may occur from time to time in the respective proportions of embodied and disembodied spirits.

(15) The probability that psychical heredity depends largely upon successive reincarnations of the same souls in the same lines of descent.

These are, of course, very sweeping statements and several of them are begging fundamental questions that have been debated for untold centuries. But they show the extensive impression Lodge's publication of *Raymond* made; even today, it is quoted as one of the most striking and challenging episodes in psychical research. And while some of the mediums with whom he was sitting had been accused of fraud while others have been declared as dubious, borderline cases, no one has ever tried to impugn the integrity and "productive efficiency" of Mrs. Leonard who supplied the bulk of the Raymond communications.

Lodge was not insensitive to criticism but very rarely changed his mind because of it. The aftermath of the *Raymond* book was a long one. Less than three years after his son's death, he lost a son-in-law; Lieutenant Langley was killed while flying in May 1918. It had been an ideal marriage and the young widow was left with a baby of only two weeks. But as Lodge wrote to his friend J. Arthur Hill: "she knows ... that he is still with her in a sense, and already he has come through; Raymond brought him very quickly." Apparently the dead flyer sent "excellent messages" at an anonymous sitting which Norah Langley had with a Miss Ortner. "Raymond was on the spot to receive him," Sir Oliver added. It seems that "Raymond" continued to act as a go-between through the rest of his father's life and was particularly active after Lady Lodge died in 1929. Mother and son were very close together and Lodge recorded in a letter of February 1, 1928:

> Raymond says his mother sometimes comes over to him at night, and hopes that some day she will remember, but at present she does not. He also constantly insists that she was with him when he was wounded, but of that she knows nothing. It seems more likely that in a state of semi-consciousness he went to her. But anyhow, she had no intimation, and the blow was unexpected when it arrived...

A year later, after a long illness, Lady Lodge died. She and Sir Oliver had been married for more than half a century and her loss was a grievous blow which he bore with the fortitude of his character. He had an In Memoriam leaflet printed, intended mainly for the family which was growing into a considerable clan. Her death, however, seemed to make his constant search for convincing and prolonged communication with the "other world" even more fervent and; unfortunately, indiscriminating. In July 1929 he had another sitting with Hope of Crewe, the "spirit photographer" whose bare-faced trickery had been exposed by Harry Price and several others. Not to Sir Oliver, however. Writing to J. Arthur Hill, he said:

> The probability to my mind is strongly in favour of simplicity and honesty, now that he has been going on so long. Surely any motive power associated with fraud would have evaporated long ago. The atmosphere of suspicion naturally attaching to all physical demonstrations greatly hampers their rational investigation.

Some seven years earlier, in February 1922, Price caught Hope cheating in a skilful and impudent manner and, in the May 1922 issue of the *Journal of the London S.P.R.* published a report under the title *Cold Light on Spiritualistic Phenomena*, reprinting it later as a separate pamphlet. Hope was defended by Conan Doyle and the Spiritualists; yet Sir Oliver wrote to Price: "I don't see how your proofs of Hope's duplicity could be more complete!" However, seven years later he appeared to have forgotten this view; or perhaps he had modified it, as he saw no theoretical objection to the idea of invisible things being photographed—"for this was already true of some parts of the spectrum". Spirit photography, he thought, was entirely a matter of evidence and if the evidence became strong enough, we might have to believe in it. In 1933 the widow of the proprietor of the British College of Psychic Séance (where Price's séance with Hope took place) admitted in an article that after the sitting her husband went through Hope's luggage and "found in a suitcase a flash lamp with a bulb attached, some cut-out photographic heads and some hairs". These basic facts were suppressed in 1922 and William Hope wasn't "laid low" conclusively until 1944 when Fred Barlow and W. Rampling-Rose proved finally that during the extensive series of experiments they had conducted with Hope all the "spirit extras" they had obtained could have been fraudulently produced.

Lodge was equally complimentary about "Margery". In December 1929, Dr. and Mrs. Crandon visited England. They refused to sit with Harry Price and laughed at the complicated system of electrical control which had been introduced by him at the National Laboratory of Psychical Research. (Margery said, somewhat ambiguously, that "the main aim was to make the phenomena control itself! (*sic*)" Price had to be content to sit with Margery away from his own premises and under quite unsatisfactory conditions of control. They were far more accommodating as far as Sir Oliver was concerned. They travelled to his home where they spent a night. Lodge recorded that they had a "good sitting" and then added:

She is quite a charming woman, and it is really absurd to have any doubts as to their genuineness. We got very good phenomena last night, under test conditions; and they are perfectly fair and above board. My daughter was here, and took control of Mrs. Crandon, and also took Dr. Crandon out of the room while one of the phenomena was repeated ...my chauffeur Walker was there, too, to act as assistant in arranging the room, etc. and putting things right afterwards. It was his first experience, and was very convincing.

I have got two good finger-prints, one of Walter, the other said to be Raymond's, but this has not yet been verified. You may be however quite certain that they are all right.

They were, of course, far from being "all right", as we have seen in our previous chapter. Nor did Sir Oliver refer later to the supposed spirit finger-print of Raymond. We do not know whether he had it checked and if he did, whether it turned out to be also one of the Boston dentist as E. E. Dudley established three years after the Crandons' sitting with Sir Oliver. I have found no reference to this unmasking of the Boston medium in Lodge's later writings; perhaps he preferred to forget them as he did several other mediums whose fraudulent activities were proved after he had in some way or other endorsed them. And of course, these painful experiences did not and need not have shaken his serene and unwavering faith in survival.

In October 1929 Lodge published his *Phantom Walls*, in which he summed up a good deal of his beliefs and dealt with the various objections to spiritualist faith. He thought that even if the Churches were losing their influence, people in general still remained deeply interested in all problems connected with the "reality of a spiritual world". This reality, he argued, was proved both by the beauty of the material world and the law and order that ruled throughout the universe, revealing an overall plan, the domination of one supreme Mind. Survival after death was a logical extension of this. As for the possibility of survival from a scientific point of view, he believed that it depended on its acceptance by men of science whether the attitude of the general public could and would be changed. If the scientists were willing to "face the facts" (for obviously the "spirit communications" and other phenomena were facts to him) even religious people would "without much difficulty adjust their views to the acceptance of phenomena generally agreed upon"—as, indeed, they had already done about the first revolutionary discoveries of astronomers, biologists and geologists. He agreed that trustworthy and crucial evidence was difficult to obtain and that scientists were naturally disinclined to start research without having some assurance in advance that they would not end up in a "quagmire of popular superstition and folk-lore".

He pointed out that animated matter was influenced by something outside or beyond itself, something mankind did not understand yet but called life or mind. And though the materialistic conception of the brain spoke of it as planning and designing a bridge or a cathedral or a work of art, it was obvious that the brain cells were nothing more than instruments "utilized for the demonstration or manifestation of the activity of some unknown mysterious purposeful entity. Mechanism is a reality but it is not all; it needs guidance." And the Universe contains far more than mechanism. Evolution is a genuine process; but there are things which no physical evolution can rationally account for. As for the mechanism of survival, Sir Oliver pointed out that even such an arch-sceptic as Thomas Henry Huxley was prepared to acknowledge: "Science seems to me to teach in the highest and strongest manner the great truth which is embodied in the Christian conception of entire surrender to the will of God." While nobody could deny the problems that the idea of survival raised (even after its acceptance), at least some of these could be solved if all existence was considered to be perpetual. There was a parallel here with energy that continued without loss, changing form but always constant in quantity—thus death was not the characteristic and fundamental thing in the universe, but "continued life". Perhaps, just as there was a constant interchange of energy between ether and matter and energy was never destroyed, it was the same with life. Lodge considered it as a "natural working hypothesis" that the interaction between life and matter was temporary while the interaction of life with the greater physical universe was permanent. In *that* sense, survival was the law to which there need be no exception. But human survival was more than that—individual survival of personality and character. To him the evidence for such survival did not depend on argument but on experience. He argued that there was a growing amount of such evidence—and that it had to be critically examined and if it stood the test, it had to be admitted. All that past arguments had done was to show that there was "nothing irrational in the idea, that we need not turn our backs on the evidence because it appears to be demonstrating something impossible. The thing is possible enough: no one has a right to say that it is impossible. Our business is to find out what is true."

He went on to point out that the frivolous or trivial aspect of some of the evidence did not militate against its genuineness. He reminded his readers that Galvani was jeered at in the early days of electricity because all his experiments showed was the jerking of frogs' legs. Yet it could make lightning flash, too. The principle of gravity, Newton discovered, could be applied to apples and toy bricks—and to the moon and planets as well. And scientists, he claimed, were beginning to accept more and more that their various disciplines were constantly developing and maturing, that like everything else, science was dynamic and not static; and that a new and nascent science like psychical research could not be expected to "attain full dignity all at once". It was the privilege of science to contemplate creation and to work it out; to realize what was happening and to dive down as far as it was possible to the innermost core of the mystery. And while there were many setbacks and dead-ends, overall progress was undeniable. A cautious optimist, a practical idealist, Lodge thought that in our century "we that were walking in darkness have caught a glimpse of a great light". He enumerated the psychic phenomena that needed investigation—the "unconscious reception of information in dreams, whether of past, present or future events"; the possibility of a similar receptive faculty's existence in the waking state; the whole vast subject of trance; the field of cross-correspondence; possession, psycho-physical phenomena, temporary materializations, phantasms and telekinetic cases. To him, work in these investigative directions would not only demonstrate survival once and for all but also have a decisive and revolutionary influence on science, philosophy and religion.

This influence was the subject of a monograph which was based on a lecture he delivered in November 1929 to the members of the London Spiritualist Alliance. Sir Oliver told his audience that he sympathized with, say, a biologist to whom the idea of demonstrated survival was meaningless if not repellent—because he had concentrated a "life interest on the material basis of life". But because facts did not fit in with present theories, scientists must not shut their eyes to them. If survival was a reality and if by actual demonstration, the continued existence of higher or mental attributes proved to be true, then life itself, even of a low grade, could be expected never really to go out of existence—though "it need not have an individual or personal existence except in its higher grades"—and the demonstration of survival, when at length it would be satisfactory and perforce would have to be accepted, must have a potent influence on science.

As for philosophy, no one who seeks to unify the universe in its widest and most comprehensive aspect (as philosophers are supposed to try) can afford not to take survival after death into account when "actually demonstrated". A philosopher, Sir Oliver argued, was someone who took all knowledge under his supervision, if not as an individual, then as a group and no fact could be outside his scope. "He must make sure that it is a fact, and then be thankful that he has found something which has hitherto eluded his system, and which may possibly contain the key to the whole." He maintained that there was much for the philosopher to learn even from existing testimony and that this "education" would be steadily expanded and enriched.

Even more, the influence of the demonstration of the survival of the human spirit, would be immensely important and fruitful for religion. Whereas a theologian may possess a "fully-developed system which satisfies him completely, so that he feels disinclined to welcome any information beyond what he already has attained", an agnostic ought to welcome any further information (provided it is trustworthy) and ameliorate his admitted ignorance by gradual acquisitions of positive knowledge—whatever the consequences. Thus the sceptic should be more open-minded than the fully-satisfied believer. Lodge was perfectly aware that the majority of people belonged to neither extreme; all were doubters to some extent and all had certain aspirations towards something better and higher than themselves; that the appreciation of goodness and of law and order was universal, some form of religion common to all mankind. But if human survival were demonstrated, it would show that life was not limited to its material forms of manifestation, that it was more than a mere function of animated matter and that its explanation was to be sought in a region outside that matter. It would establish the existence of a spiritual world; our "own hopes and aspirations would then be regarded as a faint indication or incipient example of something far more deeply embedded in the nature of things . . . which may lead us in the last resort to surpass our present attainment as far as that surpasses the attainment of the lowest forms of life . . ." The existence of a spiritual world was the preamble of all religions and realization of that existence would be a rational consequence of demonstrated survival.

Sir Oliver Lodge died on August 22, 1940 at Normanton House, where he had lived for many years. He was buried two days later at Wilsford where his wife and other members of his family found their final resting places.

He died on the anniversary day of his long and happy marriage. It was an "easy death", serene and gentle. The year before, on his 88th birthday, he had said: "I feel I have done my work here and can now enjoy leisure and watching others while I am waiting to go on to the next life; where I am confident all our affections and love will be as on this earth, with freedom from material restrictions, and scope to advance from whatever stage in development we have reached here . . ."

In spite of the wartime paper restrictions, practically every newspaper and many magazines carried long obituary notices, paying tribute to a great man with singularly few enemies.

Several years before his death he deposited a sealed envelope with the Society for Psychical Research, containing the text of a message which "he hoped to be able to communicate"— following the example set by Sir William Crookes, his friend Myers and many others.

The envelope, as the press reported at some length, contained several others, each with a different "secret".

(1) Some "childish idiosyncrasy of his, a laughable one".

(2) A formula in higher mathematics with at least one mistake.

(3) The names of two towns and a hamlet which played an important part in his career, unknown to almost anybody now living.

(4) A cryptic quotation from the verses of three of his favourite songs—and how one of these songs also played a curious part in his life.

(5) The name of a cliff near which he had a youthful adventure which, so far as he knew, was unknown to anyone now living.

Sir Oliver gave these clues to a friend of his during a talk at the Athenaeum Club a long time before his death but after he had deposited the sealed envelope at the S.P.R. He was anxious to provide positive proof for survival and he told his companion, a "well-known author of books on mystery and magic":

"I want it to be impossible for sceptics or critics to be able to find any flaws, because there are some people who will refuse even the most irresistible facts. No one in the world but myself knows the wording of the tests."

He added, however, that if the tests failed, it should not be taken as proven that there was *no* survival. His daughter Nora who was with him when he died, told a reporter that the family knew of the test message; Sir Oliver used to speak about it though he had not done so in recent months. Miss Lodge, herself a devoted spiritualist, added: "We shall, of course, faithfully observe his conditions. He certainly will communicate though not immediately and to prove a thing like this will naturally take time."

Harry Price was one of the first to comment; he said he did not think the Lodge test to be "water-tight".

"In my opinion," Price said, "the most likely medium to receive the message is a personal friend of his, through whom he received many messages from his son Raymond killed in the last war." (Price was obviously referring to Mrs. Leonard.) "But every fake medium in the world will pour in claims that Sir Oliver has spoken through them and they know the contents of the envelopes."

The spiritualists countered by saying that Sir Oliver had a sufficient knowledge of his subject to refrain from any attempt at test messages "until he had first made himself master of his new surroundings". They expected many general communications from him before any attempt was made to transmit the critical message. The spiritualists drew a parallel between the use of a new instrument that needed many trials before critical work was undertaken and spirit communications. As *The Two Worlds* put it: "It is one thing to sit in the office and use the telephone. It is quite another thing to build the telephone, establish the lines, set up a generating plant, and be sure that the way is clear, before attempting an important job." Sir Oliver himself attached far more importance to scientific accuracy than on spectacular popularity.

By early September, a fortnight after Lodge's death, more details emerged about the sealed message. It seemed that Sir Oliver wrote one message, sealed it, put the envelope inside a second one, placed that in a third and so on. Each sealed envelope carried a direction that would serve as a reminder.

"Each fresh envelope is to be opened only at intervals," Sir Oliver instructed the S.P.R. "When the right people are sitting with the medium, I shall try to give them a message. But that may take a little time—it may take as long as a year. When the message I have written is received, it will be seen to be a very trivial thing, and people may say it was not worth making a fuss. It is not a simple letter that has merely to be read. It is in one sense somewhat complicated, and in another sense so absurdly childish that I do not expect it to receive attention save possibly from my immediate friends, even if I am able hereafter to indicate its contents..."

There was an added difficulty when Mr. W. H. Salter, secretary of the S.P.R.—which had moved from Blitz-threatened London—said that until the former offices had been visited, nobody could exactly say where the sealed envelope was. Later, however, it was established that it was in a safe place and would remain locked away until the time came for it to be opened by the Council. That step, Salter said, would not be taken until the Society heard from some-

Hereward Carrington

Sir Oliver Lodge

one in whom complete trust could be placed. It was, however, possible, that a member of Sir Oliver's own family would be told what the message was.

More than four months after Lodge's death no message had been received from any medium that could be considered sufficiently important to open the sealed packet. Those that had been received, were filed carefully. More than a dozen mediums in Britain and America claimed to have had spirit communications—but none was serious enough to warrant opening the envelopes. Nor have I found any later indication about the fate of the sealed messages—though in September 1940 hundreds besieged a big spiritualist church in New York where Lodge's "wispy form" was alleged to have floated over the altar, announcing himself as Sir Oliver. The "spirit" even stated that he had decided to "spend a holiday" in America and planned to extend it in order to "convert Joseph Dunninger, president of the Universal Council for Psychic Research", an organization that had offered £2,000 for the sight of a ghost "that can be proved genuine".

Visiting ghosts, sealed messages, arguments between spiritualists and materialists—these are all trivial and ephemeral aspects of Sir Oliver's pioneering work in psychical research. No one could argue with his beliefs because they were his own and he never tried to impose them on others. He was the most tolerant man imaginable. He also lent his great prestige, his superior authority to a subject that few scientists had dared to endorse as openly and as courageously as he did. For this modern psychical research must be deeply and enduringly grateful.

CHARLES RICHET

Lodge and Richet were friends; the tall, slim Englishman found very much a kindred soul in the tall and equally prolific Frenchman. Richet was only a year older and they both had achieved a solid reputation by the time they met in their early forties—Lodge at Liverpool and Richet as professor of physiology at the Sorbonne. And they both shared an abiding interest in psychical research.

Lodge and Richet first met at the house of Myers in Cambridge and took to each other almost at first sight—though their temperaments were very different even if one discounted the national characteristics. Richet, as Lodge recorded, was a great talker and sometimes, at meal-times, his wife often had to call him back to the business in hand which was the Victorian ceremonial duty of carving. He loved to address a large company at table from its head, with his numerous family and his visitors listening to him enraptured. Lodge, too, loved to talk but he preferred the intimate dialogue, the quiet chat; he was certainly a far better listener than his eminent friend. Once when Baron von Schrenck-Notzing joined the Richet household, with Eusapia Paladino and Professor and Mrs. Sidgwick (the founder-president of the S.P.R. and his wife) also present, there was a true Babel around that dinner table. Only Mrs. Sidgwick seemed to have risen to the occasion, talking to most of the company in French, to von Schrenck-Notzing in German, to Eusapia in Italian and to Lodge in English—though even she found the rapid switch from one language to another somewhat trying. Richet's French was the sonorous beautiful tongue of Bossuet and Racine; when he addressed Lodge, he was fairly intelligible but the British scientist was lost when it came to a rapid conversation between native Frenchmen. Still, they did seem to understand each other in most essential things.

We have spoken in our previous chapter about the sittings which Lodge had with Eusapia Paladino on the Ile Roubaud Richet had leased for the whole summer. It was reached by boat from the peninsula de Giens where the salt lagoons were guarded as government monopoly and the peasants were forbidden even to take a bucket of water out of the sea.

Lodge related how Richet used to get up at five or six o'clock in the morning (they shared a big bed upstairs so he couldn't help being an early riser on these occasions himself) in order to go fishing in an open boat. (The only servants on the island were a fisherman and his wife; she acted as cook). Once Lodge accompanied Richet on this early piscatorial expedition but when he found that it was continuing almost till noon, he begged to be put ashore as he was suffering from sea-sickness. Richet, however "did not seem to be troubled by any weaknesses of the flesh". He took no food until the mid-day déjeuner at which he loved to have a lively, give-and-take argument with whoever was able to stand up to him. Lodge couldn't—but only because his French wasn't fluent enough while Richet refused to speak English.

The son of a surgeon and military physician, Charles Richet was born on August 26, 1850 in Paris. His teachers were Claude Bernard, the brilliant French physiologist, pioneer of greatly varied research into the chemical phenomena of digestion, the glycogenic function of the liver and the sympathetic nervous system, and the great Louis Pasteur himself. Richet not only followed in their footsteps but developed into one of the most outstanding natural scientists of his age whose interests were as wide as his knowledge and whose studies were just as creative as thorough. The membership of the prestigious Institut de France and the Nobel Prize were only two of the most signal honours bestowed upon him. Far beyond his physiological research he made outstanding discoveries in various fields of medicine. He had, as Schrenck-Notzing put it, a "voracious appetite for work"; by the time he was sixty, he had published over 250 scientific papers and books and his "creative intellect" dominated

French physiology for many decades.

Richet's most important discovery was the anaphylaxis which Professor Gley, one of his colleagues called "the immortal daughter of his genius". Anaphylaxis is the opposite of vaccination, of immunisation. By injecting various substances (in particular, albumen) into the blood, a certain hyper-sensibility, an extraordinary receptivity for toxic matter is created. The injection of anaphylactic blood into the circulatory system of an animal produces extreme anaphylaxis, a specific supersensitiveness of the smooth or involuntary muscles of the body to the previously introduced protein. Anaphylaxis can also be produced by diet and causes leucocytosis, an increase in the number of leucocytes—white blood-corpuscles—in the blood. The importance of Richet's discovery was strikingly illustrated by the fact that by 1912 no less than eight hundred original works were published in France and other countries dealing with the importance of anaphylaxis for medicine, surgery, forensic medicine and therapy. He was the first to initiate the fight against the fatal disease of leukaemia by showing the process by which its causes operated; and though the fight is far from having been won, without Richet's discoveries not even the proper battlefield could have been established.

Nor were Richet's achievements in experimental pathology and therapy less significant. Together with M. Hanriot he discovered *chloralose*, a powerful analgesic drug which relieved pain efficiently and quickly. He proved the necessity for a saltfree diet in treating epilepsy with bromates; demonstrated the diuretic effect (releasing urine) of substances containing sugar and treated canine tuberculosis successfully by feeding dogs with raw meat. Serotherapy—the curative or preventive treatment of disease by the injection into the body of animal or human serums, containing antibodies to the bacteria or toxins causing disease—which Roux and Behring developed into such an important and effective branch of clinical medicine was based to a considerable extent on Richet's experiments in animal physiology. He was only thirty-eight when, in November 1888, he established that the blood of animals injected with a serum immunized them against infection by the corresponding toxins. And on December 6, 1890, Richet gave the first serotherapeutical injection to a human being.

His neuropathological studies formed an important part of the work in his special field. In 1876 he published his paper about the function of nerves in cases of hysterical hemianaesthesia—the loss of sensibility to touch on one side of the body which usually also connotes the same lack of reaction to pain and temperature. The same year his paper about the condition of sensibility in ataxy cases appeared. Six years later came his researches into muscular stimulation; the biology of pain and the role of nerves in animal and human reaction to it occupied him for many years until his papers on this subject appeared in 1896. No wonder that his colleagues ranked him with Lavoisier, Claude Bernard, Magendie and Marey.

Lodge came to psychical research from the discipline of physics; Richet approached it from the scientific base of physiology and neurology. For neither of them was it an easy decision, a simple transition. As Baron von Schrenck-Notzing put it in his introduction to the German edition of Richet's massive *Outline of Parapsychology and Parapsychophysics* (1924):

When a thinker and researcher of Richet's rank in whom a severe self-critical faculty and great reserve in judgment must be presupposed, if only because of his numerous experimental investigations in the field of exact, acknowledged exploration of nature, not to mention a complete sovereign domination of scientific methodology—if such a man casts his entire authority behind the factuality of so-called occult phenomena, such a positive engagement must be particularly appreciated and valued. But in the case of the eminent physiologist the study of parapsychology does not mean just a hobby, a sideline of his leisure hours, as music may be in the case of a hardworking physician—and as, indeed, many of his opponents have claimed. No, his studies developed from a deep, honest, passionate urge to discover truth, to explore nature. And Richet had the courage to express his thoughts openly, represent them publicly, carry them to their logical extremes—all of which has been, throughout his life, part and parcel of his fundamental character.

In 1840 the Paris Academy of Sciences declared solemnly that animal magnetism did not exist and that any research in this field was a waste of time. Thirty-five years later, while still a student, Richet proved that the observations of ancient physicians were largely correct, that hypnotic or, as it was called by Mesmer and his followers, magnetic conditions were by no means universally fraudulent. His first papers about *somnambulisme provoqué*, as he named it, were published in 1875 in the *Journal de l'Anatomie et Physiologie* and, five years later, in the *Revue philosophique*. In 1881 he contributed to the latter journal a study about the stimulation of muscular reflexes during the first, initial period of the hypnotic state. Richet had few illusions about the hostility the nature of his studies and his conclusions were likely to awaken. The first of his essays began with the statement:

It needs great courage to utter the word somnambulism; the dullard credulity of the masses and the trickery of some charlatans have given this word such an ugly connotation that there are very few among the scientifically trained who do not feel reluctant to approach this subject.

And in his *Thirty Years of Psychical Research* (published in English in 1923) he added:

... The history of the sciences shows that it has often been necessary to return to notions once thought to be puerile. The very existence of hypnotism and of spiritualism shows that mere denials without examination, instead of aiding, tend to fossilize science—routine rather than the desire of progress dominating the minds of those who claim to be scientific.

It was Richet's persistent illumination of the psychic phenomena of hypnotism (or, as he called it, somnambulism) that directed the attention of French medicine to this field and its allied problems. The work of the pioneer Scotsman

James Braid (or Brade) who investigated mesmerism, proving its subjective nature and demonstrating that no magnetic influence passed from operator into subject, had been largely forgotten. So had Liébeault's remarkable achievements (he was able to produce healing effects by hypnotism on children under three years old). Richet gave the impetus to the systematic and open-minded study of hypnotism and helped Charcot, Bernheim, Beaunis and others to develop it during the years 1878-1884 in Paris and Nancy into a legitimate, comprehensive branch of science which today includes regular application in psychiatry, neurology and the treatment of many mental and physical ailments. In a whole series of publications—including *L'homme et l'intelligence* (1884), *Origine du mot magnétisme animal* (1884), *Hypnotisme et contracture* (1883) and *Les mouvements inconscients* (1886) —he gave a thorough presentation of the whole subject and his conclusions were later incorporated in the general and fundamental knowledge we possess about the hypnotic phenomena.

Though all this was at first received with suspicion and considerable animosity, he was soon able to reduce all opposition to at least reluctant acceptance. In 1890 he completed six years of exhaustive and brilliantly organized research with a large-scale work on telepathy and clairvoyance. Once again, as Schrenck-Notzing pointed out, he showed the courage of his convictions in dealing with a subject the representatives of orthodox and exact science had denounced as fakery and objectionable speculation. Once again Richet was proved to be right in his conclusions. To him—as to a growing number of his fellow-researchers—the alleged phenomena of telepathy without the intervention of the "normal" senses could not be denied; there was an overwhelming mass of proof to support their genuineness. Again, "pure" clairvoyance also seemed to occur in many cases. And while today both of these claims are still being assailed, Richet's own experiments and conclusions have never been questioned. Above all, apart from the extremely rich and varied material collected and published by the British Society for Psychical Research (of which we have spoken in the previous chapter) Richet was once again a fearless pioneer in a largely unexplored and highly controversial field. In France he certainly showed the way which methodical exploration of such a difficult subject had to follow, to achieve a fuller understanding of these psychical and mental forces, to establish a fruitful and regular methodology for extra-sensory perception. The results of his own investigations were perhaps less important in this respect than his methods; but he never gave up his patient and tenacious research in this and other, wider fields.

One of his most important works was the 800-page *Thirty Years of Psychical Research* which Schrenck-Notzing sponsored and Rudolf Lambert translated into German while the English edition was the work of Stanley De Brath. (The former was published in 1924, the latter a year earlier.) In this magnum opus Richet made a determined attempt to bring together a number of well-attested cases which he considered sufficient to convince any serious enquirer of the existence of what he called *metapsychics*. He defined it as

a science dealing with mechanical or psychological phenomena due to forces that seem to be intelligent or to unknown powers latent in human intelligence . . . My own experiments and those of others finally led me to a profound conviction that metapsychics is a real science, to be treated like all sciences—laboriously, methodically and with respect.

Even his most determined critics could not deny that this prescription could be fully applied to Richet's own work. Naturally many argued that even this great work could not convince other scientists of the same eminence that there lay under his records a "real science". It was pointed out that a good many books had been compiled before of the same kind, without results. Still, the cumulative effect might achieve in the end something which individual efforts could not.

Richet's work differed from that of many other psychical researchers in his absolute determination to accept no explanation of any of the phenomena whose existence he admitted but an extension of human faculties. In other words, he was *not* a spiritualist, he did not believe in the supernatural or survival after death. He tried to refer every case to what he called *"subjective or objective crypthestesia"*. By the first of these he meant a "hidden sensibility—a perception of things by a mechanism unknown to us, of which we are cognizant only by its effects". Richet found it easier (or at least more scientific) to believe that the power to see or hear what was happening hundreds of miles away was due to some special sensibility rather than to say "transmitted vibrations of human thought". (On the basis of his experiments and of material collected by him, he had no hesitation in admitting the existence of such power.) At the same time he defined this sensibility by saying "that the human mind has means of cognition other than our five senses". Some of his lay critics replied to this that he "simply did not possess *any* explanation of these strange happenings". Certainly, Richet himself admitted candidly enough: "we have as yet no satisfactory hypothesis to put forward." For that matter, no entirely satisfactory hypothesis has been put forward in the fifty years since he published his long and comprehensive book.

We have said before that Richet was no spiritualist. His scientific mind revolted against the whole spiritualist theory though he always did his best to give evidence favourable to it without bias. A believer in the hypothesis that discarnate, disembodied minds affected incarnate, physical minds, still bound to the body, could not share his own beliefs, he thought. "When we devote ourselves to the high task of seeking pure truth," he wrote, "we ought not to be intimidated by the opinion of the crowd, nor allured by any obscure desire for personal immortality." The spiritualists replied that there were many fine and highly-trained minds—among them his close friend, Sir Oliver Lodge—who would never allow considerations of this kind to affect them—and yet were convinced that the spiritualist hypothesis was "the only one at present that would fit the ascertained facts". (Edith Lyttelton.) Richet himself, in trying to state the hypothesis, linked it with what he considered a necessary Spiritualist tenet. The Spiritualists, he argued, believed that the discarnate mind

can manifest itself through certain privileged living

persons, by taking possession of their body (brain, muscles, and nerves); it then writes, sees, thinks and speaks as in the time when it was incarnate in flesh—the minds of the dead know things near and far, past, present, or even future.

By no means all Spiritualists and, in particular, scientists like Lodge or Crookes, would dogmatize on any of these points —many of them would consider Richet's summary of their views as going far beyond what they either claimed or stated. Richet, they said, seemed to imply that the argument rested merely on the supposed supernatural powers of a medium; powers which he said might possibly be within the grasp of a living mind—even if there was no explanation for it. Richet's critics argued that the argument rested upon a much more extended survey of the intricate facts whose implications were not easily accounted for under any theory. Even if the theory that incarnate minds could perform all the "wonderful feats" demonstrated by mediums, could produce phantoms and materializations, could read the past and produce every kind of hidden fact, could foretell the future— even if all this were accepted as within the range of man's unexplored powers, it did not account for the curious evidences of design and co-ordination in the communications of various automatists, entirely independent of each other. (Here the cross-correspondences of Lodge and his associates were being invoked.) Richet himself said: "Everything can be very simply explained if we admit that there is never anything at work but the thoughts of the medium." Perhaps he *was* oversimplifying—certainly it was not easy to postulate that the unconscious minds of several mediums would combine for many years to produce evidence of a survival—which evidence was fraudulent. This was the main argument of the Spiritualists against Richet's theory—and of course, neither he nor they could provide *more* than a theory.

We have spoken repeatedly about the comparatively restricted knowledge we still have of the workings of the human mind. Richet and his colleagues have expanded this knowledge but vast areas still remain unexplored and unexplained. Much has been done to examine, closely, skilfully and tenaciously, the amazing powers of the brain—whether under the influence of drugs or with the conditioning methods of the Pavlovian school. Freud has also shown us what propensities our unconscious possesses for dramatizing memories, desires, urges, hates and loves. But all this does not constitute a refutation of the Spiritualist theories; rather it is a statement, in often attractive and convincing, but by no means conclusive, form, of the materialistic attitude. Those who opposed Richet arrived at a different conclusion; they said that these strange functions of the mind, while they accounted for many inconsistencies and follies, still appeared to be "the instruments used by intelligences outside of them". Richet himself made a suggestion which appeared no less fantastic than that of the acceptance of survival after death:

It is possible, it is even probable, that there may exist in nature other intelligences under other conditions than the physical conditions of terrestrial life; but *they would no longer be human intelligences*. Consequently should they desire to enter into relations with us, they would pity our coarse but inevitable anthropomorphism, and in order to be understood would have to clothe themselves in human names and human sentiment.

This was a prophetic forecast of all the science fiction "aliens", the "extraterrans" which today fill thousands of pages in the works of imagination—coarse or sophisticated, hack-written or of the high standards of Ray Bradbury, Arthur Clarke and their peers. Edith Lyttelton, reviewing Richet's great book, waxed quite indignant over this premature vision of "strangers from space":

Surely, the wildest guesses of spiritualism have never been wilder (she wrote) than this theory of long and elaborate deception by intelligences so well equipped with intimate knowledge of the details of our lives than they can simulate the character, habits and memories of anyone. It is not the existence of these super-terrestrial intelligences which is an absurd hypothesis, but the necessary further one, if facts are to be explained, that they have combined to deceive us into a belief in our survival. Unintentionally the scientist has reinforced rather than refuted the spiritist theory.

Today, almost fifty years after the publication of Richet's work, this seems less evident than it was in 1923. It shows a curious parallel with the political attitude of an absolute and inevitable choice ("if you are not a Communist, you *must* be a Fascist" and vice versa). There have been a good many imaginative writers who did not exclude the possibility of survival after death while accepting the possibility of other, intelligent life-forms. Neither position has been supported by proof and therefore neither can be rejected out of hand until proof to the contrary has been forthcoming.

Richet himself was tied to his belief which he reiterated in his book that "the mind, whether human or animal, can possess the human psychological characteristics of consciousness, memory, sensibility, reason and will, only if the brain exists". This is opposed to the theory that the brain is an instrument of expression, though not by any means the only instrument, used by a being; or, more crudely put, that though we think with our brain, it is not our brain that thinks; that the brain is not identical with the man it serves— just as the unconscious, even in Freudian terms, is not the total personality of the individual. Richet cited "seeing fingers" and "a stomach that can read print" in his book— but these, too, cannot be identified with the complete personality. The mechanism of our bodies, as modern psychology has shown, does not express our whole being. Richet asked: "Will the old man who has fallen into second childhood have the self of his intellectual prime, or the self of his decrepitude? Will the self of a person who stammered continue to stammer in the Beyond?" These are questions that have been asked again and again by those puzzling about survival after death —and, like so many others, can only be answered by private conjecture and personal belief. One of these might be the contention that modern psychology has decisively shown: the mechanism of our bodies cannot express our whole being— the operative parallel being an out-of-tune or worn-out instrument that cannot do full justice to a fine piece of music.

Richet himself condemned the mental technique of looking upon our bodies as instruments for the expression of some being, rather than as the being itself. The opponents of his theories argued that if such a hypothesis (the body being the agent of some outside power or state of consciousness) was correct, then most of Richet's ideas became untenable. Yet Richet himself was frank about his own position:

> I call a halt at the facts and decline to be led beyond them. I do not condemn the spiritist theory. It is certainly premature, and probably erroneous. But it has the immense advantage of having stimulated experiments . . . There are indisputable and verified facts of premonition. Their explanation may or may not come later; meanwhile the facts are there—authenticated and undeniable. *There are premonitions* . . . abundant and formal proof has, I think, been given . . . It has been proved that a whole world of powers, *sometimes accessible*, vibrates around us.

Like so many scientists drawn into the exploration of the unseen and unknown, he felt that he could not discuss the implications of all this; perhaps because he felt that they were too great, too frightening—and incapable of any physical proof.

> We must keep clear of illusions (he added). There are great depths to be sounded. The task is so noble that, even should it fail of success, the honour of having attempted it gives fresh value to life.

In his *Thirty Years of Psychical Research* Richet attempted a comprehensive survey of the hotly contested occult problems while presenting his own richly varied experiences, summing up his metapsychical (parapsychological) life's work. His contribution, at least in his own country and in the languages into which his book was translated, helped to gain recognition of parapsychology as a scientific discipline. Myers and Crookes had done the same pioneering work in Britain while Richet himself was acknowledged as the founder of serious psychical research in France. His friendship with Lodge, with Schrenck-Notzing, with Dr. Ossovietski and other outstanding workers in the same field led to a great deal of cross-fertilization, mutual inspiration and made him an international authority whose influence stretched far beyond his own country.

Richet sat with many mediums and discovered quite a few "sensitives". Of these "Eva C."—or, to use her real name, Marthe Béraud—was probably the most famous. (Schrenck-Notzing repeatedly paid tribute to his friend for introducing him to her; the German psychical researcher later spent four years with the lady and she also sat with several others.) He classified her with those mediums who experienced some strange phenomena quite unexpectedly and "almost in spite of themselves followed the path opened before them". A physical medium of great power and versatility, she became a professional, as D. D. Home and Eusapia Paladino did. She was famous for what Richet called "fluidic emanations". Schrenck-Notzing also obtained excellent telekinetic phenomena in his sittings with her. Richet himself considered her work of the highest importance, presenting numerous facts illustrating the general processes and "supplying metapsychic science with entirely new and unforeseen data".

Marthe Béraud's career began when General and Madame Noel conducted a series of experiments with her in North Africa which lasted nearly two years. The séances were also attended by Captain Démadrille, a naval officer and Dr. Decréquy, a physician. At the end of this period, Richet and Delanne (editor of the *Revue du Spiritisme*) were invited to Algiers by the General. Richet was greatly impressed by the first experiments but as he "always distrusted first impressions" he returned to Algiers to repeat them under stronger control.

Marthe Béraud, whom Richet described as a very intelligent and lively young lady, who "wears her hair short and is a bright-eyed brunette" had been the fiancée of General Noel's son—who died in the Congo before their wedding. She herself was the daughter of an officer and there was no question of her trying to cheat or particularly impress the family of her betrothed. The Algiers experiments were held in a small, isolated building over a stable, with the window blocked up and the only door locked at the beginning of each séance. It was the only room in the building and was minutely inspected each time by Richet and Delanne. Apart from the Noels and the two researchers Marthe Béraud's two younger sisters, Marie and Paule were also present—and so was a Negress, Aisha, who sat with Marthe within the dark cabinet formed by two curtains stretched across one corner of the room. Aisha, by the way, seemed to have been present at Madame Noel's insistence—but the best results were obtained when the Negro servant was absent. Yet she, too, went into a trance and though Marthe did not like her presence (she found "in the tropical heat the odour of the Negress unbearable") in some way she drew strength from the totally passive coloured woman. It was established that "no instrumentation and no theatrical accessories" could be introduced by the medium nor could any stranger enter the room. Later when Areski, an Arab coachman dismissed by the General for theft, "confessed" that he had "played the ghost" and was taken up by an Algiers doctor, Richet angrily refuted the "impudent lie".

The materializations produced were "very complete". As Richet put it:

> The phantom of Bien Boa appeared five or six times under satisfactory conditions in the sense that he could not be Marthe masquerading in a helmet and sheet. Marthe would have had not only to bring, but also to conceal afterwards, the helmet, the sheet and the burnous. Also, Marthe and the phantom were both seen at the same time. To pretend that Bien Boa was a doll is more absurd still; he walked and moved, his eyes could be seen looking round, and when he tried to speak his lips moved.

> He seemed so much alive that, as we could hear his breathing, I took a flask of baryta water to see if his breath would show carbon dioxide. The experiment succeeded. I did not lose sight of the flask from the moment when I put it into the hands of Bien Boa who seemed to float in the air on the left of the curtain at a height greater than Marthe could have been if standing up. While he blew into the tube the

bubbling could be heard and I asked Delanne, "Do you see, Marthe?" He said, "I see Marthe completely." Aisha was far off and could be seen clearly, asleep in the other corner of the cabinet. I could myself see the form of Marthe sitting in her chair, though I could not see her head and her right shoulder . . .

There were other, even more spectacular phenomena of which several photographs were taken. A beautiful fair woman appeared and Richet was allowed to cut off some of her "very fair and very abundant hair". Marthe—or, as she later called herself, Eva C.—continued her séances for several years. Apart from Richet, she sat with Schrenck-Notzing, Dr. Geley, J. Mackwell, Dr. Bourbon and many others. The séances were held in Paris, Biarritz and Munich. Her mediumship seemed to develop and change but its intensity was the same. Richet, in face of some attacks on the authenticity of Marthe's powers, had no hesitation at all to give her repeated and glowing testimonials, though as we have seen he refused to draw any spiritualist conclusions from it. To him the materializations were emanations of the medium's body and mind, similar to the process of giving birth; they proved "metapsychical forces" but not the afterlife. Even to be convinced of such a possibility was not easy for Richet. When he summed up his experiences with ectoplasms, he made it clear enough:

There is ample proof that experimental materialization (ectoplasmic) should take definite rank as a scientific fact. Assuredly we do not understand it. It is very absurd, if a truth can be absurd.

Spiritualists have blamed me for using this word "absurd"; and have not been able to understand that to admit the reality of these phenomena was to me an actual pain; but to ask a physiologist, a physicist, or a chemist to admit that a form that has a circulation of blood, warmth, and muscles, that exhales carbonic acid, has weight, speaks and thinks, can issue from a human body is to ask of him an intellectual effort that is really painful.

Yes, it is absurd; but no matter—it is true.

In a way Richet found himself between two opposing camps —and was assailed by both of them. Like so many men with an open mind, trying to be scrupulously fair to both sides, he got the worst of both worlds. This did not deter him from continuing his experiments and researches.

We have already mentioned his sittings with the extraordinary Eusapia Paladino, with whom Carrington and Lodge had such contradictory and unusual experiences. He cited her as a classic representative of "objective metapsychics" which was material and external, as opposed to subjective metapsychics which he described as internal, psychic and nonmaterial. He ranked her with Eva C., Eglinton, Mrs. Leonard, Stainton Moses and others though he added that if he had to cite only two examples of objective and subjective phenomena he would select her for the first and Mrs. Piper for the second. Certainly he shared the study of the Neapolitan lady with a whole galaxy of scientists, ranging from Schiaparelli to Aksakoff, from Flammarion to Lombroso, apart from those we have already cited. The fact that she fell into trance without being hypnotized set her apart from many others; just as her "control" and "guide" was utterly different from the usual personalities that were such an essential part of all spiritualist activity. He was rather disappointed that Eusapia's "John King" was unable to give him the first name of his, Richet's father—just as another professional medium claimed to give a long, verbose and silly message purporting to come from his mother, ending with a pun on her maiden name. Richet remarked, fairly enough: "I absolutely refuse to imagine that the soul of my mother had nothing to say to me but this idiotic play on words..."

At Ribaud Island where Richet arranged a series of sittings with Eusapia, he designed a square table measuring "one metre each way and one metre high" with pointed legs so that it was difficult if not impossible to raise it with the foot. It weighed forty-four pounds. As soon as Eusapia touched it with the tips of her fingers, it tilted, swaying about and without the legs being touched at all, it rose up completely with all four feet off the ground. Again Richet emphasized: "All hypotheses that attempt to explain this by normal mechanics are absurd." The levitation of the table took place in half-light and Richet and Ochorowicz held Eusapia's hands and head. There were a good many other telekinetic effects. It is interesting to note that Richet came to the same conclusions about the Paladino mediumship as Hereward Carrington and Lodge did though he gave a more detailed psychological explanation of her cheating than the others—an explanation that could be applied to practically all "mixed mediumships":

> Subjective phenomena (he wrote) often occur among persons who do not use their powers as a trade, and therefore it is likely that they do not deceive; but as soon as a medium is sufficiently powerful to obtain movements without contact, he is naturally tempted to make a profession of his mediumship, and then the temptation to fraud is often well-nigh irresistible. This is the more likely because, as has already been explained, the medium in trance is often unable to distinguish between muscular movements and metapsychic phenomena. The mental state is abnormal; and in the course of an experiment mediums lose a part of their moral responsibility, their moral consciousness is attenuated, even when, as in Eusapia's case, their good faith in the normal state is obvious...

He admitted that he himself had been highly sceptical of the Neapolitan medium's powers—until he had his first sittings with her at Milan. But these convinced him—as they had other eminent psychical researchers—that, at least part of the time, she was an extraordinary source of psychic phenomena. This conviction was strengthened during the more than hundred séances in which he participated with her at Milan, Rome, Carqueiranne, Ribaud Island and Paris. Richet was a brilliant analyst of human character, seldom deceived; he recognized Eusapia for a very simple-minded woman though with an undeniable trait of shrewdness, highly intelligent but quite uneducated and illiterate. Her life was far from happy and, being generous by nature, she spent recklessly and gave away much of her earnings so that she died in poverty and neglect. He found her different from other mediums in many respects—for instance in regularly warning her sitters that a phenomenon was coming which was so contrary to the practice of fraudulent mediums or professional magicians; the graduality of her going into trance; the difficulty encountered in hypnotizing her; and the extraordinary energetic movements of her arms, her legs and body which corresponded to the telekinetic movements of objects. He did not minimize the disappointing failures and her transparent attempts at deception—yet, in the final analysis, he gave her a fair and appreciative testimonial:

> ...I have insisted on the phenomena of telekinesis produced by Eusapia because there have perhaps never been so many different, sceptical and scrupulous investigators into the work of any medium or more minute investigations. During twenty years, from 1888 to 1908, she submitted, at the hands of the most skilled European and American experimentalists, to tests of the most rigorous and decisive kind, and during all this time men of science, resolved not to be deceived, have verified that even very large and massive objects were displaced without contact.

He was equally convinced about the genuineness of many of Eusapia's materialization phenomena which he observed frequently and under extremely good conditions. (At one of these his fellow sitter was the great Madame Curie herself.) Eusapia's materializations, Richet added, had been demonstrated not only by photography but also by "metapsychic moulds".

Richet had some sittings with Eglinton (whose most famous séance was with Gladstone) but was not particularly impressed with the medium's slate-writing which he thought a skilful illusionist could have done. On the other hand, he accepted the reports of other researchers which were more favourable to him, both about luminous and materialization phenomena, not to mention levitation "in the presence of the Emperor and the Empress of Russia, the Grand Duke of Oldenburg, the Grand Duke Vladimir, and other members of the Imperial family", no doubt too august to be deceived. Richet had a good many séances with Linda Gazzera, discovered by Dr. E. Imoda of Turin, a "young girl of twenty-two, pleasant, well-educated, lively and gay" at the time Richet met her. She was first investigated by the Italian professor in the house of the Marquise de Ruspoli; during a series of séances she produced many telekinetic and ectoplasmic phenomena. Richet himself sat with her repeatedly during 1905-10. One of the séances was held in Richet's home with the medium's hands and feet firmly held, in complete darkness. The most striking event involved a heavy chest weighing some two hundred pounds which was about ten inches from Linda—it began to oscillate and crack, being displaced so violently that Richet became afraid it would fall and had to stop the experiment. During another séance only Richet, his wife and another lady were present and he held Linda's hands the whole time. (He found her more easily controlled than Eusapia for she scarcely moved at all.) At this particular sitting one of the chairs was taken from Mme Richet's friend and removed to the middle of the room, then given back to her; Richet himself received a flower that he had placed on a shelf as high as the cupboard, barely to be reached by the hand of a tall man. He was also touched from behind the curtain—"though I could not affirm that it was a hand . . ."

Linda's mediumship was characterized by a very rapid production of the phenomena; the light was hardly extinguished when objects were displaced, musical instruments were played and "various white forms appeared". At the same time the sitters felt touches "of a warm, moist, mobile, living member". When she visited Richet in Paris, his colleague G. de Fontenay took some excellent photographs—a hand and a face, "the latter seeming to be that of the face of a 'possessed' man in one of the Rubens's pictures in the Louvre". Richet was positive that Linda, being carefully searched and then re-dressed, her hands constantly held, could not manipulate cards, dolls and drawings quickly and skilfully enough to risk being photographed. More than once, the great physiologist reported, she was searched again as soon as a photograph had been taken and nothing was found. In his preface to Imoda's book on her, Richet pointed out: "The fact that the ectoplasms are not living faces is no objection; for there is nothing to prevent the ectoplasm being an image and not a living being . . . the formation of an image is not less extraordinary than that of a living human head . . ."

The most "decisive" experiment with Linda was held at Richet's house in Paris with de Fontenay, Mme. C. Richet and Argentina, the Italian nurse of one of the small Richet children, in the circle of sitters. (Richet thought that Linda would feel more at home if her own countrywoman were present.) The séance lasted only thirty-five minutes, with de Fontenay and Richet flanking the medium. Both her hands were firmly held and the two men controlled each other repeatedly that they remained so.

Even before she went into trance, there were movements of objects—the musical box started, and in complete darkness, a pipe placed behind Linda was placed in Richet's mouth. A little later, still in total darkness, it was seized and thrown into the middle of the room. Some heavy object dealt strong blows on the back of Richet's hand; some large object struck heavy blows on the table and it also struck de Fontenay. It was on this occasion that a photograph was taken showing a well-materialized hand, with the nails and all the fingers being visible; it was circled by a ribbon of "some kind of stuff" and a thin thread connected it with Linda's head. Richet summed up Linda's mediumship with an enthusiastic endorsement:

> This experiment, together with many more by E. Imoda and the Marquise de Ruspoli, place the reality of the phenomena beyond doubt.

A non-physical medium with whom Richet had a series of experiments used the name of "Stella" (no relation to Harry Price's Stella C.). She took up spiritualism "by chance" when one day, putting her hand on a table or planchette, she obtained some "curious answers".

She gave me striking examples of lucidity (Richet wrote);

I could not, however, decide whether this was telepathic or otherwise.

I made my experiments as strict as possible. In these experiments three persons were present—Stella, myself, and G., a B.Sc. and a skilful physician who had never seen Stella. I myself knew nothing at all of G.'s family. During these experiments not only did G. not touch the table, but he had his back turned to it, said no word, and made no sign. In the eight séances held, Stella gave the first name of G.'s wife, brothers, son, father and father-in-law, names of which both Stella and I were entirely ignorant. Taking a probability of $1:40$ based on there being about 40 usual Christian names of men and the same number for women, the odds against successful results by chance are $(^1/_{40})^6$, that is, 1 to 25,000,000,000, which is moral, if not mathematical certainty.

Richet, however, was fair and scrupulous enough, to warn that the calculus of probabilities had to be handled with caution. There were *some* failures and hesitations. Even so, the compounded probability was about $1:25,000,000$. Some of Stella's failures were instructive in themselves: thus, the name of G.'s child was asked for and she gave "Georgette" which was wrong for the child was a boy, called Jean. Then G. told Richet that had the child been a girl, his wife and he intended to call her Georgette—a fact neither Stella nor Richet could have known. G. asked the name of one of his dead brothers. The answer was "André but he is living." The dead brother's name was *not* André—but there was a living brother by that name. This, Richet thought, was almost more interesting than a success. Stella's mediumship was characterized by the fact that she rarely gave a precise answer to a precise question. Yet the oblique instances of what Richet called "cryptesthesia" appeared to him clear arguments against chance and accident. He related a typical example of this:

I saw Stella on the 2nd of December, during the day, and on leaving I said, "I am going to give a lecture on snake-poison." She at once replied, "I dreamt last night of snakes, or rather of eels." Then, without of course giving any reason, I asked her to tell me her dream, and her exact words were: "It was about eels more than snakes, two eels, for I could see their white shining bellies and their sticky skin; and I said to myself, I do not like these creatures, but it pains me when they are hurt." This dream was strangely conformable to what I had done the day before, December 1st. On that day I had, for the first time in twenty years, experimented with eels. Desiring to draw from them a little blood, I had put two eels on the table and their white, shining, iridescent, viscous bellies had particularly struck me. They had been fixed on the table for the removal of their hearts. I had certainly not spoken of this to Stella, whom I had not seen for some time, and she is not familiar with any one of the persons who frequent my laboratory.

I had not asked her anything about what I had been doing on the previous day, and she had no idea that her dream had any reference to me. She only saw two eels. It is none the less a remarkable instance of crypthesthesia, for her words corresponded so well with the impression strongly made on my mind, that chance can have had nothing to do with the matter.

Stella's trance-personality was called "Louise". At another séance, speaking in the name of this "secondary" ego, Richet was told: "Give Stella the statuette that is in your drawing-room." He had never told Stella that he had such a statuette; however, though it was extremely unlikely, he could not be absolutely certain that he had not done so. "I would not dare to condemn a man to death on such a belief," Richet commented, "and the evidence for a scientific conclusion should be as rigid as for a death-sentence." He did not think that Stella had ever spoken to anyone who knew the Richet drawing-room; and she may have used this phrase by chance. It showed Richet's unyielding opposition to any spiritualist theory when he added: "though all these hypotheses are unlikely, there is one still more unlikely—that an extraneous

intelligence revealed to her the existence of the statuette in
my drawing-room . . ." He was undisturbed by the fact that
so much of the evidence he gathered was trivial and even
childish; for his scientist's training had taught him to accept
even the most insignificant fact as essential to comprehensive
investigation. But, unlike his friend Lodge, he could not
accept the alternative to his own theory of crypthesthesia—
the alternative of survival after death, of "extraneous intelligences", disembodied yet conscious. Even when "pantomnesia"
or "subconscious mentation" could be excluded and chance
eliminated, he rejected the spiritualist possibility. On another
occasion he asked Stella the name of one of the women who
were his nurses. She replied "Melanie". Richet insisted that
he was not thinking of anybody called "Melanie" and that
he was "most positively sure" that the name that had disappeared from his life fifty years earlier and of which he
hadn't thought for fifty years, had never been uttered by
him. "In this case I am obliged to infer a metapsychic phenomenon," he wrote though this acknowledgment was still
within the limits of his non-spiritualist views. Nor did he
believe that the "spirits of the great" could communicate
through Stella or any other medium. In her normal state the
young girl never composed poetry; but in trance she dictated
verses "sometimes of high merit, on a subject given to her and
in a prescribed number of words". This was interesting but
Richet refused to be impressed:

> . . . I may say, without vanity, that I myself, simultaneously,
> by a kind of collaboration with Petrarch who (according to
> the table), was speaking through Stella, was able to com-
> pose four lines on a given subject in a required number of
> words; and this poetry to order was neither better nor
> worse than that of "Petrarch". I prefer to suppose that
> Stella composed unconsciously what I was able to compose
> consciously; at any rate, that it is much simpler than to
> suppose the intervention of Petrarch.

He was quite willing to admit that Stella possessed some
"cryptic sensibility" that enabled her to know or discover
whatever her normal sense could not have told her. And

Richet argued that even if there was no explanation or accounting for this "sensibility", the facts themselves were no less real because they could not be scientifically explained. He rejected chance as the general and exclusive answer. For, as he put it:

If I make an experiment on the atomic weight of silver and get 108.4 I do not attribute the result to chance. Why should I do so when, on asking Stella for the name of Mr. N.'s son, she answers (correctly), "Jean"?

Apart from his massive survey of psychical research, Richet devoted a number of shorter works to telepathy and clair-voyance. His "Experimental Studies" were widely translated —Dr. Schrenck-Notzing published an excellent German version in 1891—and Richet summed up a life-time of experience and experiment in *Notre Sixième Sens* which appeared seven years before his death. At seventy-eight he had no hesitation to declare that while his aim in writing this book was modest, he had no illusions about it being "daring". For he declared firmly and clearly that a sixth sense did exist—a sense of which the organs were still unknown, whose existence was still denied by the majority of the learned and the laymen alike. Its manifestations were both varied and strange; and one which he had established to his own full satisfaction both by observation and experiment.

It seems to me (he wrote in the introduction to his book)... that the reality of a sixth sense (in its vastest and most mysterious connotations) cannot be denied any longer. One might still contest the facts of objective (or mechanical or physical) metapsychics, one cannot any longer question the fundamental fact of subjective (or mental) metapsychics, the perception and reception of notions by our intelligence which are not communicated by the normal senses.

His intention was to turn psychical research and, in particular, mental mediumship into a new branch of physiology, making it as much of an exact science as its raw material permitted. He was still opposing the spiritualist theory but he was going rather further in drawing the conclusions from his researches than he had done before.

Richet's fascinating book began with the definitions of the sixth sense—summing it up as "the mysterious sensibility which, in some fugitive moments, in an imperfect manner, reveals to us a fragment of reality". He spoke of the vibrations surrounding all human beings, some of which could be perceived by our normal senses while others could not, ranging from magnetic to high frequency electric currents, from ultra-violet and infra-red to radiation, from gravity to ultra-sonic. He gave a historical summary of the discoveries of all these forces, provided their definition and terminology, the vast variety of experience and observation that led to their establishment. Then he passed to the long and arduous work that established the reality of the sixth sense. Here he dealt with what he called "hallucinations of reality", especially with premonitions—both of death and other events. The premonitions of death he divided into "isolated" and "collective" examples. Again, he eliminated coincidence as far too unlikely. "It was only once in my life," he stated, "that I dreamt of fire—and it happened that on that very day my wife and my daughter were in grave danger of being burned alive!" And the mathematical calculations of probabilities supported this elimination; accident and coincidence were statistically so small that the evidence of premonitions, of the *hallucinations véridiques* was overwhelming.

He classified the incidents and experiments supporting the reality of the sixth sense, dealing both with his own experiences and with the incidence of telepathy and clairvoyance under hypnosis, with experimental monitions. He described psychometry, the clairvoyant or telepathic research connected with objects, the reproduction of drawings and texts by telepathy and surveyed a number of mental mediums or "sensitives". These included Madame Briffaut, the Polish Jew Bert Reese, the American Madame Piper, the British Mrs. Leonard, the young Dutch student Vandam, the Austrian psycho-graphologist Raphael Schermann (whom we shall meet later), the Polish engineer S. Ossowiectki, the Russian Sophia Alexandrovna, the German Kahn, and the French critic and writer Pascal Forthuny. While he did not claim equal powers or even equal integrity for all these men and women, he was certain that they all possessed a varying measure of paranormal powers or abilities. He examined the phenomena usually related to the sixth sense, detailed what he considered the necessary conditions for properly conducted experiments, went to considerable trouble to refute the main objections while exploring the frequence and rarity of the manifestations of the sixth sense and presented some hypothesis as to its mechanism—varying from telepathy, to pragmatic cryptaesthesia, from a "vibration of reality" to the spiritualist and the hyperaesthesic. He made a determined attempt to classify the "vibrations of reality" which appeared to trigger off the functioning of the sixth sense, the role of symbolism and association and ventured some forecasts as to its future. Then he summed up his general conclusions. He believed that the so-called "veracious hallucinations", that is, impressions received by other means than our existing senses and subsequently proved to be true, offered in themselves sufficient proof for the existence of the sixth sense. The experiences of Mrs. Piper, of Ossowiectki, of Kahn and Pascal Forthuny were, to him, the most striking among those he discussed. To deny its existence, Richet argued, would entail refuting and proving false all these demonstrations of its workings, one by one and in their totality.

The sixth sense (Richet wrote) is far more complex than we have supposed. There are even, perhaps, more than six—there maybe a sixth, a seventh, an eighth sense. The phenomena are of a frightening diversity. How could one put in the same category the case of Madame Wheatcroft who saw, simultaneously with her son, the "phantom" of her husband cross the room; the case of Mrs. Piper who "saw" how Uncle Jerry had nearly drowned some forty years earlier; or Ossowiectki's achievement who read a stanza by Rostand, sealed in an envelope, which no one present knew?

All these "lucidities" are irregular, abnormal, whimsical.

Any collection made of them is bound to be widely different, totally gratuitous; yet they all tend to establish the same fact on an undeniable basis.

We have dared to speak of "vibrations". Certainly this offers a hypothesis; but according to the classic rules of general physics all forces, all the energies of Nature are communicated by vibrations, by waves. In the final analysis the external world is nothing but the totality of actual or past vibrations. Perhaps this term may furnish us with an indication as to the method to use in this field of study. Can we intercept by some screens or metallic cages the transmitted vibrations? It does not seem so. But it must be tried—as Cazzamali did. Is it possible to strengthen and develop the sixth sense by the chemical vibrations acting upon the nervous system? For instance, by peyotl, hashish, opium, alcohol?

How many new problems to study! What is the influence of age, sex, nationality and, above all, heredity upon the sixth sense? All these questions should be the subject of special and detailed monographic studies.

Richet forecast in these few sentences a whole new special branch of physiological and psychological research. Some of his suggestions have been taken up recently by the tests with hallucinogenic drugs while others, especially in the field of hyperaesthesia, still remain to be organized. He was a true pioneer, envisaging more than forty years ago the possible direction of psychical research in a combination with physiology, neurology and other, "exact" sciences rather than a spiritualistic, irrational tendency. He himself preferred his theory of "vibrations" to what he considered the far more fantastic—one that presupposed the human soul, roaming across the universe "where it did not encounter any obstacles to search and find (!) the distant reality and then returning, after such an excursion, to reveal it to our consciousness..."

The sixth sense, he concluded, was the one that led to the cognition of a "vibration of reality"—a vibration which our normal senses cannot perceive. Just as we are constantly bombarded by cosmic rays, by infra-red and ultra-violet rays, by innumerable intangible and invisible waves and particles, which however can be measured and even utilized by the appropriate apparatus, there are other forces, waves, vibrations that are "received" by our sixth sense. This is highly developed in the "sensitives", atrophied or suppressed in the majority of people. That such a sense existed, he did not doubt at all. It presupposed a special sensitivity—or a whole spectrum of "sensibilities" which were still unexplored and mysterious—able to obtain such fragmentary notions of reality which the "normal" senses cannot provide.

To prove his contention, Richet elaborated:

There are multiple and decisive proofs.

(1) First of all, the precognative hallucinations, sufficiently numerous and precise so that it is impossible to ascribe them to accident or coincidence. Myself alone have gathered so many premonitions of death or of less important events that I was forced to the conclusion: a clear link of cause and effect existed. Therefore the naïve hypothesis of coincidence must be rejected even though it is put forward regularly. The "explanations" of the sceptics are much more improbable and complex than the theory of the sixth sense.

On the basis of these observations alone it is possible to say that there are many occasions when an event of the exterior world impinges upon our intelligence without passing through our normal senses.

(2) However, there are better proofs than observations— direct experiences.

The sensitives, if one experiments with them, prove by their clairvoyance, their lucidity, that on many occasions a veil is lifted and that a portion of the truth, inaccessible to the normal sense, reaches them, penetrates to them.

Let us take a very simple comparison.

If one stretches a rope across a road and a cyclist, passing there during the night, is tripped by it, falling at the exact point where the rope is fastened, no one would claim that he has fallen by accident. In the same way I cannot believe that when Mrs. Piper touched an armchair and said: "This was the gift of Aunt Annie" (having never been in that particular house nor known anything about the family) this could not have been an accident. There is no coincidence or accident in all these experiments which have been repeatedly conducted with the great mediums or sensitives.

Richet also denied the possibility of fraud as far as his researches into mental phenomena were concerned. Certainly, if one insisted on extremely severe and exact methods, physical mediumship still demanded further proof and left room for doubt. Ectoplasm, materializations, spirit lights, raps, levitations, spirit finger-prints and footprints, being touched by hands or pseudopods, "walking phantoms"—all these phenomena took place mostly in darkness and could be faked if only one or two dishonest, fraudulent people were present. But with the mental phenomena, with the researches into the sixth sense none of this applied. There were far too numerous subjects, far too frequent experiences. Everything happened in full light. Any control required was accepted and supplied. If there was any trickery, it was very easy to discover and discount it.

Thus, Richet concluded, both fraud and coincidence had to be eliminated—which only left the sole explanation and interpretation of the sixth sense.

Unfortunately, he hastened to add, all this was simply a statement of fact—not an explanation.

To explain this new fact (he added), so unlikely and unfamiliar, all the theories put forward until now are ridiculous and impotent. But whatever these hypotheses are —telepathy, the interference of spirits or the abnormal hyperaesthesia of the normal senses—we must in the final analysis admit the existence of a sixth sense, that is, a communication of knowledge by the impact of unknown forces. We still know very little about the limits, modalities, mechanism, organs of this sixth sense. But however obscure and mysterious, this does not mean that its existence remains unproven.

All science has two phases. The first is the ascertaining of facts. The second is the explicative theory. In this particular subject we are still only at the first stage.

But Richet believed that the day would come when a theory could be not only put forward but become the accepted one as to the laws governing the sixth sense. For his own part, he was content that he had proved its existence— to his own, exacting satisfaction. He summed up his whole work:

The world of reality around us constantly emits vibration. Some of them are perceived by our senses; others, which we cannot perceive sensually, are revealed by our technological apparatus; but there are still others, unperceived either by our senses or by our machinery, which have an impact upon certain human intelligences and which reveal fragments of reality.

And there exist others, just as surely, which neither our senses nor our technological apparatus nor the sixth sense of the sensitives are capable of perceiving and communicating.

The mechanical world which we know, atoms, electrons, stars, planets, animals, microbes, chemical reactions, heat, electricity, may be only a tiny part of reality. Other forces of quite different nature are in constant action around us. Who knows whether these other, non-material worlds do not govern our destinies!

Perhaps we shall never know these forces nor shall our descendants know them. But this is no reason to deny their existence.

To me it seems that the sixth sense is a small (extremely small) window that opens into the world of these mysterious powers.

In these paragraphs—as in others, throughout his voluminous writings—it is the poet and the visionary who speak; both of them were very much part of Charles Richet's complex and many-sided intellect. He was deeply interested in psychical research, in the labyrinth of the occult and this interest was echoed in the fables he loved to write. Some of these were miniature essays in philosophy; others served as polemics to present whatever views he had about a vast variety of subjects; still others were reflections of his time and its problems on polished and artistic form. He wrote a drama called *Circe* and a two-volume novel (translated into a number of languages) entitled *The suffering of others*. It was a novel with a message but with a deeply-felt central theme that preoccupied him again and again. Richet was a practical idealist and much concerned with poverty. Today he would be in the forefront of the ecological fight against pollution and the lunatic waste of our global resources. But in this novel—first serialized in the Brussels *Indépendance Belge*—presented, graphically and dramatically, the problems of world poverty, the needless and heart-breaking suffering of millions, the thousand different forms and causes of want. Then it proceeded, to detail, dramatically and persuasively, a possible solution—the application of capital, abundantly available, in the most effective and equitable manner to eliminate hunger and want. It was, like a good deal of Richet's writing, a practical utopia and in many ways a forerunner of today's visionary yet by no means far-fetched science fiction. The novel, first in its serial and then in its book form, caused a considerable sensation. Above all, it was an impassioned and closely reasoned defence of peace.

Richet was profoundly convinced that war was the most terrible scourge of humanity—a conviction he shared with Flammarion, with Lodge and many other friends and colleagues who also shared his life-long interest in matters psychic. He refused to accept the age-old urge that turned man against man, nation against nation in futile attempts of domination; like Norman Angell, he set out to prove that the victors were losers in equal measure with the vanquished, whatever temporary advantages and glories they gained. He became an early recruit of the international peace movements, the supporter of Bertha Suttner's movement. His great fear was a world conflict and long before 1914 he devoted a great deal of his time and energy to try and prevent one. Thus the eminent physiologist, the most versatile natural scientist who

Raphael Schermann

Charles Richet

Baron von Shrenck-Notzing

was also a poet and a visionary, added cultural history and sociology to his interests. His *The Past of War and the Future of Peace* (which Bertha von Suttner translated into German in 1912) presented his views in a most impressive and convincing series of arguments. Perhaps the most striking sections of this great book were the devastating portraits he painted of the great mass-murderers and conquerors Attila, Alexander the Great and Caesar. But neither did he spare Napoleon whom he described as un unhappy wretch, the scourge of France and of the whole of mankind. Stripping Bonaparte of what he called his "mendacious fame", he showed him as brutal and arrogant, an outrageous liar, an aggressive scoundrel, an unscrupulous adventurer who sowed the seed of hate and despair, made his country the most unpopular in the world and butchered eight million people. Had he lived a few years longer, no doubt he would have found the same characteristics in an even more "productive" warlord, responsible for the death of thirty million human beings, Napoleon's German emulator, Adolf Hitler.

In 1914 Richet visited Berlin and delivered a lecture—as he did in a number of other German cities—stressing the need for a rapprochment between Germany and France, which he thought the only way to prevent a world war. He did not know how close the holocaust was. When war came, he refused to join the chorus of hate which was equally clamorous on both sides of divided Europe; nor did he agree with the harsh provisions of the Treaty of Versailles and the other, rather vindictive treaties that stored up such a frightful desire for *revanche* in Central and Eastern Europe. He worked tirelessly for the creation of an effective instrument of arbitration and international organizations that would be able to prevent conflicts. He was a supporter of the League from its inception though by no means blind to its shortcomings and inherent weaknesses.

It was during the war that he wrote his *General Cultural History of Mankind,* one of the most brilliant surveys of a vast field. While it traced the rise of humanity from primitive barbarism to a more highly organized and promising status, it also set out to show what enormous setbacks war had caused throughout history, what political, social and economic disasters have resulted from the conflicts that were provoked by stupidity and greed. He also dealt at length with the significance of science for cultural progress. The book could not be published during the war but appeared in the early twenties as a courageous testimonial of peace, of international understanding and tolerance. Richet was sufficiently optimistic to believe that science would be able to raise the cultural and material standards globally and would make war impossible. He wrote, of course, before the menace of the atomic and hydrogen bombs cast its shadow over our world though he did hint at the possibility of weapons that would by their very destructiveness act as deterrents. However, he believed that if such weapons of mass destruction were ever invented (and he did not doubt their feasibility) there would be an overwhelming temptation to use them sooner or later. Therefore means had to be found to outlaw them from the beginning. "If the twentieth century does not wish to bring about a general decline," he wrote, "it must surpass its predecessors; but all efforts will be in vain if society does not grant the scientist, as the priest and missionary of truth, the necessary measure of independence, tranquillity and prestige." He did not set the scientist above everyone else, did not believe that a world entirely run by science would be perfect—but he thought that a synthesis between what was to be later called the Two Cultures was perfectly possible and eminently desirable. In his own person he provided a perfect and eloquent example of such a synthesis.

Though his scientific and political activities were immensely varied, Richet remained singularly faithful to his basic ideals. Again and again he set out to prove and to champion the domination of spirit over matter—whether in psychical research (seeking to prove the autonomy of the spiritual in connection with matter in experimental disciplines) or in international affairs where he sought a new spiritual form of life, a new philosophical system that would combat the madness of war, the creeping or erupting menaces to human freedom and the plague of totalitarianism. Whatever he wrote, lectured, examined or advocated was part and parcel of his fundamental *Weltanschauung* which remained remarkably consistent throughout his long life.

This consistency and this harmonious and enduring synthesis made him an archetype of a man in whom spirit and intellect are at peace, whose thoughts and actions are without any dichotomy, whose sense of reality is particularly fruitful. He had little patience with abstract intellectualism or with the irrealities of purely utopian ideologies. One of his most penetrating books was *L'homme stupide* in which he managed to say something new and original about a much-discussed subject. Though he attempted neither definition nor classification, he dealt, tolerantly and wisely, with the stupidities of alcohol, opium and nicotine; with the idiocies of wealth and poverty, of slavery and feudalism. He tackled the fields of war, fashion, semantics, superstitions; passed in a brief review cruelty to animals, the barbarian destruction of works of art, the martyrdom of pioneers, the protective tariff systems, the short-sighted exploitation of the soil (long before the present-day conservationist movement) and many others. He did not claim for his book the status of a scientific study though a great scientist himself; he was content to present some wide and varied thoughts and examples. Several of his chapters had very little to do with stupidity, and stretched the meaning of the world to unnatural lengths to create a tenuous connection between subject and matter—but none of it was unimportant or uninteresting. His whole life, as Schrenck-Notzing pointed out, was a fight against the blind mechanization and urbanization of the world. He emphasized a spirituality that was above and beyond the individual; the need to achieve a higher ideal of culture, to maintain physical well-being and mental health.

To psychical research he gave a prestige and solidity which it needed badly. Many of his colleagues when assailed for "chasing spooks" summoned his example in support and explanation. He was never grudging in his praise of the work of others and always scrupulous in giving credit wherever it was due. I have found no record of any serious dispute with his equals though he was quick to refute any slur on his motives and integrity. He had the universal respect of his fellow-researchers; at one time Harry Price, the British "ghost-hunter" actually thought of transferring his Laboratory from London to the *Institut Métapsychique* in Paris with which Richet was closely connected. The negotiations came to a halt but their failure had nothing to do with Richet's and Price's mutual respect for one another, which endured until the Frenchman's death. Price had met him several times and delivered a lecture under his chairmanship at the Third International Congress of Psychical Research in June 1927. Richet had friendly and, in some cases, very close personal and professional relations with F. W. H. Myers, with Baron von Schrenck-Notzing, with Sir Oliver Lodge, with Sir W. Barrett, with Lombroso and countless others.

As a physiologist and poet, as a psychical researcher and a sociologist, he was a courageous and unflinching seeker of truth, trying to create new and lasting values. He made a decisive contribution in freeing hypnotic and occult phenomena from the limitations of primitive superstition helping them to become acceptable and accessible to serious scientific study. Of the great pioneers he was perhaps the most universal genius.

BARON VON SCHRENCK-NOTZING

When Baron von Schrenck-Notzing, the neurologist, published his *Phenomena of Materializations* before the first
world war, it caused a general uproar in German scientific
and academic circles. His medical colleagues sneered and
scoffed while the general public was fascinated. The scepticism, as Thomas Mann pointed out rightly, was not true
scientific doubt but a rigid rejection of all the experienced
phenomena which Schrenck-Notzing reported with absolute
good faith. It took many years before the general hostility
lessened. World War One with its shattering disasters on the
battlefield, with its millions of casualties was certainly an
important factor. "Human spirit," Mann told an interviewer
in 1923, "seemed to have changed in its very essence and was
more inclined to accept or at least take notice of the mystic,
occult phenomena." When Schrenck-Notzing published the
second edition of his great work at Christmas 1922, the broad
masses approached with an entirely different mental outlook
the mysterious experiences described in it. They no longer
sneered or belittled it; though this did not mean that they
necessarily gained a peaceful and balanced view. It was more
like a new fatalism, a quiet *laisser faire-laisser aller*. Even this
could not represent a final attitude. Between the extreme
explanations a golden mean had to be found. German science
which had represented until the early twenties the stiffest
orthodoxy, was filled to a certain extent by a liberal spirit;
the English and the French went even further. Here the
example of Richet and Flammarion were particularly
important.

Thomas Mann, the future Nobel Prize laureate in literature, was introduced to Baron Schrenck-Notzing by an artist

who had come to draw his caricature. Not long afterwards he was invited to a séance at the Baron's laboratory.

There was a fairly large gathering (Mann related). A Polish painter, myself and men and women of various professions. The medium was a young boy named Willy Schneider who was put in a trance. But first the room, the darkened chamber and cabinet were searched just as diligently and minutely as the medium himself, who was dressed by two of the sitters in a woollen one-piece garment.

The control was also carefully divided; I pressed the knees of the medium between mine while two others held him fast so that he could not move. Music accompanied the séance—rather primitive music. One member of the company, a well-known zoologist whom I would have never suspected of interest in such complex problems, played the mouth-organ and a music-box was also played, repeating the same melody endlessly. We waited for a long time while Dr. Schrenck-Notzing pleaded with Minna—the mysterious entity through whom the medium performed his manifestations—to come forward and give a sign. The music went on. Suddenly a handkerchief lying on the carpet rose, hovered in the air, flew at a sharp angle to the edge of the table and then fell on the ground again. There was half-light in the room; the shining diadem on the medium's head and the luminous bands hanging from his séance garment were the only centres of light.

Then came another phenomenon. There was a bell in the middle of the room which no one could touch—the sitters formed a magnetic circle, holding hands closely—and now it began to move, its clapper vibrated and it began to ring. Wearily, the medium leant his head against mine. Now, in order to make control more complete, those present changed places, there were new groupings; the experiment was repeated in different forms and the telekinetic phenomena followed each other...

Mann's experience was typical of hundreds, even thousands of séances which the eminent neurologist conducted with a number of mediums. He, too, belonged to the select company of pioneers which numbered Lodge, Richet, Flammarion, Crookes—and Mann was quite right when he pointed out that Schrenck-Notzing's position was perhaps even more difficult than that of his colleagues, the scepticism and derision he encountered through so much of his life even more disconcerting and frustrating. Mann himself was probably close to the Baron's own ideas when he set out his own interpretation of what he had witnessed. The eminent author of *Buddenbrocks* told my father in the long conversation they had in April 1923:

"Two-thirds of the people to whom I related all this told me that it must be trickery or hallucination; but I know that the time will come when they'll change their views. I only refer to what a French scientist said about these phenomena: 'I do not maintain categorically that there was no trickery only that the possibility of trickery was excluded.' This is a more honest and correct attitude." And, in answer to a question as to a scientific explanation, Thomas Mann added: "We can only achieve it by trying to get closer to the secret psychophysical emanation of the medium which caused these phenomena. We must first and foremost realize the truth that true science had never lost touch with the occult phenomena. We are faced with cases of materialization—cases in which energy is gathered and organized outside the body of the medium . . . I think humanity must resign itself to the fact that these phenomena can never be examined with the methods of exact science. This seems to be the playful magic of organic life which produces real facts but lures the curious human mind like a will-o'-the-wisp into mysterious distances . . ."

At this point the novelist and the psychical researcher parted company. Perhaps Mann was afraid to become too deeply involved; but his friend, Schrenck-Notzing, had no such inhibitions and his work made him one of the most persistent and outstanding pioneers of occultism.

I met the Baron in 1923 when he came to Hungary to encounter members of the Budapest Metapsychical Society and have some sittings with a strange and controversial Magyar medium, Laszlo Laszlo, who later turned out to be a psychotic criminal and cheat.

My father, as a writer and criminologist, was much interested at that time in the relationship of crime and the occult.
Both William Torday, a retired Hungarian civil servant
who was president of the Hungarian Metapsychical Society
and Laszlo Laszlo came to our apartment fairly often and my
mother gave a dinner in Schrenck-Notzing's honour at which,
a boy of fifteen, I was allowed to be present. I was fascinated
by his calm dignity, his air of authority which, however, was
softened by an unexpected twinkle in his eyes. I thought that
Torday, a deaf and rather fragile gentleman, was fawning
unduly upon him, desperately eager to obtain his endorsement for Laszlo, his pet discovery. He boasted that control at
the séances of his society was so strict that "even Baron von
Schrenck-Notzing . . . admitted that we could not go beyond
it". He also referred to the German psychical researcher's
work when he claimed that the "teleplasm" which Laszlo
produced was "examined microscopically and found to contain the same elements which the Baron had discovered in the
teleplasm obtained by him". He invoked Schrenck-Notzing's
support for his own spiritualist theories.

I wasn't admitted to the séances but my father attended
one; he was much less impressed but was polite enough not
to argue with Torday. A couple of months later the scandal
exploded when Laszlo Laszlo made a detailed confession of
his trickery. It turned out that Schrenck-Notzing's works
provided much of the direct "inspiration" for his cheating
and that he was even impudent enough to use the visiting
celebrity as his unconscious and unwitting accomplice. (This,
of course, was Laszlo's contention.)

"I read Schrenck-Notzing's book about Eusapia Paladino
and the other famous mediums," Laszlo told my father, "their
trances and phenomena. The photographs showed the emergence of teleplasm. I doubted the genuineness of these from
the first moment . . . I decided to show up this Schrenck-
Notzing whom they considered such a great and infallible
man . . . I offered myself as a medium. I went into a 'trance'
and became the bearer of ghostly messages. I knew what I was
expected to say—I learned some passages from Schrenck-
Notzing's book, records of such conversation séances—and

repeated them. Of course I wasn't asleep or in a trance. I just acted it—as if I were in torment, groaning and struggling with spirit forces. This stage lasted about a month. Then the members of the Society asked me whether I could persuade the spirits to materialize through me as they did in the photographs in Schrenck-Notzing's book . . ."

Laszlo Laszlo obliged. His trickery was so successful that he was beginning to receive invitations from Paris and Berlin and Schrenck-Notzing himself agreed to come to Budapest and sit with him. (The real purpose of the Baron's visit was to deliver a lecture on the Schneider brothers but Laszlo's colossal conceit wouldn't admit that.)

What happened, was told in Laszlo's confession though this must be taken with several grains of salt:

One Sunday evening Schrenck-Notzing arrived in Budapest. He was received triumphantly by the Society at the station; I was asked to be present and introduced to him as a "world marvel"; we drove in the same car to the Hotel Gellert. At the hotel where I was employed as a resident electrician, they were a little surprised at my arrival as a "world marvel". I had repaired some faulty fuses in the morning; they say that I am quite good at my work. They could not make out how I could be an electrician in the morning and a super-medium in the evening!

Next day a luncheon was given in Schrenck-Notzing's honour at the same hotel. I was placed next to him. He asked about my work, my education, my past; I sensed that with German thoroughness he wanted to find out my mental and moral abilities. After lunch he retired and we agreed that I would also rest; next evening the experiments were to begin at Mr. Torday's home; a whole series of experiments for Schrenck-Notzing wanted to find out whether I was really a "marvel" or not . . . At seven next evening Schrenck-Notzing and about seventy other people gathered in Torday's flat.

The usual severe control began; it was even stricter than before. All I was given was a wooden stool. I realized that

I couldn't do anything—conditions were too bad. Nor did
I know Schrenck-Notzing. I had no idea how he would
behave during the séance, whether he was a "believer" or
not, whether he moved and fidgeted a lot. I decided to make
the first séance negative and use it to observe Schrenck-
Notzing. But I produced a "spirit voice" for him when I
became "entranced" and greeted him with a little speech:
"Welcome, our brother," I said, "welcome to a man who
serves the truth, a pioneer of science whose reward will not
be on this earth but the heavenly laurels!" Then I started
to moan again and after three or four minutes of this I
declared that the forces of the medium were not sufficient;
it was necessary to wait until the powers developed completely. Perhaps by tomorrow or the day after, we could
see some phenomena.

We broke up then and though the sitting was negative,
Schrenck-Notzing was satisfied. And I had watched him; he
did not move much, he sat close to me . . . I, too, was satisfied
with him. I decided to produce "results" next day. I prepared a head. I folded it up quite tiny and before they
started the examination, I slipped it into Schrenck-Notzing's left pocket. He was sitting near me so that his pocket
was only a couple of inches away. The search was naturally
negative. The trance began. In the red light I reached out
from under the black curtain, and picked Schrenck-
Notzing's pocket. I took the plastic head between my teeth,
I opened it up and when the curtain was drawn aside, the
"horrible ectoplasm" appeared. Schrenck-Notzing even
touched it as I was moaning terribly. He released it at once
and, turning to the others, said: "It's ice-cold. It's a wonderful, genuine materialization . . ."

At the end of the séance Schrenck-Notzing congratulated
me and invited me to Munich; he promised to establish
me as the leading medium of the world. I thanked him.
Next day I produced my teleplasm once again from his
pocket; this time there was a head and a hand. Once again
he was terribly impressed. I think he still wonders how
the grease-spots came to appear on his coat—for I had

soaked my material in goose-grease to make it easier to swallow afterwards . . .

Much of Laszlo's story was probably sheer invention; there is no trace in any record of the German psychical researcher inviting him to his laboratory or promising to work with him. Several months after Laszlo's unmasking and vainglorious confession, Schrenck-Notzing published a pamphlet about him which showed how balanced and sensible his judgment had been from the beginning:

This fraudulent medium (he wrote) used various methods and as a practised magician he loved to surprise. He was skilful in adjusting himself to any given situation and his audacity often involved him in the danger of exposure . . . While in the alcove, Laszlo could only cheat if his hand was somehow free. I immediately noticed the faulty control whenever the curtain was closed which always happened at his request, his hand was from time to time released so that he had a chance to get out the objects he had prepared or to hide them again. If he had been seated outside the alcove or if his hands and feet would have been held from the beginning of the séance, no frauds of such magnitude could have occurred. He could never have worked them with his mouth and tongue alone. At the end of the sitting he often threw the tiny parcel under the desk or some other piece of furniture only to collect it later. This was possible because the séance room was overcrowded with furniture.

The motives for the systematic fraud carried on for more than a year can be largely found in Laszlo's psychology. His psyche was not such an obedient, blind instrument as it was believed at first. Laszlo is a born psychopath, with a certain moral apathy, unreliable, egotistic, vain, mendacious, always in financial difficulties, easily yielding to bad influences, ready to rob others of any credit he could claim for himself, scribbling pathetic letters in a fantastic style, crammed with polysyllabic words to his numerous "fiancées". Passionate in dreaming about wealth, unscrupulous in his ways and means. Now he glories in the role of a hero unmasking the spiritualists, explaining the materializations phenomena, running to newspapers and making largely lying and contradictory confessions.

Some severe critics said that this was a classic case of hindsight. But Schrenck-Notzing had warned Torday *before* Laszlo's exposure about his doubts in a letter which the President of the Hungarian Metapsychical Society ignored and suppressed. "As for the Laszlo-experiments," Schrenck-Notzing wrote, "I must accept unreservedly your methodical procedure, your scientific earnestness and unselfishness. But I definitely advise you against publication in the near future —the results are not sufficiently mature for this and certain details are obscure . . . The experiments are not convincing enough and show definite contradictions to other experiences . . ."

He could not be more explicit for, after all, he had no proof of Laszlo's deception apart from his own views and observations. And Torday rushed into publication which, in turn, led to disastrous consequences, the splitting of the entire Hungarian Metapsychical Society and the discrediting of psychical research in the country. All this could have been avoided if he had followed Schrenck-Notzing's wise advice— for nobody could accuse the Baron of not being circumspect and thorough in *his* own methods and in publicizing his results.

We have encountered Schrenck-Notzing in every previous chapter of this book—he was one of the sitters of Paladino, a colleague and fairly frequent collaborator of Lodge and an even closer friend, translator and supporter of Richet. He also knew Lombroso well. A physician and psychologist, he married a rich lady (her family was linked to the giant I. G. Farben enterprises) and this enabled him to devote most of his time to psychical research—unlike his friends, Lodge and Richet, who had another, practically full-time scientific and academic career to follow but rather like Carrington and Harry Price. But neither of these two had the means and facilities which the Baron possessed. Neither of them could boast of such a handsome palace as the Schrenck-Notzing home near the Karolinenplatz in Munich, built for him by the famous Bavarian architect Gabriel von Seidl which also housed his library and laboratory. A tall, handsome and impressive-looking man, he was a fit tenant for such an aristocratic home and his wife Gabriele (daughter of the Wurttemberg industrialist and member of the Reichstag, Gustav Siegle) who survived him by twenty-four years gave an added charm and dignity to No. 3 Max-Josef-Strasse.

Schrenck-Notzing spent almost forty years in psychical research, investigated countless mediums, published a large number of books, edited a series of reviews and reports and travelled widely in search of psychic phenomena. He distilled his life's work into the huge volume entitled *Materializations Phenomena*, first published in 1914 and issued in a second, considerably enlarged edition in 1922. In over six hundred pages he offered a contribution to the "mediumistic teleplasty" as he called it. It remains a standard work as far as methodology, scientific discipline and the exploration of physical mediumship are concerned—and with the dearth if not total disappearance of physical mediums it may well be the classic cornerstone of twentieth century psychical research. It covered the period of 1909-21. The mediums involved were Eva C. (the name Schrenck-Notzing gave to Richet's Marthe Béraud), Stanislawa P., the young Polish girl, Willy Schneider of Braunau, Austria, Frau Marie Silbert of Graz, Einer Nielse of Copenhagen, Franek Kluski and a number of other private mediums. Schrenck-Notzing's experiments with Willy's brother, Rudi Schneider, followed later and were only interrupted by the Baron's death in 1929.

Characteristically, Schrenck-Notzing's book was both a defence and an attack. His epigraph was Faraday's: "Nothing is too marvellous to be true." By 1914 he had spent twenty-five years in psychical research and he felt that after four years' work with Eva C. he could no longer refrain from publishing the results. He cited Lombroso and Flammarion, Richet and Crookes in his support—and pleaded with the reader to approach his work in the same spirit in which he had written it—uninfluenced by the existing, dominant views, undeterred by the numerous failures and disappointments which studded the history of occultism. In the introduction to the second edition, Schrenck-Notzing had to defend himself against the numerous attacks the previous publication had provoked, especially the theory of "rumination" which some sceptics put forward—a theory according to which the medium swallowed certain substances and regurgitated them to produce the phenomena. Patiently and carefully, Schrenck-Notzing destroyed this theory in connection with Eva C. (Much later Harry Price was to unmask a medium who did use this unusual process but her phenomena were completely different and much cruder than Marthe Béraud's.)

By the time his work with Eva C. began, Schrenck-Notzing had sat with many other mediums. During sixteen years he had a number of séances with Eusapia—the first of them in 1894 in Rome which he organized and in which Richet, Lombroso and the Russian Danilewski participated. As we have seen, he was also present during the séances Richet directed in the summer of 1894 some of which were also attended by Lodge, Sidgwick and Myers. In May and June 1898 and in February and March 1903 he brought the Neapolitan medium to Munich in collaboration with Professor Flournoy of Geneva and a number of German scientists. He followed these up in May 1896 in Rome, in March 1898 in Naples, in April 1902 in Rome and Naples, in March 1903 once again in Rome and finally in April 1909 in Genoa and Nice. By and large Schrenck-Notzing was far more sceptical about Eusapia's mediumship than Richet, Lombroso or Carrington and it was only after Eusapia's death that he published some of his findings which were, on the whole, critical though he did not reject totally the possibility of a mixed mediumship. And he was fair enough to admit that other researchers had far more positive yet severely controlled results with Eusapia than he.

Schrenck-Notzing was introduced to "Eva C.", Richet's Marthe Béraud, after she had moved to Paris in 1908. The séances stretched from May 1909 until June 1914, practically to the outbreak of the First World War and were held in Paris, Biarritz, St. Jean de Luz, Munich (during three months in July, August and September 1912) and La Baule. The war naturally cut off the medium from the experimenter but the séances with Eva C. were continued until 1921 by a committee of the British Society for Psychical Research in which Dr. Dingwall, Everard Feilding, Fr. Fournier d'Albe, Whateley Smith and others participated; among the French scientists in the period 1916-21, apart from Richet, de Fontenay, Flammarion, Dr. Gustave Geley, Dr. Montalescot, Professor Boirac and other eminent persons sat with the lady for varying periods of which Madame Frondoni Lacombe's was the longest (September-November 1916).

It is interesting to observe Schrenck-Notzing's work with Eva C. through the comments of Richet. For one thing, Richet did not think it necessary to disguise the medium's name while the German researcher, for reasons of his own, scrupulously observed her incognito. Richet was particularly impressed by his German colleague's findings about telekinesis as the first stage of materialization and had nothing but high praise for the experimental methods he used with Marthe Béraud. He agreed with Schrenck-Notzing as to the development of the first lineaments of materializations which they both observed as a kind of pasty jelly or liquid emerging from the mouth or breast of the medium, organizing itself by degrees, acquiring the shape of a face or limb. Much of the German researcher's careful work helped to confirm Richet's own with Marthe Béraud which began in Algiers and also covered many years. The French scientist summed up the 1909-14 Schrenck-Notzing investigation (some of which was conducted in co-operation with Madame Bisson, Marthe Béraud's close friend and patron) by paying warm tribute to his colleague:

In these experiments (Richet wrote) which lasted over four years and were conducted with admirable care and patience, minute precautions were taken against fraud. At each séance the cabinet was closely searched. Eva was completely undressed and in presence of the experimenters clothed in a close-fitting garment covering her from head to foot. Her head was covered by a veil of tulle sewn to the other garment. Her hair, armpits, nose, mouth, and knees were examined; in some cases even examination *per rectum et vaginam* was resorted to. As the materialized substance frequently comes from her mouth, syrup of bilberries was administered, whose deep colouring powers are well known, but notwithstanding this the extruded forms were absolutely white. Experimental rigour was even pushed to the point of giving her an emetic before a séance.

The light in front of the curtain was sufficient to allow large print to be read. Behind the curtain were a red and a white light that could be put on at will. Three cameras, one being stereoscopic, were focused on the cabinet ready to be worked at a signal; sometimes there were as many as nine. Eva, having been undressed in full light and clothed as described above, was brought into the cabinet and the curtains were drawn, the light reduced and the experiments began.

Under these circumstances it seems physically impossible that any fraud could occur. The notion that an accomplice could enter is absurd; the hypothesis that Eva might bring various objects with her is equally ridiculous.

... The phenomena of materialization produced were most striking.

Essentially they consist in a luminous and plastic emanation proceeding usually from her mouth, sometimes from her navel (when alone with Mme. Bisson she was completely nude); sometimes from her breast; sometimes from her armpits. It is a whitish substance that creeps as if alive, with damp, cold, protoplasmic extensions that are transformed under the eyes of the experimenters into a hand, fingers, a head, or even into an entire figure...

... These remarkable experiments by Schrenck-Notzing and Mme. Bisson confirm yet once again the phenomenon of ectoplasm. The phenomena ... bring fresh evidence on the formation of ectoplasms, evidence that is of high theoretical importance. The word "ectoplasm" which I invented for the experiments with Eusapia, seems entirely justified . . . a kind of gelatinous protoplasm, formless at first, that exudes from the body of the medium, and takes form later.

Richet himself attended a number of séances organized by Schrenck-Notzing and had nothing but the highest praise for his colleague's painstaking thoroughness and scientific dedication.

As for the Baron himself, after filling some 270 pages with detailed descriptions of his own researches during the five years and giving equally full summaries of British and French sittings with Eva C., he devoted another eighty pages to a retrospective summary of Eva C.'s mediumship.

He dealt fully with the negative aspects and with the manifold theories of trickery which the critics of Marthe Béraud's mediumship were only too ready to produce. And here, being concerned solely with Schrenck-Notzing's work and stature, we can only face up to the same difficulty that is common to all occult phenomena. Whatever we can say about them is inevitably second or third-hand for we have not attended any of these séances. Nor can we deny the good faith and honesty of the sceptics—most of these were among the members of the British Society for Psychical Research, notably the redoubtable Dr. Dingwall and some of his colleagues—who produced a whole series of highly involved hypotheses *how* the trickery could have been worked.

Marthe Béraud or Eva C. was purely and simply a materialization medium. She produced ectoplasmic or, if you like, teleplasmic substances which were often formless but sometimes developed into portraits of actual people, faces, heads or even full figures. These had certain remarkable features in common; they were primitive, rather like bad magazine art, they were creased and crumpled like two-dimensional representations of the human face and body which had been folded up or subjected to some physical process of mangling and pressing. This naturally led to the accusations that they had been prepared by the medium or her accomplices, introduced into the séance room, produced at the proper moment and then removed again—for, apart from one or two tiny paper fragments nothing was ever found during the hundreds of sittings that could be called in the slightest way suspicious.

The possibility certainly exists; Schrenck-Notzing himself points out how much the materializations resemble creased and folded paper or, in many cases, fabric. There was absolutely no indication that Eva C. was bringing phantoms from the other world, that these "apparitions" had anything to do with flesh and blood or the astral body. They were, more or less primitive representations of actual persons, ranging from the late M. Bisson to the very much alive M. Poincaré, from President Wilson to Ferdinand, King of Bulgaria. They were actually so crude and so easily identifiable that no professional magician or illusionist would have deigned to use them.

The only difficulty was that no one could offer any valid explanation as to *how* these images were produced, *where* they came from and *where* they disappeared to. Was Mme. Bisson Eva C.'s accomplice? Not even Dr. Dingwall seemed to think so—in his report he spoke highly of her character, her dedication, her unselfish friendship for the medium and her profound interest in psychical research. Mme. Bisson was not a spiritualist and it was difficult to establish any possible motive for her. Nor was she present at *all* séances; good phenomena occurred on several occasions when she was absent. In addition there was the difficulty of the veil which enclosed Eva C.'s head. Dingwall produced a theory: he thought that the objects emerging from the medium's mouth were made of wax which was reduced to a liquid state at the body temperature, penetrated the veil and then was solidified by quick breathing upon it, lowering the temperature to 25 or 30 degrees. The trouble with this ingenious theory was that the wax, passing through the veil, would have inevitably left some traces—and none was ever found. And if Eva's hands were tightly controlled, how could she shape the wax into the varied and complex forms in which her ectoplasmic phenomena so often appeared? Schrenck-Notzing also dealt with the regurgitation/rumination theory according to which she hid the substances she produced as materializations in her stomach or in her windpipe and regurgitated them when needed. The German psychic researcher pointed out that this was a particularly important question because the British committee investigating Eva C. thought it the only possibility of trickery and hesitated to endorse the mediumship fully because it felt it could not exclude it.

Schrenck-Notzing who, of course, had a thorough medical training, dealt with the physical and physiological elements of regurgitation and rumination in great detail. He explained that it was completely impossible to produce this by a simple act of will. In most cases when some object, a fragment of food etc. is regurgitated, it is from the oesophagus and not from the stomach. If it has already passed that far down, it is bound to have undergone certain modifications and these are inevitably identifiable. While it is possible to produce vomiting by psychological stimulation (the sight or the imagined sight of something nauseating) this is quite exceptional and is never *selective*. In other words, if a medium wants to regurgitate, he will have no guarantee that whatever comes up is something he can utilize for his trickery. There is also a hysterical or nervous regurgitation, a pathological vomiting but this is always connected with some easily observable illness which is accompanied by the dilation of the pupils, a slow pulse, headaches, dizziness etc., caused by a hyperaesthesia or hyperalgesia of the stomach lining or some similar organic trouble. All these symptoms are impossible to hide. In order to refute once and for all that Eva C. suffered from any such condition or would have been able to produce the necessary "inner motions" for regurgitation, Schrenck-Notzing asked two eminent French specialists to examine her. Drs. Beauprès and Vallet made a thorough radiological and clinical examination and found the lady completely normal; nor were there any signs that she had practised, for twelve whole years, such "interior acrobatics" as the sceptics charged against her.

Schrenck-Notzing concluded that Marthe Béraud had never at any time taken any objects with her into the cabinet which would have helped her to produce the ectoplasmic phenomena. While in the earlier séances she was only examined before and after the sittings and was not held fast during the actual experiments, from October 1912 onwards her hands were always held outside the curtains—and yet the phenomena not only continued but became even more varied and interesting.

The German scientist, like his friend Richet, was no spiritualist. He believed, however, that Eva C. and other mediums had an extrasensory ability of creating matter—or at least exteriorizing it—in the form of ectoplasm.

> ...it cannot be denied (Schrenck-Notzing summed up) that the participants of a séance have a certain imaginative influence upon the nature and content of the phenomena. But in the final analysis it is the subconscious of the hypnotized medium that must absorb and digest the once perceived idea of the phenomenon. Then, having gathered sufficient psychopsychical energy in the body, this idea is transformed and expressed, i.e. objectivized by a biopsychic projection ectoplasmically across a certain, severely defined distance. The phenomena of Eva C. must be therefore conceived as an ideoplastic ability of the medium's constitution—until now unexplored... In the process of materialization there are two factors involved; first a simple spontaneous exudation and formation of a sometimes phosphorescent or auto-luminous material of transitory character and secondly a shaping of this material into various forms, images and living organs. The psychophysical emanation of the teleplastic basic substance is the pre-condition of the ideoplastic process—showing certain analogies with the radioactive brain-currents of Kotik...

This is pretty heavy going but I have deliberately given a literal translation of Schrenck-Notzing's prose. He was no great stylist but scrupulously and teutonically intent on the exact meaning, the perfect word. It may not be amiss to paraphrase it into lay language. The five years of experiments with Eva C. convinced him that the phenomena were genuine and that the charges of fraud or hallucinatory mistakes were untenable. He came to believe that the mental processes of the participants in these sittings had a direct bearing on the results—that, in a way, the medium drew from the minds or the subconscious of the sitters some inspiration or impulse for the production of these phenomena. These were, in turn, absorbed and digested by her own subconscious which was able to do this in a hypnotized, trance condition. Once she had done this, she transformed the images and ideas into matter—by the use of some force or energy within herself which was both psychical and physical. (We have spoken of the most striking parallel examples that occur in individuals who are *not* mediumistic—in particular in women who have a strong wish for children and, unable to bear them, produce false pregnancies, with every visible, physical symptom of the actual, real conditions. Mediums appear to be able to do this repeatedly, transiently and more or less "to order".) The idea becomes tangible, the mind produces matter in a bio-physical projection which Richet has named ectoplasm. This can be "cast off" from the medium's body across a certain distance though this distance appears to be limited and strictly defined. Eva C., at least, was able not only to create matter and project it outside her body but to shape it, make it plastic, rather like a sculptor taking wax, clay or some other pliable substance and giving it whatever shape he or she wishes or is required. Schrenck-Notzing did not claim that this ability of a medium's constitution has yet been explored or understood—all he stated was that it existed, that its authenticity has been established, that there was overwhelming evidence as to its genuineness and frequency. The material which the medium produced was non-permanent, was spontaneously projected and shaped, was usually phosphorescent or had a luminosity of its own. It was able to move even when it became separated from the medium's body to which it was usually—at least in the initial stages—connected by some tenuous thread or rope-like appendage. It could adopt a great variety of forms, resembling limbs, shapeless lumps, even images which looked like rather primitive drawings or paintings. It could even develop into living organs. Schrenck-Notzing found another parallel here, between the electric currents of the brain which had been measured and linked to the thought processes and the ideoplastic processes.

All this, he emphasized, was pure theory, a hypothesis

which the existing facts supported but did not prove to full scientific validity. "These purely hypothetical references," Schrenck-Notzing wrote, "only serve the purpose to remove the observed facts from the realm of the miraculous, of the spiritualist doctrine and transfer them into the field of natural events following certain laws, indicating the direction which may perhaps lead to the possibility of an explanation."

Highly cautious and circumspect, the Baron was still far too fanciful for most of his colleagues. He was derided and attacked, vilified and abused because he lent a considerable scientific reputation and the prestige of highly respected achievements in neurology to what was considered unworthy of any "serious" scholar. Yet Schrenck-Notzing gave the answer to all these attacks when he quoted Johann Kepler's famous and haunting question: "Is the whole visible world perhaps only the sheath of an invisible world of forces?"

In her most interesting, highly readable and stimulating autobiography *Zum anderen Ufer* (To the Other Shore), Dr. Gerda Walther, psychologist, philosopher phenomenologist psychical researcher and writer on a great variety of scientific subjects, devoted several chapters to her work with Schrenck-Notzing whose assistant she was during the last eighteen months of the Baron's life, and whose work she continued for several years, alone or in conjunction with others. The book contains especially valuable and authentic data on the mediumship of the remarkable Schneider brothers, the "stars" of the so-called Braunau Circle.

Braunau or Braunau am Inn is a fair-sized town in Upper Austria, about thirty miles north of Salzburg. The town has a rail junction, breweries and tanneries; one of its suburbs, Ranshofen, contains a large aluminium plant. It is also the birthplace of Adolf Hitler (a distinction which the Braunauers would probably like to forget). It has been also the home of one of the most remarkable families in psychical research—the Schneiders.

The father, Josef Schneider, was a compositor, a very intelligent, much-respected and quiet, exceptionally well-mannered man—though he ruled his family with firm authority. His wife, a gentle unassuming woman, had borne twelve children of whom six, all boys, had survived. They were named Karl, Hans, Fritz, Willi, Franz and Rudi. Four of them were mediumistic, though Hans and Karl possessed this faculty only to a very slight degree while Willi and Rudi were destined to become two of the most famous and most discussed mediums in Europe if not in the world.

No one has offered any valid explanation why the Schneider boys should have developed psychic faculties. No traces of abnormality could be found on either side of the family. Yet Willi showed signs of mediumship at the age of fourteen and Rudi at eleven.

One evening (as Harry Price wrote in his Rudi Schneider monograph) Herr Schneider's friends were holding a séance with Willi when "Olga" the trance personality who then spoke through Rudi's brother, said that the power was not good and that she wanted Rudi to "assist". But the boy's parents objected on the grounds that Rudi was only eleven years of age. Rudi was then asleep in bed. "Olga" said nothing but a few minutes later the door opened and Rudi, deeply entranced, entered the room and took his place in the circle.

As Dr. Walther related, it was Captain J. Kogelnik, a retired naval officer, who discovered the Schneider brothers. He was much impressed with the first edition of Schrenck-Notzing's *Materializations Phenomena* and wrote to him about the improvised and informal séances at the Schneider home. The Baron visited Braunau and rented a room in the small town of Simbach, on the western, Bavarian bank of the River Inn, opposite Braunau; he asked Kogelnik to "educate" Willi to the function of a scientific medium. This Kogelnik undertook gladly though later he and his wife withdrew from the Braunau circle—not because they doubted the Schneider boys' authenticity but because they felt that the sittings could no longer offer anything new or important to them. It was through these experiences that the Kogelniks reached a deep Christian faith that went far beyond spiritualism.

Schrenck-Notzing's work with Willi began in October 1919 with a series of séances in five different homes, some were held at the Baron's Munich laboratory. Later, when he was not yet sixteen, Willi was partly supported by the Baron who spent several years on detailed experiments with him. In the second edition of his monumental work, Schrenck-Notzing devoted some forty pages to these experiments (up to January 1922) and published a page of photographs showing a number of "teleplasmic manifestations".

After finishing school, Willi studied to become a dental technician and undertook to work for a year exclusively for Schrenck-Notzing. He moved to Munich where he lodged in the home of a lady, much interested in occult phenomena. "Thus it was possible . . ." wrote Schrenck-Notzing, "to keep any harmful influences away from him and to follow closely his psychological development and the occasional, spontaneous psychic phenomena during his stay in Munich."

Willi was subjected to a regular and thorough medical examination which included intelligence tests and psychological checks. The Baron gave a detailed analysis of the young boy's character:

Lively reflexes. Psychogenic squint, especially when depressed. Field of sight shows normal limits. No disturbances in the area of sensibility and motility. School record and general development correspond to social milieu; it must be emphasized that his father's intellectual interests and knowledge—especially with regard to the history of his home-town and occultism—are far above the usual lower middle-class standards.

Willi's general knowledge is normal considering his schooling. His memory is good average. A soft, kind-hearted character, obedient, modest; he easily gains the affection of those who know him well. His work as dental technician has been highly praised both by his former and his present employer; a diligent and trustworthy worker. Will-power underdeveloped. Easily impressionable; irritable. Changeable moods; unmotivated, over-sentimental sadness and nostalgia changing suddenly into gay abandonment. Inclination to masquerades, dancing and acrobatic performances. Love of nature. Abstract thinking rudimentary but imagination lively. Great ambitiousness. Strongly marked sympathies and antipathies towards people which play a great part at the séances. His self-importance strongly stimulated by earlier séance-successes in spiritualist circles. Some capriciousness; idiosyncratic dislike of certain kinds of food. Frightened by his own phenomena. Lack of self-discipline combined with stubbornness. Inclined to be spendthrift, desire of easy-going, expensive way of life. Actions more influenced by emotions than by reasoning. Deep, dreamless sleep, especially after séances. Often day-dreams. While fully conscious but somewhat absent-minded he sometimes sees clouds and head-like formations; also full figures in white garments and veils; i.e. similar to those observed during séances. No actual hallucinations...

The Baron's long analysis of Willi's character and psychological make-up (which continues for several pages in his book) shows how thoroughly enumerated the young boy's good and bad qualities were. He was equally thorough in organizing the sittings, keeping records, establishing the most rigorous control, doing everything humanly possible to exclude all fraud. During five months there were never less than five, usually seven to ten participants at the sittings, including university professors, physicians, writers, psychical researchers. The conclusion Schrenck-Notzing reached concerning 56 séances held between December 3, 1921 and July 1, 1922, in which 94 people took part, was clear and definite:

No single participant noticed the slightest suspicious manipulation by the medium or anybody present and the collective impression of all witnesses can be summed up by saying that Willi Sch. could not have produced the phenomena through the known mechanical means, i.e. fraudulently. Doors were locked before the sittings so that there was no possibility of any accomplice gaining access during the darkness to the laboratory. In addition, the most important materialization processes took place in the centre of the semi-circle, immediately under the eyes of the observer, at a distance of 40 centimetres to one metre, in the light of a lamp with a red bulb, standing on the table.

Any person separated from the site of the manifestations by the circle of participants would have been unable to influence them in any way. Finally, in the case of many phenomena, the nature and evanescence of their appearance, their flowing, changing and fantastic shapes and their mode of development until they reached their final form, argue against any possibility of a fraudulent production of them—even if one would assume that one of those present would have tried to deceive his fellow-observers . . .

Professor Schrenck-Notzing believed firmly in Willi's mediumship and so did those who participated in the séances; at least, no voice was raised questioning the method of controls or alleging any fraud. Yet the phenomena were greatly varied—raps, cold winds, black shapes, materializations of heads, hands, arms, levitating of various objects—the whole range of the usual séance "productions".

In May 1922 Harry Price and Dr. E. J. Dingwall (then Research Officer of the British Society for Psychical Research) visited Munich and took part in sittings. They had three successful séances and the British visitors returned to London, fully convinced that Willi Schneider had genuine psychic powers. Willi was invited to England at the end of 1924 by the British S.P.R. and gave a number of séances; this visit, though a few striking telekinetic phenomena were witnessed, was not particularly successful—probably, as Price thought, because of "the strangeness of the country or the people or the unfamiliar surroundings of the séance-room . . ."

Not long afterwards Schrenck-Notzing and Willi parted company through one of those arguments or misunderstandings common enough between a medium and his "patron". Willi went to Vienna and put himself under the guidance of Dr. Holub, head of the famous Steinhof asylum. During the brief period the well-known alienist worked with Willi various new phenomena were witnessed in addition to materializations, telekinesis and the usual "repertoire". Dr. Holub died suddenly and left Willi at a loose end. But Frau Dr. Holub offered him a home, the experiments continued and in April, 1925, Harry Price was invited to take part in them. He had again three séances, one of which was quite spectacular, returning to London well satisfied with his visit. A short time afterwards Schrenck-Notzing and Willi made up whatever differences they had and Willi signed a two years' contract with the Baron, undertaking to continue the experiments with his original sponsor. In October, 1925, Harry Price found him in Braunau when he visited the Schneiders for the first time. There were three séances at the family home; the sitters included Professor Karl Gruber and the writer Georg von Hildebrandt and the phenomena were both striking and successful.

Not long after these sittings Willi Schneider practically retired from mediumship. His powers had begun to wane and although there was another series of experiments with the Baron, it was evident that his psychic talents were almost exhausted. He worked hard at his dental studies and his mediumship became a secondary consideration.* His "mantle" had now fallen on his younger brother, Rudi.

Like Willi, Rudi had also been more or less "adopted" by Schrenck-Notzing who worked with the boy with shorter or longer interruptions until his (the Baron's) sudden death in January 1929. Rudi was a healthy and robust youngster, more interested in cars, football and, later, his sweetheart Mitzi Mangl (who became his wife) than in psychical research. Yet his work with the Munich researcher produced excellent results, more or less on the lines of Willi's. In December 1925, not long after Price's second visit to Braunau, Herr Schneider himself wrote with pardonable parental pride that Rudi had been producing phenomena "which very few mortals had ever got to see. In yesterday's sitting there were at least thirty appearances of an almost six-foot high phantom. At one time there were two such phantoms. One of them touched a member of the circle. Materialized hands were seen in innumerable profusion. Telekinetic phenomena were observed at a distance of more than two yards." Father Schneider seemed to hint that Rudi was an even greater, more brilliant medium than his older brother.

A few weeks later Professor Gruber who had attended a

* Willi died, after a long illness, in his native town in 1970.

series of séances at Baron von Schrenck-Notzing's Munich laboratory, reported enthusiastically that "Rudi produced magnificent phenomena. A hand appeared and took a ring from Baron von Schrenck-Notzing's finger." (Gruber was, according to Dr. Walther, in line to become the Baron's successor. But he died, tragically, in 1927.)

While in 1926 and 1927 the mediumship of the Schneider boys was under attack by several people—among them Dr. Dingwall, the American journalist W. J. Vinton and Dr. W. F. Prince of the Boston S.P.R.—Schrenck-Notzing was observing good phenomena during the same period at Munich, under perfect conditions of tactual control. Later the Baron introduced the system of electric control invented by the jeweller Karl Krall who, after conducting a long series of experiments with the famous "talking horses of Elberfield", had settled down in Munich-Harlaching and installed a most sophisticated laboratory. This system controlled the medium and immediately signalled every break in the circuit. (Later Harry Price used the same system but extended it also to all the sitters.) Schrenck-Notzing and Karl Krall planned to have a long series of sittings in their respective laboratories using this virtually fool-proof control. But within a few weeks of each other, both Baron Schrenck-Notzing and Krall died.

This is not the place to tell the remaining story of Rudi Schneider's mediumship; I have dealt with it in my Harry Price biography and, in some detail, in my book *Companions of the Unseen*. There is a whole shelf-full of books about the remarkable Braunau boys. In the end Rudi settled down in Weyer/Ennstal as owner of a driving school. His powers as medium became weaker and weaker—just as it was the case with his brother Willi. He no longer held any psychical séances, especially as his wife much preferred to have a "normal" businessman for her husband than a controversial figure of psychical research. Much of Schrenck-Notzing's material about his mediumship was edited by Dr. Walther and published posthumously; Rudi himself considered briefly writing his memoirs but his Mitzi was firmly set against it for she was afraid that their publication would once again bring unpleasant and persistent publicity. Rudi died, suddenly, on April 28, 1957, from a brainstroke, in his forty-eighth year. With him the long and fascinating story of the Schneider mediumship came to an end.

In 1912, 1913 and 1916 Schrenck-Notzing had three series of séances in Munich with the Polish medium Stanislawa P. The young girl was nineteen when their collaboration began, having been discovered a year earlier by a Warsaw psychical researcher while she was working as cashier in a shop. Her "control" was "Sophie", a childhood friend who died young and who "appeared" to her in the very moment of her death. It was this "telepathic hallucination" as Schrenck-Notzing called it, that started Stanislawa's career as a medium. By 1911 she was producing whole phantoms in strongly dimmed white or red light while she was fastened at the ankles and neck to the chair and wall. Later the "phantom" and the medium were visible at the same time. Her Munich séances were less productive—though various ectoplasmic fragments appeared under perfect control conditions; on several occasions in July 1913 the emergence and disappearance of the teleplasm was filmed. Stanislawa was also a telekinetic medium who moved objects from a considerable distance. Like Eva C., she also produced ectoplasm while her face was covered in a veil; Schrenck-Notzing concluded that the two mediums had a good deal in common. The young Polish girl was searched both before and after the séances though she would not permit, for obvious reasons, vaginal and anal control. However, the Baron had little or no doubt about the authenticity of these phenomena. While her hands were clearly visible, holding on to the curtain, a "handlike append-age" appeared, performed various movements and gestures, took objects offered to it, held them and cast them off again.

Another medium with whom Schrenck-Notzing had some séances was the Graz widow, Frau Maria Silbert, mother of ten children of whom seven survived. The lady was 54 when the Munich researcher visited her in her home, a white-haired, kindly, thoroughly normal-looking woman who refused to derive any profit from her mediumship; she believed that she would lose her gift immediately if she turned it into a business.

Her clairvoyant talent was discovered in her youth; the first materializations phenomena began when she was eight years old. But her regular mediumship began only when her husband, a revenue official, died in 1914. Her "control" was called "Nell"—and supposed to have lived in Nuremberg in the fifteenth century as a scholar. While "Nell" always refused to answer any questions of a financial nature or anything that would bring material benefit to the sitter, he had a remarkably high score in forecasting the immediate future. Maria Silbert was also famous for telekinesis—in her case the lifting and moving of heavy objects—for raps and touches, for materializations, for direct communication by writing, for the disappearance and reappearance of objects and similar phenomena. During the séance which Schrenck-Notzing had with her in April 1921, he was deeply impressed by the variety and intensity of the manifestations of all which took place under a strong light. "My total impression," the Baron wrote in his book, "was that Frau S. is a strong physical medium highly suitable for scientific investigation ... As to the necessity or advisability of examining the question of fraud in her case, this seems to be senseless in view of the nature and variety of the phenomena; it would be totally impossible to produce them fraudulently under the same conditions. Nor is there any possible motivation for the medium for she never expects nor accepts any compensation for her work. She is a deeply, sincerely religious person who considers her mediumistic talent as a gift of destiny bestowed upon her for purely idealistic purposes..."

In any case, Schrenck-Notzing did not have the opportunity to have a regular series of experiments with Frau Silbert though he gathered a number of reports by other reputable researchers for his book. Harry Price who visited Graz some five years after Schrenck-Notzing's single séance was not very much impressed by Frau Silbert's telekinetic phenomena but

found the raps quite remarkable—for these could be produced at command. He concluded that the "raps were paranormal and that they could not be reproduced normally *under
the conditions*". It seemed, by the way, that those who
criticized or attacked the Austrian medium did it at their
peril—for they all came to grief, either economically or
through some personal, physical mishap!

Price was equally or even more sceptical about Einer Nielsen, the Danish medium with whom he had an entirely
negative séance in Copenhagen. Schrenck-Notzing also had a
single sitting with him in August 1921 during the Congress
for Psychical Research which was held in the Danish capital.
Nielsen was then twenty-six, a tall, sturdy-looking young man
who worked as an assistant in a bookshop. He was highly
regarded by spiritualist circles while others accused him of
fairly primitive tricks. The séance was held in the villa of
H. E. Bonne, a wealthy Danish industrialist in Prastrub,
near Copenhagen; apart from Schrenck-Notzing and several
regular members of the Nielsen circles, several Norwegian,
Swedish, Danish and Icelandic university professors were
present and so was Madame Bisson, Marthe Béraud's (Eva
C.'s) patron and friend. Nielsen and the two people who were
to be his immediate controls were all searched carefully. The
séance lasted over two hours and Schrenck-Notzing's general
conclusion was that though the phenomena he had observed
could be granted a "subjective power of conviction" they were
not objective proof. He insisted on a second sitting which was
more successful; his final judgment was that Nielsen, like
Eusapia, probably had a mixed mediumship. This was supported by the controversy that erupted soon after Schrenck-
Notzing's visit to Copenhagen which produced the usual
violent split between supporters and opponents with neither
side convincing the other.

But then, Schrenck-Notzing himself did not escape such
attacks, charges and insinuations—some of which were highly
slanderous. Like Richet, he always managed to preserve his
dignity and did not seem to descend to the level of some of
his vituperative enemies though he did not exactly turn the
other cheek. Dr. Walther gave a very fair and balanced

estimate of his psychological make-up, his abilities and his limitations.

Schrenck-Notzing was a typical representative of the generation of scientists of late nineteenth century (wrote Dr. Walther in her autobiography)—because he believed that one must ascribe the highest demonstrative force to natural scientific experiments that can be repeated as often as desired—and this in all fields. Though he had an open mind for everything new in sexual pathology, in psycho-therapy and in the acknowledgment of hypnosis as reality and as an important therapeutic factor and became in the end a pioneer in parapsychology, throughout his life he never advanced beyond this over-estimation of experi-mental research. The ideographic description of historical individual cases, the ontological development of the essen-tial as a method that would be of equal validity and better suited for the research disciplines outside the natural sciences—this he never realized. Thus in parapsychology, too, he was primarily concerned with experimentation, with the most tangible, concrete experiments—that was, probably, why he had a predilection for the "physical" phenomena, for materializations and telekinesis. His ideal was to be able to produce under the most perfect control conditions possible, which removed all suspicion of fraud in the opponents, always the same phenomena in the desired quantity—just as the physicist and the chemist are able to do it in their laboratory. He could or would not realize that because the phenomena were at least governed by un-controllable, psychological factors, many delicate details, perhaps even essential elements had to be lost. For others the sameness of the "offerings" at the séances, going on for months, for years, would have become in the long run boring. But not for Schrenck-Notzing; he wanted to present these matters to new and new, well-known scientists, con-vince them by visible proof—because then they had to agree with him, had to acknowledge the results of his re-searches and consequently had to champion him! Unfor-tunately he was often deceived in this hope. The scientists who seemed to be completely convinced during the séances and perhaps for a while afterwards, acquired doubts afterwards or pretended that they had not been fully convinced, had perhaps overlooked something. Only too often they evaded in the end the unequivocal commitment.

This is, of course, a recurrent difficulty which we have encountered repeatedly in the careers of the Pioneers of the Unseen. Dr. Walther invokes the example of Sir Oliver Lodge who, she thinks, would have certainly received the Nobel Prize if he had not "compromised" himself by his preoccupation with psychical research. Of course, Lodge's commitment, as we have seen, was to a spiritualist faith while Schrenck-Notzing was at great pains to emphasize that though he considered the phenomena he observed often as paranormal, he did not accept them as proof for survival after death. Still, it was true that especially younger scientists may have been anxious not to support even such cautious theories lest such a stand should have an adverse effect upon their careers. Nor was there in these matters any difference, as Dr. Walther pointed out, between the bourgeois, capitalistic and the Marxist scientists of our century.

Schrenck-Notzing was a completely independent man—his marriage had made him financially secure after his earlier years which were by no means overly prosperous. According to Professor Alexander Pfänder, with whom Gerda Walther studied and who knew Schrenck-Notzing well, the Baron had been a modest, dedicated researcher; when his wife brought him a considerable fortune, he was surprised to notice how humble people became and how they besieged and courted him. This, Pfänder thought, caused him to lose his sense of proportion and he became somewhat dominating and overbearing. This may have been true, Dr. Walther thought; but anybody who insisted on his rights and expressed his opinions freely and frankly, found the Munich professor always ready to listen. Though he had a stubborn streak, he tried to do justice to the arguments that were presented calmly and objectively—especially when he noticed that his opponent did not seek personal advantages. Unfortunately in psychical research, where vanity and blind prejudice often prevail, there were only too often such personal, selfish considerations.

One of Schrenck-Notzing's main local enemies was a redoubtable lady called Mathilde von Kemnitz (née Spiess) who later became rather better known as Mathilde Ludendorff, the wife of the Kaiser's principal military strategist and, at least temporarily, Hitler's early associate. Frau Mathilde who had a totally confused and extreme philosophy—it was she who dragged the ageing Ludendorff into all kinds of ludicrous adventures—hated Schrenck-Notzing. The Baron told Dr. Walther with a smile that at the single séance to which the lady came he made the mistake of treating her as a scholar—instead of flattering her as a woman and this, apparently, she never forgave him. (Mathilde's most popular lectures were those in which she spoke about "erotic revival" though no one was quite sure what she meant.)

The Baron spoke fairly good French but had little or no English and it was Dr. Walther's duty to conduct his English correspondence and to interpret when visiting firemen from the Anglo-Saxon countries arrived—which they did fairly often. He insisted on keeping abreast of the foreign publications relevant to his field of research and published a good deal of material from abroad in the *Zeitschrift für Parapsychology* (Journal for Parapsychology) which he had taken over, retitled from Aksakoff's *Psychic Studies* and was editing. He kept painstaking records of the séances—as his massive *Materializations Phenomena* proved. Unless he travelled abroad, there was a separate secretary engaged to whom the Baron or other participants in the séances dictated the descriptions of the various phenomena as and when they occurred. These were, of course, timed and provided an immediate and constant report of what was going on. The second part of these records consisted in the evaluation of the phenomena, comments and remarks which were added later. Sometimes it happened that these evaluations were changed by Schrenck-Notzing at a later stage, when he had acquired additional data. Some of his opponents accused him of "doctoring" evidence. This, as Dr. Walther emphasized, he never did. The chronological record remained strictly unaltered—only the commentaries and judgments did if new developments and discoveries warranted.

Schrenck-Notzing was always prepared to introduce new techniques, more advanced apparatus if these improved the conditions of research. The séance room in the laboratory had a second door and the Baron's opponents often criticized him that this gave access to possible accomplices. He became tired of these charges and had a book-case filled with heavy volumes built into the doorframe from the outside. Now his enemies charged him with even more cunning: they said that this was a movable book-case that might swing round at the touch of a finger. Dr. Walther then suggested that heavy surgical tape should be placed around the door on which the participants could make their own marks, making sure that it remained undisturbed. The door was both locked and bolted from the inside.

During the Eva C. séances the medium usually sat in a darkened cabinet; but in the later experiments Willi and Rudi Schneider and the others sat in front of it. The cabinet itself was formed by a heavy black curtain, divided in the middle. The mediums were always held by one or two people and were under electric control, while constantly visible in good red light—thus it would have been very difficult if not impossible for them to cheat. The sceptics thereupon maintained that some accomplice had to be hidden in the cabinet. Again, it was Dr. Walther's suggestion which Professor Schrenck-Notzing adopted, that a double floor should be built in the cabinet so that if anyone entered it, there should be an immediate warning light switched on—like in a telephone booth which is lit up when you step inside.

By the time Gerda Walther began working with the Baron, the sittings had become highly formalized—they followed always the same procedure for he thought that this would add to the exactitude of the research. The séance room (usually inaccessible) was opened, the participants were invited to search it thoroughly; the mediums, the secretaries, even Schrenck-Notzing himself submitted to the same search if requested. Then the doors were locked and bolted, sometimes even sealed from the inside. The medium undressed (if required, even removing his underclothes) and put on the special pyjamas which were connected with the electrical control apparatus and had phosphorescent (luminous) stripes. The sitters took their places, the controller opposite the medium whose hands he took after both had put on the metallic gloves which were always wired into the control apparatus. The medium put his feet into the sack-like control slippers and placed them on the control plate; the controller held his feet and legs between his own. Some of the scientists were given places immediately next to the controller and were able to place their right hands upon the clasped hands of medium and controller while their left hand held the right hand of their neighbour. Thus chains were formed. The circle usually consisted of five or six people. On the opposite side of the laboratory, to the left of the curtain, sat the person in charge of the experiment who handled the rheostat which could dim or brighten the red light. Schrenck-Notzing always refrained from control as he did not want to be accused of "helping out". Behind him were tables with luminous objects; he was completely hemmed in and could only rise if his neighbour left his place. Sometimes there was a second chain of people behind the first one, also linked; the sitters at both ends placed their outside, free hands on the shoulders of those sitting in front of them. The experimental space in front of the cabinet was separated from the participants and the mediums by a gauze screen, about sixteen inches high, divided into four sections and equipped with mesothoric luminous strips. At the right-side edge its frame was fastened to the chair of the medium so that he could not possibly push it away with his foot which was outside the screen. The position of the medium was carefully regulated at every séance so that he could not reach the circular little table in front of the cabinet which was marked with a luminous spot in the centre.

The séances usually began about nine p.m. When the chain was formed, the lights were put out and all kept quiet until, in about five minutes, the medium went into his trance. (All these arrangements referred to Willi and Rudi Schneider though Schrenck-Notzing used them, with small variations, with his other mediums. Of course, when he visited the laboratories of other researchers he generally had to submit to whatever methods *they* used.) Neither of the Schneider brothers was hypnotized; both of them were supposed to be put automatically into a trance state by their respective controls who spoke in a quick whisper through the medium's mouth. This usually happened through an audible gasp or similar sound. "Olga (or 'Uina') are you here?" was the customary question of the controller whereupon the medium's foot signalled a loud "yes"; then came the whispered greeting: *"Gott zum Gruss!"* "God greet you!" This was also the beginning of the characteristic *hyperpnoea*, the increase in the depth and frequency of respiration, producing a panting effect which was a Schneider "speciality". The frequency rose from 12-14 per minute (which was Rudi's normal breathing) to as high as 350. (This resulted in irritability and tension of the muscles and changes in the function of the brain which were examined in considerable detail by Dr. Osty in Paris.) Now the sitters were allowed to speak; the gramophone which "Olga" loved —she preferred strongly rhythmic music—was started up. As Dr. Walther reported this remarkable "lady" and the Baron often had arguments as to which records to play. Olga liked marches, a strong beat while Schrenck-Notzing would have loved to have classical music by famous performers. Olga usually won. She claimed she produced the phenomena with the "power" she drew from the medium's body (sometimes with help from the sitters when it needed intensification) and this was helped by the strongly rhythmic music and the "swaying", "swinging" of the participants. This was a "thickening" (Verdichtung) or concentration of power— though it was never explained what "Olga" meant by it. She seldom spoke during the hyperpnoeatic periods.

Dr. Walther gave a vivid picture of the average séance with "Olga":

In good sittings the curtain in front of the cabinet began to move after fifteen or thirty minutes; even in a dim red light this was easy to tell by the tinkling of the small bells fastened to it and the swinging of the luminous strips. Then it billowed like a sail and resisted when someone tried to press it back. (This was now and then allowed to one of the sitters.) Sometimes it blew as far as the first row of the participants. Then usually a number of telekinetic phenomena followed: a handbell was swung "by itself" above the table, sometimes over the heads of the participants and cast behind the second row; a small luminous rubber dog, like a baby's toy, flew around, squeaking; a waste paper basket was levitated and was placed, upside down, on the head of a sitter. (This was a special distinction granted to visiting scientists; in my presence, for instance, it happened to Professor Driesch.) This was all easy to follow for all objects were painted with luminous paint; in good séances the red light shining above the cabinet and the numbers of the electric control apparatus gave sufficient illumination.

After an hour or an hour and a half there was generally a pause of ten–fifteen minutes. The medium woke up, the white light was put on, the sitters moved to the adjoining room where soft drinks were served—some smoked. In good séances Rudi did not feel any exhaustion even after the wildest phenomena. But when "Olga" toiled in vain to "thicken" the "power" and still not the slightest phenomenon was produced, he often complained after the séance of headaches and lassitude.

After the interval the séance proceeded exactly as at the beginning. Once again there occurred, though more quickly, telekinetic phenomena; but sometimes there were immediately materializations. I often felt as if the whole atmosphere would be charged with power (not unpleasant but somehow "demonic"). It worked best when the music was swinging; so that for me the "Bavarian Parade March" is closely associated with the appearance of a prehensile organ, something like a not-too-large, three-fingered hand which moved through the opening of the curtain to the middle of the table, seized something, drew it behind the curtain or swung it to and fro. Sometimes one was allowed to hold one's own hand at the curtain and felt a light touch; exceptionally though very rarely, directly through the uncovered, visible materialized structure. Either during the first part or later, it happened often that a perfect knot was tied in a handkerchief or it was lifted from below. Quite often we discovered after the séance such a knot at all the corners of the curtain.

Both Dr. Walther and others who participated regularly in the séances found it somewhat surprising how tensely and impatiently Schrenck-Notzing awaited the phenomena, with what a deep excitement he followed their course. Significantly, the Baron was a passionate hunter who leased his own shooting in the Carpathians; his trophies were proudly displayed on the wall of the entrance hall of his palace. So it must have been the hunter's passion that dominated him when at last the desired phenomena appeared; just as if he had been waiting for a sixteen-pointer in some primeval forest.

Others found the phenomena rather boring if they attended many séances and found that they were always the same, endlessly repeated. "Olga" went so far that once when there was a "voice medium" sitting in an intimate circle she declared that she was "sick and tired" of the Schrenck-Notzing "circus". This may have been unjust; the Baron believed in the quantitative importance of evidence; still, some of his associates found it surprising that he spent some forty years specializing on this one group of phenomena. He was perhaps less interested in telepathy, clairvoyance, psychometry for he considered that these could not be proved—at least not to his own satisfaction—under laboratory conditions. Indeed, mental mediumship though in some circles considered to be far more "respectable" was far more difficult to establish; repetition was rare and the same medium may produce quite contradictory evidence.

Schrenck-Notzing had his own circle of friends and collaborators though in some respects he was a "loner" who did not depend on others for advice or guidance. The nearest to a "father figure" in his life was General Josef Peter, an inspector of the Prussian artillery and a specialist in heavy armaments. He left the army in 1904 because of a serious illness but survived to the ripe age of 89, dying in 1939. His interest in occultism—especially in survival after death—began very early though he could not be openly and officially connected with it as long as he was in the Army. (It would have been "unbecoming" for a Prussian officer.) He joined the Society for Scientific Psychology (founded in 1889 by Baron Carl Du Prel whose writings had influenced him deeply); a body that was in spite of its name, basically the equivalent of the British Society for Psychical Research. Gradually it developed into a purely spiritualistic direction and Schrenck-Notzing who frequented its meetings, found this little to his liking. So, in 1905, he founded his own Society for Parapsychology, which lasted until only a short time after the Baron's death. Du Prel's society, however, survived until 1941 when the Nazis banned it. Schrenck-Notzing and General Peter remained friends in spite of their different approaches and the General attended many séances with Willi Schneider, acting on some twenty-five occasions as the chief controller. He also took part in some fifteen sittings with Rudi Schneider. He was fully convinced of the Schneider brothers' genuine powers. Though he was known as a spiritualist he told Dr. Walther repeatedly in the final years of his long life that he did not find the proofs for survival sufficiently convincing; it was still, at least partly, a matter of faith.

Another member of the Schrenck-Notzing circle was the well-known Munich neurologist and psychiatrist, Dr. Ferdinand Probst who attended some 36 séances with Rudi Schneider and was the main controller at all but two of them. It was Probst who introduced into the discussion of the Schneider mediumship the important theories of Dr. Morton Prince about the dissociation of personality. Whether he was convinced that with "Olga" and "Anton" the two "trance personalities" of Rudi Schneider such dissociation actually occurred, would be difficult to decide on the evidence available. But the Munich psychiatrist did not hide his regret that the Baron, through his impatience, his lack of understanding for the "trance personality" (whatever it might be) sometimes hindered rather than helped the phenomena. He also seemed to assume that he could exert his own will to make the séances fruitful—though Dr. Probst was the first to declare that Schrenck-Notzing could not possibly be an accomplice in any fraud—not only because of his character but because of his position at most of the sittings. Probst was also somewhat dismayed by the Baron's habit of making Rudi, in his "waking" condition responsible for whatever happened during the trances and occasionally he reproached him strongly when the phenomena were too slow, too sparse or did not occur at all.

One of the bitterest arguments in which Schrenck-Notzing became involved was the "Kraus-Weber case". "Karl Weber" was the pseudonym of a former schoolteacher who arrived in Munich in 1924 and offered himself to Schrenck-Notzing as a research subject. He claimed that by highly-developed yoga powers he could levitate (without going into a trance), perform telekinesis and produce materializations. In 1927, at the Paris Congress of International Parapsychology the Baron reported on the "levitations" though, shortly before, "Weber" had been unmasked in Vienna and had confessed that "all his phenomena were fraudulent". The Austrian researchers, among them Professor Thirring and the Countess Wassilko-Serecki (the patroness of Eleonora Zugun, the "Devil Girl") had sent prompt and detailed reports to Munich. Schrenck-Notzing, however, adjudged Weber's as a "mixed" mediumship and refused to withdraw his lecture nor did he mention the Vienna episode. Later when all this was established, he appeared in an unfavourable light and he was accused of vanity, overweening ambition and misleading presentation of the facts. Early in 1929 Weber offered his memoirs containing "all the revelations" to the Baron for a fairly high sum—as a kind of blackmail, saying that he would sell all rights and would refrain from publishing in the future. Schrenck-Notzing was supposed to buy the manuscript sight-unseen. Dr. Walther discovered, by accident, that "Weber" sent a copy of his "memoirs" (while he was still negotiating with the Baron) to the Munich scientist's bitter enemy, Count Carl von Klinckowstroem, giving him permission to make extracts which he could use as he pleased. Schrenck-Notzing refused to be blackmailed; but without "Weber's" knowledge he was able to obtain a copy of the notorious fabrication and was still working on a refutal and clarification at the time of his death. He intended to publish the "Weber" case together with the pamphlet he had written about Laszlo Laszlo—both as "Forged Miracles", a study about the psychology and phenomenology of fraudulent mediumship. In the end "Weber" found a buyer in Mr. Malcolm Bird of the American Society for Psychical Research who intended to publish it with Schrenck-Notzing's commentary—but here again the Baron's death intervened. "Weber" however, continued with his "sensational revelations" long afterwards and, as Schrenck-Notzing was dead and his widow did not wish to become involved in any argument with such a dubious character, it wasn't until Dr. Walther's memoirs were published in 1960 that an unbiassed and truthful account of the whole unsavoury attempt at blackmail was given. In her book she had dealt with all the ridiculous claims of the ex-medium in considerable detail and offered convincing proof of how little truth there was in his allegations. Schrenck-Notzing was eager to witness phenomena—but he was too experienced and too upright to be taken in by even the most skilful trickster.

After her husband's death—Schrenck-Notzing died of acute appendicitis which developed into septicaemia—the Baroness retained the services of Dr. Walther and Miss Henseler, his two secretaries, to deal with the posthumous correspondence and the publication of his unprinted material. Major Rudolf Kalifius who was in charge of the Braunau circle, offered to continue the Baron's work in his Munich laboratory and was even prepared to give up his army career if he were guaranteed a minimal income. But the Baroness thought that this would only be meaningful if some very famous scholar, a university professor took charge or at least supervised the work. Unfortunately no such person could be found. She felt that her husband's opponents would mount new attacks and there would be no one to counter these with the sufficient authority. For a considerable time it was Dr. Walther alone who had to defend her late employer's record and the mediumship of the Schneider-boys. (This came under particularly violent attack when Harry Price charged Rudi with cheating though other

British researchers denied the validity of these charges; the very complex story has been told several times and is summed up in my own *Companions of the Unseen*.) She also began to edit Schrenck-Notzing's literary "estate". The first book appeared late in 1929 and was a collection of the Baron's most important parapsychological studies, already published, which were completed by a bibliography and divided according to subjects. There was an introduction by Professor Hans Driesch. Another dealt with Rudi Schneider and his phenomena. Here a selection had to be made of an enormous amount of material, including the séance reports, Schrenck-Notzing's commentaries, the letters and comments of some of the sitters, critical attacks and the Baron's responses to the charges. It was a difficult task and when it was finished, the publication costs (to be covered by the Baroness) were found to be too high so that the manuscript had to be shortened by about one third. This necessitated the omission of quite a bit of pertinent details and led to certain objections by those who did not know the complete material on which the final version was based. Dr. Walther visited Braunau repeatedly, met all the people concerned in order to form her own judgment and made friends with the Schneider family, especially with Rudi. She was fascinated by the young man not as a kind of "performing animal" but as a human being. While Schrenck-Notzing had refused resolutely to have Rudi (or Willi) psychoanalysed because he thought this might destroy his mediumship, put an end to the phenomena whose genuineness he was, above all, intent to prove—his former secretary who was developing into an independent psychical researcher and writer about psychical matters wasn't so sure. It was necessary to accept "Olga", the trance-personality and control of the two boys as an independent entity. "Olga" was insistent that Rudi only provided the "power" and it was up to her to use it, to work with it. When the Baron, during a negative period, tried to hypnotize Rudi and give him post-hypnotic commands, he failed completely. Instead he went into a trance and a furious "Olga" denounced the Baron for unwarranted interference.

Whatever the shortcomings of the Munich researcher, his

contributions to psychical research are solid and considerable. He may have occupied himself with a comparatively narrow range of phenomena, he may have been unsympathetic to any spiritualist interpretation and little interested in the mental side of mediumship—yet by his patient, tenacious work he established a general pattern for research into materialization phenomena and that strange world in which mind is able to create matter. Even his most determined adversaries were unable to claim that *all* these results were fraudulent or inconclusive. He was a true pioneer and his great book remains a peerless classic of its kind.

CESARE LOMBROSO

It is not an unusual destiny that people become celebrated for the wrong reasons; that their fame is inextricably tied to some thought, gesture, idea or action that is only incidental to their real achievement or is based on something totally irrelevant. Lord Sandwich obviously did other things apart from ordering a cut of meat to be placed between two slices of bread; Machiavelli was not in the least Machiavellian; Raleigh's cloak, Drake's bowling, Nelson's blind eye, Washington's cherry-tree—all this flotsam and jetsam has little to do with the mainstream of history or progress. But once stuck with a label, however incongruous, the centuries add to the adhesive power rather than help its removal.

Cesare Lombroso is stuck for ever with the criminological concept of the "Lombroso type". Though he himself was far less positive about it than his disciples and imitators, the phrase has been repeated parrot fashion ever since the publication of his first study in 1876 when he was forty. It was followed up by the monumental *L'Uomo delinquente* in 1889 and *La Donna delinquente* (1893).

Born in Verona of a Jewish family, Lombroso studied at Padua, Paris and Vienna; at thirty-two he was professor of psychiatry at Pavia, then became director of the lunatic asylum at Pesaro and later filled the chairs of forensic medicine and psychiatry at Turin where finally he held the professorship of a science he created himself: criminal anthropology. *Criminology* as a branch of social psychology was practically Lombroso's invention. The school which he headed accepted whole-heartedly his discovery (or alleged discovery) of a criminal type, the "instinctive" or "born" criminal—a creature who could be recognized by certain external facial, physical, even moral "birthmarks". If you possessed these, you were foreordained to commit crimes. You were the member of a separate and distinct genus of the human species; the personality of such a human monster could be identified by inherent moral and physical traits. These did not necessarily appear all in the same individual but generally existed in conjunction and thus constituted the type. Lombroso based his theory on a long investigation and combination of a number of criminals in various prisons. The traits which he thought to have traced in an overwhelming proportion of these cases included various brain and cerebral abnormalities, receding foreheads, massive jaws, prognathous chins, a-symmetrical skulls, long, large and projecting ears (*ad ansa*), rectilinear noses, strongly marked wrinkles (even in the young and in both sexes), abundant hair on the head but little on the cheeks and chin, feline, cold, glassy, fixed, ferocious eyes and "bad, repellent faces". There were a number of other "marks of Cain" which Lombroso claimed he had discovered—the great width of the extended arms (*l'envergure*, as the French called it) combined with extra-ordinary ape-like agility; left-handedness and ambi-dextrism in equal measure; superior eyesight but much less acute sense of smell, taste and sometimes of hearing. "In general," as Lombroso wrote, "the born criminal has projecting ears, thick hair and thin beard, projecting frontal eminence, enormous jaws, a square and protruding chin, large cheek bones and frequent gesticulation." Apart from these physical character-istics there were, according to the Lombroso school, marked psychological ones: moral insensibility, a dull conscience, a general freedom from remorse; low intelligence that leads to lack of proper precautions both before and after the crime, hence resulting in early detection; a strong vanity with pride taken in "infamous achievements rather than personal appearance".

Lombroso, like his colleagues Giovanni Bovio, Colajanno and Enrico Ferri (not to mention his son-in-law, Guglielmo Ferrero, the famous historian) was strongly influenced by Auguste Comte and therefore apt to look for biological causes behind all mental facts; an early behaviourist whom Pavlov would have hailed as a fellow-traveller, a complete materialist. When his first book was published, fully illustrated, a French scientist remarked plaintively that he could have made a similar selection from the portraits of famous generals or members of the Académie, showing the same physical traits. Another, more general objection was made by the champions of free-will—for if Lombroso's theory were accepted, no congenital criminal (if such a person existed) could be punished. How could he help committing crimes if his heredity robbed him of all control over his actions? The "instinctive" criminal should have to be classified with the lunatic. It was pointed out that if the face of a criminal betrayed him, that of an honest man should be a guarantee of his uprightness. And there were thousands of examples when the stamp of honesty on a face turned out to be counterfeit while an ill-looking fellow with huge ears and prognathous jaw was impeccably law-abiding.

The argument raged for many years—and, in a way, is still unfinished. Lombroso's deductions have been based on rather small statistical samples and insufficient premises—yet his work was epoch-making in criminology and he surpassed all his predecessors by the wide scope and systematic nature of his researches. While criminals may not be recognizable by facial and other physical characteristics, they do, by and large, show a higher percentage of physical, nervous and mental anomalies than non-criminals. Whether these are due to heredity or to environment or a combination of the two is a moot question and not yet decided. A child growing up in a Negro ghetto is more likely to turn to crime than one in an upper middle-class household—though the drop-outs, the rebels and anarchists of the nineteen-sixties often come from such backgrounds. The criminologists themselves differed considerably as to the acceptance or rejection of the Lombroso theories; but no one would say that his work had been useless or that at least some of his conclusions have not remained valid. To him the habitual criminal stood halfway between the lunatic and the savage. Today, with prison visitors, probation officers, remedial training and a whole host of penological and post-prison institutions and reforms, we seem to be getting nearer to Lombroso's practical suggestions. He proposed that offenders should be classified from the beginning, that the "born criminal" should receive a different kind of punishment from the offender who is tempted into crime by circumstances—that crime should be accepted as both a medical and social problem.

Lombroso also spent considerable time on the problem of genius and madness. His *Genio e follia* was published in 1877, his *L'Uomo di Genio* eleven years later. Here his biological principles were applied much less successfully. To him the eccentricity of genius was its prime factor; the greater a human being the more different, the more extreme he must be, he argued. He thought that genius was a morbid, degenerative condition—presenting analogies to insanity and not altogether alien to crime. But if genius is the highest conceivable form of original ability, utterly different from talent, it can be completely normal as long as it remains on this lofty level. Not that genius has ever been defined to universal satisfaction, however many epigrams have been coined about it. The identification of the great men with a generative spirit leads us back to the original, Roman meaning of the word and may well be the nearest answer to an insoluble problem.

If the criminal and the genius were subjects of large-scale historical and statistical examinations with perhaps questionable conclusions, there was one chapter in Lombroso's life that had an immediate, practical application and that has made him one of the benefactors of his country and of the world. He was still in his early thirties when he discovered that the terrible scourge known as *pellagra* was due in Italy to peasants eating diseased maize which contained a powerful poison. Thousands of lives were saved though it was only later, with the development of vitamin research that this problem was finally solved—when it was found to be due to a vitamin deficiency which nicotinic acid or niacin could stave off. But until Lombroso's discoveries, pellagra remained totally incurable—millions suffering weakness, depression, diarrhoea, scaly skin and thick tongue, no appetite, though no identifiable infection either. Even as late as the nineteen-thirties, there were thousands of pellagra deaths in the southern states of America, their cause unrecognized. Here, certainly, the Turin professor blazed the trail.

It was essential to sketch Lombroso's professional background in order to understand the tremendous spiritual upheaval which his involvement in psychical research represented. In many ways he resembled Arthur Conan Doyle's fictional Professor Challenger: a complete sceptic, a fiercely aggressive materialist, a total abnegator of free will. In his *After Death—What?* which was published not long after his own death in 1909, he faced this squarely:

> When, at the close of a career (he wrote)—richer in fierce logomachy and struggle than in victory—in which I have figured as a champion of the new trend of human thought in psychiatry and criminal anthropology, I began investigations into the phenomena of spiritism and afterwards determined to publish a book on the subject, my nearest friends rose against me on every side, crying, "You will ruin an honourable reputation,—a career in which, after so many contests, you had finally reached the goal; and all for a theory which the whole world not only repudiates, but, worse still, thinks to be ridiculous."

There are strong echoes here, of course, of Lodge's predicament though Sir Oliver seems to have taken opposition more calmly and less personally. Certainly Schrenck-Notzing's battles against those who belittled and pitied him for becoming involved with "hocus-pocus" and Richet's recurrent clashes with academic science also present close parallels. And like his friends and colleagues, Lombroso also had no hesitation in proclaiming his beliefs:

> But all this talk did not make me hesitate for a single moment. I thought it my predestined end and way and my duty to crown a life passed in the struggle for great ideas by entering the lists for this desperate cause, the most hotly contested and perhaps most persistently mocked-at idea of the times. It seemed to me a duty that, up to the very last of the few days now remaining to me, I should unflinchingly stand my ground in the very thick of the fight, where

rise the most menacing obstructions and where throng the most infuriated foes.

And one cannot in conscience blame these opponents, because spiritistic phenomena, as commonly conceived, seem designed to break down that grand idea of monism which is one of the most precious fruits of our culture, retrieved by so sore a conflict from the clutches of superstition and prejudice; and because, furthermore, when contracted with the precision of experimental phenomena—always accurately tallying with each other in time and space—spiritistic observations and experiments, so frequently varying with different mediums, according to the time of day and according to the mental state of the participants in the séance, notwithstanding their frequent repetition and reinforcement by accurate mechanical instruments, and however carefully sifted out by the most severely scientific experimenters (one need only name such men as Crookes, Richet, Lodge, James, Hyslop), are always wrapped in a dim atmosphere of uncertainty and show a tinge of medieval science. But note this well, that, however doubtful each separate case may appear, in the ensemble they form such a compact web of proof as wholly to baffle the scalpel of doubt.

One felt that he must have taken a very deep breath when he finished writing the first, practically endless sentence of this paragraph—trying very hard to be as accurate and definite as if he were writing about contaminated maize or the relationship of madness and crime. And succeeding even while failing. For he had no hesitation in admitting:

In psychical matters we are very far from having attained scientific certainty. But the spiritistic hypothesis seems to me like a continent incompletely submerged by the ocean, in which are visible in the distance broad islands raised above the general level, and which only in the vision of the scientist are seen to coalesce in one immense and compact body of land, while the shallow mob laughs at the seemingly audacious hypothesis of the geographer.

His entire scientific education opposed him to spiritualism.

All his life he had defended the thesis that every force in nature was a property of matter and what was "miscalled the soul", an emanation of the brain. For years he resisted every invitation to attend a séance. Then, in 1882, he witnessed some extraordinary phenomena for which no scientific explanation could be found—though they occurred in hypnotized or hysteric individuals.

As a neuropathologist he was called to examine a fourteen-year-old girl, daughter of a distinguished intellectual whose troubles began with the first signs of menstruation. These were at first typical hysterical symptoms: vomiting, dyspepsia (during one month she could only swallow solid food, during another only liquids), convulsions and a severe state of hyperaesthesia so that she believed a wire placed on her hand to be as heavy as a bar of iron. In another month blindness developed with

hysterogenic points on the little finger and on the rectum, which, when touched, exhibited not only convulsive movements, but motor paresis in the legs, with exaggerated spastic reflex movements, contractions, and muscular energy increased to such a degree that the pressure of the hand on the dynamometer caused a rise from 32 kilograms to 47.

But there were more spectacular things to come. Somnambulism appeared—not in the *sleepwalking* sense of the word but as a hysterical state of automatism. During this the girl became unusually active in domestic work, showed great affection for her parents and an extraordinary aptitude for music. Later her character changed—a "virile audacity and immorality". (Possession?) Lombroso found the most extraordinary of all the fact that when she became temporarily blind, *she was with the same degree of acuteness* (which he carefully measured with the Jaeger scale) at the point of her nose and the left lobe of the ear. Lombroso blindfolded her and yet she was able to read a letter which had just arrived addressed to him; she was also able to distinguish the figures on a dynamometer. Equally curious was the reaction to the stimuli upon her "improvised and transposed eyes". When a

finger was approached to her ear or her nose or the examiner
made as if he were going to touch it or a ray of light was
flashed upon it from a distance with a lens, she became keenly
sensitive to all this and irritated by it. "You want to blind
me!" she cried and recoiled. With an instinctive simulation
she even lifted her forearm to protect the lobe of the ear and
the point of the nose—and remained in this position for ten
or twelve minutes.

Her sense of smell was also transposed; even the strongest
ammonia thrust under her nose did not produce the slightest
reaction—while a substance even with the weakest odour
if held under her chin, excited a quite special simulation. If
it was pleasant, she smiled, winked, breathed more rapidly;
if it was distasteful, she quickly put her hands up to that part
of the chin and rapidly shook her head. Later the sense of
smell became transferred to the back of the foot(!); when any
odour displeased her, she would thrust her legs right or left
while her whole body writhed; when it pleased her, she
remained motionless, smiling and breathing quickly.

All this was still within the physiological phenomena of a
hysterical condition. But what began Lombroso's gradual and
reluctant conversion to a more open-minded attitude towards
occultism were the phenomena of precognition and clairvoyance which he now observed in the young girl. She foresaw
"with what I would call mathematical exactness and sometimes fifteen or sixteen days previously" the day of her cata-
leptic fits—the hour in which they were to occur and the
"particular metal to be used in checking them". This, in
itself, may be described by sceptics as an elaborate hoax—*if*
these fits were play-acting then obviously the girl could choose
the time and day at which to produce them. Lombroso, however, did not think so; and he recorded that the girl predicted
events that would happen to her father and brother—and
these came true two years later. She clairvoyantly saw from
her sick-bed her brother behind the scenes of a theatre, more
than half a mile away from their home.

This particular case induced the criminologist to collect
others and he amassed quite a wide variety of similar cases—
transposition of sight and hearing to other parts of the body,

hyperaesthesia, clairvoyance and telepathy. Lombroso studied some twenty subjects who were, in his view, successful in transmitting thought, able to divine the name of a paper, a number etc. Twelve of these, he noted, were neuropathics and these he found the most rapid and most precise telepaths. At first he developed the theory that thought, being a phenomenon of movement, could be transmitted over short or long distances. But then he discovered a fault in his own theory: for as the forces of vibratory motion decreased as the square of the distance, even if transmissions of thought could be still explained over short distances, how could those between two distant points affect the mind of the percipient without being dissipated on the way? Especially as the brain is not an instrument fixed on an immovable base and therefore the starting and receiving points were by no means stable.

One of the most remarkable clairvoyants Lombroso was able to study at first hand was Dr. C., a distinguished young scientist and at the same time a neurotic who had suffered since puberty from grave symptoms of hysteria due to some hereditary defects. He had noticed at an early stage that he possessed powers of premonition. He frequently announced to his mother the arrival of a letter or a person whom he had never seen before and yet described minutely. His most spectacular and most practical exploit was the foretelling, on February 4, 1894, of the great fire at the Como Exposition (which actually took place on July 6th of the same year.) He was so insistent about this that some members of the family hastened to sell all the shares they held in the Milan Fire Insurance Company—thus avoiding a considerable loss for after the fire the claims were so huge that the market value of the shares fell to one third of the original. Strangely enough, as the date of the fire drew closer, he felt less and less certain about it—although when he was in a trance he kept on repeating it, up to the morning of the day when it happened.

Again, this particular case inspired Lombroso to make a large collection of prophetic dreams and precognition cases, ranging from the historic dream of Jacopo Alighieri, Dante's son, which led to the finding of the thirteen lost cantos of the

Divine Comedy, the dream of a Lieutenant Perrino who saw, most vividly, his own capture and murder by a band of outlaws; the dream of a servant girl in which her dead lover told her the winning numbers of a lottery which came up promptly and a whole host of others. Lombroso, still uncertain as to the interpretation of all this varied (and often trivial) material, concluded:

> There is enough in all these observations to enable us to conclude that there exists an immense series of psychical phenomena that completely elude the laws of psychophysiology, and that have solely this feature in common and this certainty—that they take place more readily in individuals subject to hysteria, or who are neuropathic, or who are in the hypnotic or dreaming condition, just at the moment, in fact, when the normal ideation is more or less completely inactive, and in its stead the action of the unconscious dominates, which is more difficult to subject to scientific examination of any kind.
> In short . . . cases are cited and verified in which there are manifestations (even exaggerated) of a function whose organ is as completely inactive as if it were lacking.

Having convinced himself he overcame one chief block— the objection that spiritistic, parapsychological phenomena could not really exist because they were contrary to physiological laws. Though he could not deny this conclusion he did not like it very much. He still had to override a considerable reluctance to agree to attend, in March 1891, a séance with that redoubtable medium, Eusapia Paladino—the Neapolitan lady who had played such an important part in the careers of Carrington, Lodge and Richet.

The séance took place in a Naples hotel, in full daylight and Lombroso stipulated that he was to be alone with Eusapia. It was, from the point of view of Eusapia, an unqualified success. "Extremely heavy objects" flew through the air without contact and Lombroso agreed to investigate the phenomena.

Three months before his death in October 1909 Lombroso gave an interview to the American *Hampton's Magazine* which dealt with Eusapia and summed up almost seventeen years of their long association. As we have dealt with the lady in considerable detail, we are more concerned here with his general conclusions than with a repetition of the observations and experiences which he shared with so many other prominent psychical researchers. Once again he repeated his conviction that mediumship was a "new form of hysterical attack".

... Just as the creative frenzy of genius is, in my opinion, an equivalent of the psycho-epileptic paroxysm . . . At the time a genius conceives a poem or picture, certain of his brain-centres work all independently of the rest of his body, is a sort of detached nervous explosion of the intellect, caused by an abnormal concentration of the brain... Mediumship contains many of the same elements.

Lombroso, like his colleagues, had no illusions about Signora Paladino's inclination to cheat—the mixed nature of her mediumship. Yet there was, for him at least, "too much material, too many authentic instances, to worry about the possible trickery. However doubtful each separate case may appear, in the *ensemble* they form such a compact web of proof as wholly to baffle the scalpel of doubt."

He was asked whether he believed that "these things" were due, possibly in part, to the spirits of the dead, but in part also to the abnormal state of the medium?

"Yes," Lombroso replied unhesitatingly. "And we are so much the more led at the very outset to believe that all the spiritistic phenomena take their rise in the abnormal state of the medium since many of these phenomena always take place in the vicinity of the medium, especially on the left side, and since the phantasmal arms and hands issue with more facility from her body and her garments, and the spectral forms appear, for the most part, above her head or that of her control standing by. Further, the rarer and more important the phenomena are (for instance, the appearance of phantasms) the heavier is the trance of the medium. Indeed, when movement of objects occurs, even at some distance away from the medium, like movements at the same moment are noticed in him or her. And, as soon as the phantasm appears, there is frequently noticed (for instance, in the medium Fairland, who was sewed into a hammock to allow the registration of variations in his weight) a gradual diminution of his weight, till it reached sixty-six pounds. Normally, he weighed one hundred and thirty-two pounds, and the moment the phantasm disappeared, his weight began to increase."

From this Lombroso deduced that the body of the "spectral appearance" was formed at the expense of the body of the medium. This, he maintained, was confirmed by the circumstance that in the first materializations of mediums many of the "spirits" they evoke bear a certain resemblance to the face or the limbs of the medium or "even to the whole of his or her person"—something, he added, that must have given even further support to the suspicions of trickery.

The interviewer asked him whether ghosts actually had weight?

"Certainly," Lombroso replied. "It has evidently been so proved—and that many, many times. Colonel Alcott, for instance, was experimenting with the medium Compton in 1874 and observed that when the young girl-spirit 'K' appeared, the body of the medium disappeared. Then he tied (and sealed with sealing wax) a string passing from the aperture of the medium's ear to the back of the chair in which she sat. Out of the invisible then stalked the spirit which was at first found to weigh seventy-seven pounds, later fifty-eight and still later fifty-two pounds. In the meantime the medium had disappeared but reappeared as soon as the spirit had gone, yet without pulse or breath..."

He went on to explain that the mediums seemed to give their actual physical weight to the "phantasms". In one of Eusapia's levitation séances it was noticed that *her lower limbs* were lacking; "John", her control explained that it was he "who had caused them to dematerialize in order that her weight might be less for the levitation". At the Paris series of sittings which both Richet and Lombroso attended, it was found that during the levitation of a table the weight of Eusapia diminished by just the amount the table weighed, returning to the normal amount after the levitation had ceased.

It was largely through Eusapia that Lombroso worked out

certain theories about the spirit world, though he used the experiences of other psychical researchers and material provided by other mediums. He concluded that, especially under the influence of anger or offended vanity, they developed a "dynamometric force" which could reach as high as one hundred to one hundred and ten kilograms and often attained to eighty or ninety—the force of a very strong man. While it was impossible to measure the velocity by which they moved through space, this, could be as high as twelve hundred miles per hour. In one case it had been proved that the "flying brothers of Bari" moved almost thirty miles in fifteen minutes. They *did* resemble human beings; they could be photographed without being visible and could leave fingerprints on a photographic plate. One of their peculiarities was that they were apt to "comport themselves as gaseous bodies under certain special tissues" and Lombroso, with some others, put forward the hypothesis that their molecular constitution resembled that of radio-active bodies.

He added:

That is, they behave beneath their spirit clothing as we radio-active humans do; and hence we have a right to think they may be made up of the same molecules that we are. In a way, ghosts exist physically just as surely as we do. But the phantasm has the negative property, so to speak, of dissolving under the influence of strong light, as wax is melted by heat . . . We see by this how it is that phantasms do not manifest themselves in the daytime. They have other weaknesses. The intelligence of these discarnate personalities, even in the case of those who were in life of strong intellect, being now deprived of their own organism and being obliged to make use of the brain of the living, is but fragmentary and incoherent. When a long time has elapsed since their death, disembodied persons seem to be dazed and confused in revisiting the familiar scenes of earth. You would say they were embarrassed in reinvesting themselves with old habits. Many are sincere, but the greater part are rude and unseemly jesters, allow themselves to be influenced by suggestion into accepting for true that which never occurred. Many spirits remember nothing of their past. Numbers of them cannot locate themselves properly except in the circle of their intimate friends and acquaintances.

This is, of course, a convenient explanation of the huge amount of drivel that has poured out during hundreds of thousands of séances; an alibi for the "ghost" who appears to his or her offspring and is unable to tell its own name. Lombroso was writing before the general acceptance of psychoanalysis and so he did not consider that the "rude and unseemly jesters" might be simply the ids of the mediums. Often enough a female medium, gentle, well-behaved and even prim in her "waking" life indulges in language during her trances which would put a navvy to shame. This may be the "rude and unseemly jester"—it may also be her subconscious revolting against repression. (In cases of medieval or even modern "possessions" all exorcists have noticed the shocking language the "demons" are apt to use.) Some of the spirit controls are very much aware of the bad impression they make and at least one of them faced the problem squarely when he said:

"To put ourselves into communication with you, we must penetrate into your sphere, and we sometimes become as careless and forgetful as you are. That is the reason why we make mistakes and are incoherent. I am as intelligent as I ever was, but the difficulties of communication with you are great. In order to speak with you it is necessary for me to re-enter the body and there dream. Hence you must pardon my errors and the gaps in my speech and memory..."

Many spirits, as Lombroso and several of his colleagues noted, made communications that were "unworthy of them". The Italian criminologist pointed out the parallel with the dreams during which many of us firmly believed we have composed something memorable—"but when we awake and write it down, it excites our pity". The discarnate individualities, he added, sometimes write with their own proper signatures. Often they use a formal, lithographic hand—because when a medium is in trance the right hemisphere of the brain appears to be dominant. Many times the words were written with the letters reversed—as *latipsoh* for *hospital*. This led to an enormous number of errors and also to involuntary blunders in the spirit communications. Hence also the "very natural and proper uncertainty or doubt which some spiritistic messages awaken in cautious minds".

Obviously, Eusapia had provided her fellow-countryman with the most striking and convincing phenomena—even though Lombroso had also been fully aware of her less attractive qualities. But he summed up these experiences with the quote from Dante:

> "Always to that truth which has an air of falsehood, a man should close his lips, if possible; for, though blameless, he causes shame (to himself by telling what fails of securing credence)." In good sooth, it is the best of advice for one who wants to lead a quiet life, especially in the academic world, which has a propensity to dissimulate and deny intractable facts which do not admit of common and universal explanation, such as these very facts that people are so shy of accepting, of an operant force that survives death.
> And yet I repeat—although it is dangerous to do so—that no other explanation applies to these facts (since the action of the medium is in many cases insufficient to account for them) except this: The dead are still endowed with power (or, rather, assume it under the stimulus of the medium) sufficient to impart those ideas and perform those feats which the powers of the medium and the experiments in the séance do not suffice to explain.

Though with a number of qualifying reservations, this was a clear enough declaration of spiritualist faith—on a scientific, experimental basis and not that of religion for Lombroso had no intention of drawing any dogmatic and moral conclusions from his researches.

By his training and scientific inclination, Lombroso shared the ambitions of many of his colleagues to try and measure psychic phenomena by physical apparatus. We have already mentioned the experiments with the loss and gain in weight which had been observed in the sittings of Eusapia and other mediums. Lombroso introduced two Regnier dynamometers during one series, placing them on a table about three feet from the medium and asking Eusapia to exert the greatest pressure she could. The indicator rose to 42 kilogrammes, in full light, during a single manipulation. Out of the trance state Eusapia was never able to reach more than 36. There was, of course, no physical contact between her and the instrument; he asserted that she saw her "John" (her regular control) pressing in his hands the dynamometer which, in her ignorance, she called "the thermometer". An interesting fact observed was that while her hands were held tightly by Lombroso and a colleague, she was wringing them, trying to turn them towards the dynamometer. The pupil of her eye contracted and her breathing grew deeper.

During the February 1907 sittings Lombroso placed a Marey cardiograph in the cabinet, some three feet from the medium who had her back turned to it; her hands, as usual, were controlled by two of the experimenters. The cardiograph was connected to a pen running upon a cylinder covered with lampblack. The connection was made by a tube traversing the walls of the cabinet. The writing pen was located some twenty inches from the left lateral wall of the cabinet and about a yard and a half from the medium. Now "John" was asked to press the button of the cardiograph. A few minutes later the noise of the pen running over the cylinder was heard. The result was two groups of curves, rapidly decreasing. The first covered about 23 seconds, the other about 18 seconds. The tracings indicated either a state of exhaustion or else "weak volitional energy". As a control, one of the experimenters pressed for one second uniformly and rhythmically on the button producing an entirely different, completely regular pattern.

Other experiments involved an electroscope (which registered a certain radio-activity in the trance state), an apparatus which registered movements of the medium, manometers, scales, styluses and cylinders—the basic purpose being to see to what extent and in what form the mediumistic energy could affect all these while excluding all possibility of normal contact, of direct exercise of pressure or energy. Summing up the

Eusapia phenomena, Lombroso enumerated about forty different kinds which he divided into five main classes. These ranged from "meaningless oscillations and movements of the table", to "displacement of the chairs of the observers"; from levitation to raps and blows at a distance from the medium to apports, from "touchings, handlings and pressures of invisible hands" to luminous points, from radio-active action on photographic plates to "apparition of forms having the human appearance, or character." He also listed, quite dispassionately and objectively, her "tricks":

Many are the crafty tricks she plays, both in the state of trance (unconsciously) and out of it—for example, freeing one of her two hands, held by the controllers, for the sake of moving objects near her; making touches; slowly lifting the legs of the table by means of one of her knees and one of her feet; and feigning to adjust her hair and then slyly pulling out one hair and putting it over the little balance tray of a letter weigher in order to lower it. She was seen by Faifofer, before her séances, furtively gathering flowers in a garden, that she might feign them to be "apports" by availing herself of the shrouding dark of the room. It would seem, also, that she had learned from certain prestidigitators some special tricks; for example, that of simulating human faces by movements of the two hands wrapped with a handkerchief so as to look like a turban. And yet her deepest grief is when she is accused of trickery during the séances—accused unjustly, too, sometimes, it must be confessed, because we are now sure that phantasmal limbs are superimposed (or added to) her own and act as their substitute, while all the time they were believed to be her own limbs detected in the act of cozening for their owner's behoof ...

As a psychologist and physiologist, Lombroso made a full clinical study of Eusapia which few others interested in psychical phenomena were able and had the opportunity to do. There was nothing abnormal in her appearance, except a lock of white hair that surrounded a depression of the left parietal wall—which was caused either by a blow with a stewpan her stepmother administered or a fall from a window at the age of two, according to which story Eusapia preferred at the moment. Her physical characteristics had been examined and recorded with minute care, whether it was the asymmetry of her cranium or her blood pressure, her sensitivity to pain (greater than normal), the hyperaesthetic zone which with her was concentrated in the ovary or the general weakness (or paresis) in the limbs of the left side.

Psychologically there were many interesting and contradictory elements. While she was not very good at precognition she had singular telepathic powers; twice when people were presented to her as admirers but in reality were her secret enemies, she repulsed them with brutal directness, without even looking at them. She frequently failed in good sense and common sense but had a subtlety and intuition of the intellect in sharp contrast to her almost total lack of education. She was ingenuous to the extent of allowing herself to be imposed on; on the other hand, both before and during her trance states, she sometimes exhibited a slyness that in some cases became downright trickery and deception. Her visual memory was extremely keen. Her morbid characteristics sometimes amounted to hysterical insanity. She passed rapidly from grief to joy, had strange phobias (for instance, she hated staining her hands); extremely impressionable, she was subject to dreams even in her mature years. When she was angry, especially when her reputation as a medium was questioned, she could be so violent and impulsive as actually to fly at her adversaries and beat them with her fists.

Yet these tendencies, Lombroso added, were offset by a singular kindness of heart; she spent most of her earnings on the poor and on children; she felt deep pity for the old and the weak and those who suffered. She was also constantly in trouble for rebuking and attacking people who maltreated animals which she considered a heinous sin.

She had the individual habit of giving notification before and sometimes after the beginning of the séance of what she proposed to accomplish. But afterwards she usually could not remember what she had promised or whether she had actually achieved it—and often she failed to do so. At the beginning of the trance her voice was hoarse and all her secretions—

sweat, tears, even menstrual blood—were increased. She became almost insensible to pain, heat, noise. When she was about to enter into a trance state, she lessened the frequency of the respiratory movements, just as fakirs did, passing from 18 inhalations to 15 and 12 a minute, while her heart beats increased from 70 to 90 and even to 120.

Lombroso gave a vivid picture of Eusapia's trance stages which, he found, in some ways resembled those of other mediums he had sat with:

> ...The hands are seized with jerkings and tremors. The joints of the feet and the hands take on movements of flexure or extension, and every little while become rigid. The passing from this stage to that of active somnambulism is marked by yawns, sobs, perspiration on the forehead, passing of insensible perspiration through the skin of the hands, and strange physiognomical expressions. Now she seems a prey to a kind of anger, expressed by imperious commands and sarcastic and critical phrases, and now to a state of voluptuous-erotic ecstasy.
>
> In the state of trance she first becomes pale, turning her eyes upward and her sight inward and nodding her head to right and left; then she passes into a state of ecstasy, exhibiting many of the gestures that are frequent in hysterical fits, such as yawnings, spasmodic laughter, frequent chewing, together with clairvoyance and a word often extremely select and even scientific, and not seldom in a foreign tongue, with very rapid ideation, so that she comprehends the thought of those present even when they do not express it aloud or utter it in a mysterious manner ... Towards the end of the trance, when the more important phenomena occur, she falls into true convulsions and cries out like a woman who is lying-in, or else falls into a profound sleep, while from the aperture in the parietal bone of her head there exhales a warm fluid, or vapour, sensible to the touch ...
>
> ...After the séance Eusapia is overcome by morbid sensitiveness, hyperaesthesia, photophobia, and often by hallucinations and delirium (during which she asks to be

watched from harm), and by serious disturbances of the digestion, followed by vomiting if she has eaten before the séance, and finally by true paralysis of the legs, on account of which it is necessary for her to be carried and to be undressed by others ...

From her and from other psychics he drew the conclusion that the phenomena demanded a tremendous concentration and expenditure of energy. Yet Lombroso did not think that the projection and transformation of this energy explained *all* the phenomena.

... it is entirely too easy a solution to suppose (he wrote in his *After Death—What?*) that, when the transmission of thought at a distance occurs, the cortical movement constituting thought is transmitted afar by the ether to a certain brain predisposed to another; that (as Ochorowicz puts it) the molecular motion of the brain (which is thought) is propagated around the thinker in the shape of ethereal vibrations, and, meeting a second brain, is again transformed into the original molecular movements and inscribes upon this brain the thought of brain Number One; and that, as this force is transmittable, it is also transformable, and, from being psychic force, becomes motor force, and *vice versa*, especially since we have in the brain certain centres the special function of which is the presiding over movement and thought, and which, when they are irritated, as in the case of epileptics, provoke now violent movements of the joints and now the great inspirations of genius.

Lombroso rejected the purely mechanistic explanation because he thought that while, in the case of telepathy and thought-transference, it could perhaps account for the transmissions over short distance, it would not provide the answer to the riddle of telepathic communications from one hemisphere to the other. Nor did it explain how this vibratory motion—called the "sightless courier of the air"—could pass to the organ of the percipient without waste, keeping its long geographical parallelism of thousands of miles.

If the "exteriorization of motivity and of sense" which

some researches ascribed to the medium, explained many phenomena—seeing things at a distance while the medium is in the dark, with his eyes closed, feeling the pricks and pinches administered to the phantasms, the transportation mentally and sometimes bodily to a distant point and so on—it still could not explain the development in the mediums of force and energy much greater than their natural resources nor the formation of phantasms totally different from their own bodies. There was also the inexplicable though authentic simultaneity and contemporaneity of certain psychic phenomena.

During a séance in Milan with Eusapia Paladino while the medium was at the climax of her trance, the image of a woman appeared to Lombroso's right who spoke a word to him. Eusapia was asleep in the centre of the room; near and above the distinguished criminologist the puffed-out curtain was blowing and swaying while at the same time on the left a small table in the cabinet was moving about and a small object was brought over the table by invisible means in the centre of the main room. On another occasion while the anthropologist was "being caressed" by a phantom, two other sitters—Princess Ruspoli and Dr. Imoda—were both touched by other hands. These phenomena raised the question in Lombroso's mind how the psychic force of a medium could not only be transformed into motor and sensory force but simultaneously act in three different directions, with three different purposes? If it was impossible for a sane, normal, alert man, with senses undimmed, to turn his attention into three different directions at once, how was this possible for a medium "in a state of evident insensibility"?

It was, perhaps, a rhetorical question, for the eminent criminologist was not attempting to answer the questions which have remained unanswerable. But he pointed out that there were things happening at the séances which seemed to take place *against the will of the medium*. A typical Italian example of this was recorded by him when he dealt with the limitations of mediums:

Having heard it asserted that during a séance at the resi-

dence of the Duke of Abruzzi the table set about beating
time, with all four of its feet, to the tune of the royal march,
I said jestingly that at Turin even the tables and John King
(Paladino's "control") were monarchists. But I had hardly
finished the sentence when the table began to protest the
contrary, and with such resounding raps and blows that they
could be understood even by profane outsiders inexpert in
the typtological code. And when I said, "Oh, John, aren't
you a monarchist, then?" he denied it vigorously with the
usual two raps,—did so in several séances. It then occurred
to me that possibly the idea might have emanated from
Eusapia, as especially the Neapolitan populace is warmly
attached to the monarchy. Being quite intimate with her,
I led the conversation up to the subject, and the poor little
woman, who in her adventurous life has too often, and not
always joyously, come into touch with princes and kings,
reaffirmed that she had no opinions in politics, that she was
not interested in kings, and that the government that she
would prefer would be one that took thought for the poor,
nor did she ever in her subsequent talks contradict herself.
And not even to the Duke of Abruzzi, who remunerated her
magnificently for the séance, was she grateful for anything,
grieving that his Highness had not presented her his visit-
ing-card and did not show her those cordial manners that
others always exhibit. Hence we see that the monarchical
manifestation did not emanate from Eusapia, nor from
John, but was, on the contrary, in opposition to their pre-
dilections.

Probably Lombroso welcomed the slight comic relief of
contrasting republican and monarchist "entities"; but he
found other proof of a third will intervening in spiritistic
phenomena, belonging neither to the medium nor to the
sitters but opposed to all of them.

At one séance Eusapia said to one of the members of the
circle, identified only as "Signor R": "This phantom is going
to be for you," and immediately afterwards went into a deep
trance. Before long a beautiful lady appeared; her arms and
shoulders were overlaid with the edges of the portières but

their outlines could be still seen. Her head was covered with a
veil of finest material; she breathed against the back of R.'s
hand, ran her hand through his hair and gently bit his fingers.
In the meantime Eusapia uttered prolonged groans, to mark
her painful effort; but the groans ceased when the apparition
vanished. It was seen by two others present and returned
several times. Though both Eusapia and "John" consented,
when they tried to photograph it, the "lovely lady" refused
and twice broke the photographic plates nor would she con-
sent to have the imprint of her hands to be taken—contrary to
Eusapia and "John". However, at the last séance a "hand was
heard dipping itself in the liquid in the cabinet" and R. obtained a block of paraffin with a complete imprint. Unfortunately, he did not keep his prize long—a "fluidic hand
reached out from the curtain and broke it into small pieces".

Later it was discovered that this was the phantom of a
living person—a former mistress of R. who had broken off
their affair and who had "a great interest in not leaving proof
of her identity".

Lombroso went on asking questions, demanding "rational"
explanations for the phenomena which he witnessed himself
or which others recorded whose testimony he was willing to
accept—for he realized that he would have to depend on outside, trustworthy and respectable support for his own observations.

. . . what shall we say of the cases (he asked) in which she
(Eusapia) is slowly lifted with her chair, from the floor without making any effort with her feet, not merely without any
support, but against the will of the controllers, who rather
seek to hinder her from rising?

. . . how can we explain the medium's seeing in trance, in
a dark room, with closed eyes, everything that takes place
before, behind, and around her, whereas awake and in light
she can see only what takes place before her and on each
side?

. . . how explain . . . the following occurences? Eusapia is
almost illiterate, spells out a printed page with difficulty,
and does not understand handwriting unless it is read and

explained to her. Now in a séance at Turin there entered the circle a young man with a bracelet in his pocket, and she not only divined that it was for her, not only succeeded by the aid of a fluidic hand at a distance of three feet from his hand in groping about his coat and extracting the bracelet from his pocket and clasping it on her own arm (her hands being all the while firmly held by controllers), but, on being asked what else the young man had in his pocket, replied, "A letter, and that letter contains a request." ... Now how could she, an illiterate person, not merely read the letter, but make a rapid summary of its contents?

... how explain the impromptu and very beautiful sculptures of Eusapia who is entirely ignorant of the art of Pheidias?

... But especially inexplicable as a part of the action of the medium are certain features or functions that rarely manifest themselves during trances but yet do so occasionally—such as vision and audition at a distance, the presentiment of the future, the knowledge of diseases, the chemical sense for medicinal substances and the instinct for remedies ...

Lombroso remarked that the majority of the medium's actions were automatic—shown by the stereotyped character of their gestures, the uniform reproduction of the same, often graceful movements. This automatism was especially plain in the case of the writing medium because his hand was writing while his mind was elsewhere occupied. He tried to suggest a physical explanation for this—according to him almost all of the phenomena of mediums originated on the left side or were perceived on the left even when they came from the right. This left-handedness or sinistrality was temporarily transmitted even to the controllers. Hence, he argued, it followed that in the trance the work of the right hemisphere of the brain prevailed, the one "least adapted to psychical work" which participated least in the activity of consciousness. (We know, of course, that any individual only uses one of the hemispheres of the brain at any given time; that the left side is controlled by the right hemisphere and vice versa. Experiment with left-handed people has proved this clearly. Any damage to one of the hemispheres causes a switch-over as the other until then unused half is drawn into action.)

But what "automates this automaton? How reconcile with the automatism of the medium his multiplex activity and his artistic productivity?" The Italian researcher believed that outside intervention was required; and this was exactly what the "spirit" provided—a "spirit" that was for the most part powerless by itself but acquired power by associating itself with the living body of the medium under trance conditions. It could not be explained by the unconscious action of the medium—for Lombroso proved, at least to his own satisfaction, that in many cases what the medium produced could not be drawn from his subconscious, did not exist in his memory. (The argument still rages about this and many of the cases of clairvoyance, clairaudience, speaking in "unknown tongues", producing mediumistic examples of art and literature have been questioned in our more sceptical or perhaps technologically and psychologically more advanced age.) Lombroso had no doubts on this score—to him only the intervention of disembodied entities could explain the greater part of the phenomena; the complete answer could be found only by integrating the mediumistic force with another force —which "although it is more fragmentary and transitory, yet acquires, by identifying itself with the medium, a greater potency". And here he passed the final Rubicon that separated the materialism from spiritualism, doubt from the acceptance of the unseen—for he stuck out his neck by summing it up, once and for all:

And this force, authenticated by the tradition of all ages and all peoples and *by experimental observations* (my italics) is pointed out to us as found in the residual action of the dead.

Lombroso had no illusions about the dangers he was running, the risks he was accepting when he repeated that he could think of no other explanation applicable to the facts which he had observed. He believed that the dead were still endowed with power (or assumed it under the stimulus provided by the medium)—a power sufficient to impart ideas and perform feats which the powers of the medium and of the participants in a séance did not suffice to explain.

It did not worry him that the replies given to questions at these séances were quite frequently "vain and false and most often in flat contradition to the culture of the medium and the sitters". Nor did his faith weaken because the appearance of phantoms was often totally different from their living images. All this could be explained—"although the explanation naturally excited a shudder in the learned scientist"— only by admitting that the presence of the entranced medium often induced the appearance and the activity, more or less vigorous, of "beings or personalities that do not belong to the living—but which for the nonce take on their semblance and assume of their functions".

Lombroso did not believe in pure, disembodied spirits— for one thing, he argued, these would be beings of which we could form no conception—but he believed that these phantasms or entities had a physical substance so subtle and refined as to be both invisible and imponderable, except under special circumstances. The parallel he used was that of radio-active bodies which had the power of emitting light and heat without apparently losing any weight whatever. He quoted his friend and colleague Oliver Lodge who, in his presidential address to the S.P.R. compared materializations to "the mollusk that can extract from water the material for its shell; or to the animal, that can assimilate material for its nutriment and convert it into muscle, skin, bone or feather." Thus, Lodge continued, the "living entities" that ordinarily did not manifest themselves to the sadly limited human senses (even though they are in constant touch with our psychic world), are able temporarily to use the terrestrial molecules that surround them "for the purpose of building up a kind of material body capable of manifesting itself to our senses".

Both men, if one interprets their rather complex reasoning correctly, believed that the "phantasmal bodies", the spirits or ghosts, belonged to a different state of matter, the radiant state. Writing in 1909 Lombroso was relating the materializations to the work of the Curies who, six years earlier, had received the Nobel Prize for their discovery of radium and polonium; to him his theory had "at length got solid footing in science". He went even farther:

> ... (this) is not only the sole hypothesis that can reconcile the ancient universal belief in the persistence of certain phenomena of life after death with the postulates of science which holds this truth to be self-evident, that without an organ there can be no function, and that there can be no functioning of an organ without loss of weight, but is also the only hypothesis that harmonizes with the phenomena we have under our eyes in spiritistic experiments.

It was, of course, the ancient and recurrent dream of all men of science who had pioneered the exploration of the unseen—a dream, that unfortunately is today farther from reality than it had been sixty years ago. The dream that belief in the occult can be reconciled with experimental science, that by the mass of evidence and the introduction of clinical and laboratory methods into the séance room materialism and spiritualism could be brought to some kind of co-existence if not complete union. When Lombroso was having his séances with Eusapia and others, there seemed to be no lack of physical mediums, the emphasis was on the physical rather than on the mental phenomena (though, unlike Schrenck-Notzing, the Italian *savant* was equally interested in both)—and Lodge, Lombroso and their fellow-believers felt that they were on the verge of a great break-through, a tremendous and decisive discovery. Lombroso himself invoked the fact that human senses possessed a very limited extension of perceptivity compared with the action of "possible external forces". Sound and light existed far beyond the limits within which our ears and eyes were able to function. The Turin professor argued that materializations, whether for a short or a long time, no longer remained "completely incomprehensible and unreducible to the grand laws of monism". Then he added, seemingly at a tangent: "At any rate, the thing has been proved over and over again." Thus, he seemed to say, the fact that something cannot be explained under the terms of existing knowledge, does not invalidate its authenticity; because something

puzzled our finite consciousness and understanding, if sufficient quantitative evidence was available, it could not be rejected.

Lombroso knew—as did practically all the pioneers of
occultism—that the evidence was often fragmentary, contradictory and trivial. It was almost always subject to attack and
some of these attacks were viciously personal, imputing to the
men of science who, in the view of their opponents had betrayed the cause of rational thought, the lowest and most
despicable motives. (Many of these were sexual innuendoes;
the Victorian mind was usually inclined to think the worst of
any male's "animal nature".) He went on quoting example
after example of what he considered incontrovertible proof,
either from his own experiences or from those whom he considered above all suspicion—and, somewhat defiantly, he pro-
claimed his faith in the afterlife and in the active link of the
dead with the living "pointed out to us by the traditions of all
times and of all peoples and by experimental observation".

Lombroso collected a large number of cases of "spirit
doubles", examined hundreds of "spirit photographs" and
analysed the proofs for the preservation of identity after death
as revealed by mediums. He himself was involved in a striking
poltergeist case at his home-town, Turin, in the winter of
1906.

The phenomena began on November 16th in a little inn on
the Via Bava, kept by a man called Fumero, with a series of
strange noises, heard both in daytime and at night. It was
found that some full or empty wine-bottles were being broken
in the cellar. More frequently, they would descend from their
places, roll along the floor and pile up against the closed door
so that they seriously obstructed the entrance when it was
opened. In the sleeping quarters on the upper floor (linked
by a staircase with the servants' room near the small, public
room of the inn) clothes were twisted up and some "transferred themselves" downstairs. Two chairs while "walking
down" were broken. Copper utensils, hanging upon the walls
of the servants' dining room fell to the floor and slithered over
long stretches of the floor, sometimes being bent or broken. A

spectator put his hat on the bed of the upper chamber; it vanished and was later found on the rubbish-heap of the courtyard below.

All these were typical poltergeist phenomena; as usual, no one could find any "normal cause" for them. The police came and investigated—in vain. A priest was called but while he was performing the service of exorcism, a huge bottle full of wine shattered at his very feet. A vase of flowers that had been brought into the inn, descended on to a table from the moulding over the door where it had been placed—without any mishap. Two large bottles of fruit-brandy being distilled were broken in broad daylight. Five or six times—while the police were actually present—a small ladder, leaning against the wall in the main room of the inn, was slowly lowered to the floor. A gun moved across the place and was found on the floor in the opposite corner. Two bottles flew down from a high shelf with some force. They were not broken but they bruised the arm of a porter.

Crowds gathered and police gave the Fumero family to understand that they were suspected of staging all these "miracles" in order to attract custom. After that, the poor people decided to suffer in silence. They pretended that Professor Lombroso had visited them and that the plague had ceased—for they were being mercilessly teased and ridiculed.

About this time Lombroso did hear of the case and decided to study it in detail.

I made a minute examination of the premises (he reported). The rooms were small. Two of them served the purpose of a wine-shop; one was used for a servants' eating-room, and was connected by a small stairway with a bed-chamber above. Lastly, there was a deep wine-cellar, access to which was obtained by means of a long stairway and a passage way. The people informed me that they noticed that whenever any one entered the cellar the bottles began to be broken. I entered at first in the dark, and, sure enough, I heard the breaking of glasses and the rolling of bottles under my feet. I thereupon lit up the place. The bottles were massed together upon five shelves, one over the other. In the middle of the room was a rude table. I had six lighted candles placed upon this, on the supposition that the spiritistic phenomena would cease in bright light. On the contrary, I saw three empty bottles, which stood upright on the floor, spin along as if twirled by a finger and break to pieces near my table. To avoid a possible trick I carefully examined, by the light of a large candle, and touched with my hand all the full bottles standing on the shelves and ascertained that there were no wires or strings that might explain the movements. After a few minutes two bottles, then four, and later others on the second and third shelves separated themselves from the rest and fell to the floor without any violent motion, but rather as if they had been lifted down by some one; and after this descent rather than fall, six burst upon the wet floor (already drenched with wine) and two remained intact. A quarter of an hour afterwards three others from the last compartment fell and were broken upon the floor. Then I turned to leave the cellar. As I was on the point of going out, I heard the breaking of another bottle on the floor. When the door was shut, all again became quiet.

Lombroso returned another day and the unfortunate inn-keeper whose stock of wines was being depleted rapidly told him that the same phenomena were happening with increasing frequency. In the servants' room a small brass colour-grinder had jumped from one place to another and, striking against the opposite wall, was twisted out of shape—something Lombroso could check himself. Two or three chairs had bounced around with such violence that they were broken—but without hurting anybody standing by. A table was also broken.

The professor then proceeded to examine all the people in the house. There was a tall lad of thirteen, a waiter, "apparently normal"; also a head-waiter who seemed to be equally "ordinary". The innkeeper himself was a veteran, a soldier who had fought in a good many battles and who had threatened "the spirits" with his gun in his exasperation. He obviously liked drink and since the poltergeist infestation had started, indulged himself even more than usual. His wife was a small woman of about fifty, lean and slender. She told Lombroso that she had been, since infancy, subject to neuralgia, tremors and "nocturnal hallucinations"; she had undergone a hysterectomy. Lombroso suggested to her husband that he should send his wife away for a few days. She went to Nole, her native town—and though she began to suffer from hallucinations, voices heard at night, movements, persons no one else saw or heard, all plagued her—she did not cause any poltergeist phenomena while she was away. Nor did anything happen at the inn during this time. But as soon as she got back, the performances started again, at first with particular fury though later more mildly. The "repertory" was the same —kitchen utensils, chairs, bottles, broken or displaced. Again, Lombroso suggested that she should leave for another period.

On the day the woman left (she was in a state of great excitement and had cursed the alleged spirits), all the dishes and bottles that had been placed on the table were broken and fell to the floor. If the family was going to dine, the table had to be prepared in another place and by another woman, because no dish touched by the mistress remained intact. Hence one naturally suspected that she had mediumistic powers, or would have done so had it not been that during her absence *the phenomena were repeated in just the same way.* That is to say (to be specific) a pair of shoes of hers that were in the bed-chamber, on the dressing-cloth, came downstairs in broad daylight (half-past eight in the morning), traversed the servants' room through the air, passed into the common room of the inn, and there fell down at the feet of two customers, who were seated at a table. (This was on November 27.) The shoes were replaced on the dressing-cloth and continually watched, but did not move until noon of the next day; and at that hour, when all were at dinner, they disappeared entirely! A week afterwards they were found, with heels to the floor, under the bed of the same chamber.

Another pair of ladies' shoes, placed in the same chamber, on the dressing-cloth, and carefully watched, disappeared and were found only after the lapse of twenty days (folded

up as if they were to be packed in a trunk), between the
mattresses of a bed in the same chamber that had been
turned upside down in vain *two days after the disappearance.*

Obviously Lombroso's theory that the innkeeper's wife
caused all the trouble and that her absence would cure it, did
not work. She was recalled from her native place—and the
phenomena continued with the same frequency as before. A
bottle of fizzy lemonade, for example, passed over a distance
of twelve or fifteen feet in full daylight and in the sight of
everybody, slowly, as if carried by a human hand—it travelled
as far as the servants' room (the door of which was open) and
then fell to the floor and was shattered.

At this point the innkeeper dismissed the boy-waiter. When
he left, all the phenomena ceased. Yet though adolescents are
often involved in poltergeist phenomena—either providing
"the motive force" or, as in the majority of cases, cleverly fak-
ing the various effects—this, according to Lombroso, could not
apply to this particular "haunting". The boy was certainly
nowhere near the cellar when all those bottles shattered in
Lombroso's own presence. Nor could he have been involved
in many of the other telekinetic phenomena. He was not a
hysteric and when he moved to another inn, there was no
further incident.

Lombroso investigated a number of other cases, poltergeist
outbreaks and hauntings. He tried to evolve a general theory
in connection with them but found it difficult. In some cases,
as he pointed out, there was the active intervention of a
medium—but in the majority, especially those of longer dura-
tion, even of centuries, there was no such intermediary. In
these cases "the action of the deceased shines forth conspicuous
and unique, verified by typtological communications or by
apparitions ... observed and recorded by the most ancient
people and preserved by all nations in their popular
legends ..."

How did this square with his theory of the "spirits" needing
the physical equipment of a medium to manifest their presence and their powers? Some put forward the theory which

Lombroso records without comment, that the "spirits" drew the material of their incarnation from the animals and plants of a deserted house which they were haunting. This explanation was offered to him several times by mediums in trance. Others affirmed that all haunted houses, even those that are free from mediumistic influence, have been under the influence of "distant and invisible psychics". The Italian criminologist doubts these and points out that the evidence quoted in support of this theory is rather that of "the doubling of the mediums, who transferred themselves to a distance for a brief moment and for a few nights, rather than cases of haunted houses"—in other words, teleportation. In any case, such "transfers" are exceptional phenomena, not frequent occurrences as those in connection with haunted houses and so no rule can be deduced from them. Telekinesis almost always takes place in the immediate vicinity of the medium—rather more frequently on the left than on the right side—and loses all active potency beyond eight or ten yards. The fact that so many of the hauntings and poltergeist infestations are linked to cases of violent death (suicide or homicide) was particularly striking. "In general," Lombroso remarked, "we may suppose that the phantasmal bodies of persons who suffered violent death, as in these old castles and halls, would exhibit a greater activity and energy, which they evidently do." (He did not seem to think it necessary to offer any explanation why this should be so—though of course, it is the traditional view.)

By and large he believed that many hauntings and poltergeist cases had remained unrecorded and were soon forgotten:

It is very curious to note how in these latter days it is possible to examine and verify so many recorded facts of this kind, whereas for almost two centuries scarcely one was observed, except among the lowest strata of the population, who were not, we may say, in communication with the cultivated classes. The latter, at any rate, since they did not believe in the phenomena, even when they took place directly under their eyes, took no pains to examine them or make known their existence. Hence all memory of them was lost. Today they take place, are perceived, and are studied, although, indeed, they are readily forgotten and encounter incredulity and derision.

Thus, in the Fumero case, if I had not persisted and returned to the place, it would have been believed that, with the first appearance of the police or of myself, the phenomena had disappeared, and they could easily have been attributed to trickery, thereby completely diverting from them the attention of investigators.

Thus Lombroso thought that the eighteenth and the nineteenth centuries were equally unfavourable to the investigation of occult phenomena—because those qualified for such an investigation were too materialistic and too much concerned with "reason" and the ordinary people who did not have these qualifications, were afraid or too embarrassed to report them. This is a rather broad generalization for the interest in the "spirit world", in hauntings and apparitions, in mesmerism (as the early experiments in hypnotism were called) certainly was very much alive during the eighteenth century and spiritualism itself was born in 1849 with the mediumship of the Fox sisters. The supernatural actually exercised a lingering and baleful fascination as shown by the witch-trials and burnings which were still quite numerous in the first half of the eighteenth century. However, Lombroso was right when he said that a multitude of extraordinary and inexplicable events and phenomena were never properly investigated—partly because the necessary scientific apparatus was lacking and partly, especially in the pragmatic and rational nineteenth century became such investigation was considered a disgraceful and wasteful occupation for any man of science.

Like his eminent colleagues and friends, Lodge and Richet, Lombroso also faced squarely the derision and even hate of the scoffers who, at the very least, accused him of being deceived by "the most vulgar class of swindlers".

Certainly, he replied, very often the first impression of the pioneers of the occult is that "all this medium business" is a question of trickery. This was the explanation, he added, that suited best the taste of the mass of people "since it saves thinking and studying, and makes the common man believe he is a more conscientious observer and more skilful than the man of science". Certainly, no group of natural phenomena (for he was quite convinced that the occult phenomena deserved this classification) lent itself more readily to fraud and doubt than that of spiritualism. All the most important events always took place in darkness—and no experimenter could resign himself to the acceptance of events and facts that could not be properly controlled and observed. The mediums themselves, whether consciously or not, often resorted to deceit; indeed, there was a general inclination within them for fraud. The majority of them were hysterics and when they felt their powers ebbing, they inevitably wanted to supplement them by artifice. Some, being extremely suggestionable (as they all are) engaged in trickery because some hostile person present urged them secretly. (Eusapia told Lombroso at Genoa: she felt that some one "secretly ordered her to cheat and felt impelled to obey". This may sound, to some, a most bare-faced lie, an impudent attempt at an alibi; but the Italian criminologist had ample experience with criminals of all sorts and prided himself on being able to separate falsehood from truth.) Lombroso set up the case for the prosecution with no evasion or disingenuity:

Let us not speak, then, of false mediums, hireling impostors, and jugglers by profession, who swarm in localities and countries where the belief in Spiritualism is most widely diffused. There is a regular literature of this subject, especially an American literature, that makes us acquainted with a whole arsenal of special weapons and apparatus used, it is said, by mediums in their cunning juggleries; such as false beards, masks, garments of finest muslin, phosphorescent substances, chairs containing hollow places from which the medium slyly draws forth his masks, or else with springs which, unbending, allow him to simulate true levitation.

...Add to this the fact that no movement at séances takes place except in the immediate vicinity of the psychic, and especially in contact with her skirts, which makes some suspect artifice. Then it looks suspicious that the fluidic element gathers strength in the darkness and behind the material stuff of draperies, such as the portières of the medium's cabinet, from which so frequently come the materializations.

Again, when we seek to give precision to mediumistic manifestations by special mechanisms, the mediums often purposely cause them to deceive us—not to speak of the fact that often, in experimental work, under identical conditions we do not get identical phenomena. (Thus some few mediums can operate in the light, while the greater number cannot.) Add that most of them show a vulgarity in strange contrast with the manifestations, apparently supernatural, of which it is supposed they are trying to give a demonstration, although even these manifestations often exhibit a vulgarity not seldom mingled with obscenity, in too sharp contrast with their pseudo-divine character.

Well, Lombroso says, these objections are not without weight—yet he proceeds in his attempt to deal with them. As for darkness—doesn't the photographer need darkness to develop his plates? Does that make his work less genuine? He cites Richet that this analogy might help to understand how light might inhibit the development of occult phenomena. There have been mediums operating in full light. Even Eusapia Paladino produced some of her impressive phenomena in full light. While some mediums are so cantankerous that at first they deliberately make the instruments react wrongly, this is due to the fact that by and large they hate innovations, are averse to new mechanisms. "And so, for that matter, is the whole human race," Lombroso adds in an aside. He quotes the examples of half-a-dozen mediums who were most severely controlled, their hands and feet tied, their bodies netted in a circuit of electricity, enclosed, naked, in a woollen sack or a net—and yet they "performed".

There have been physical experiments, the Turin professor continued, "that have the gravity and importance of all experiments made, as they were, with exact instruments, especially since they were controlled, or authenticated, by the photograph". True, spirit photographs have often been fraudulent and Lombroso was fully aware of some of the methods used to obtain them—but suspicion inevitably was weakened when some of them were made "before a special commission of experts and men of indisputable fame". (Alas, this is not a clinching argument. We have seen how outstanding scientists have been fooled by unscrupulous and clever fakers. Still, Lombroso himself was convinced by the evidence which his colleagues Aksakoff, Finzi, Carreras, Volpi and Zöllner had gathered.)

Nor does telepathy, in his view, account for certain phenomena, though those "who shy at the hypothesis of the spirits of the dead as operant psychical agents" have tried it as an explanation. How could mediums draw from the minds of the sitters knowledge which they (the sitters) did not possess themselves? And, quoting James Hyslop, Lombroso asked: "How could the successive appearance before mediums of various communicators—five, six, ten times, with accurately individualized personalities" be explained by telepathy? The very fact that there are errors in the communications, he argued, excluded the hypothesis of telepathy—being accounted for by the difficulties that beset beings who endeavoured to develop "their powers in the new sphere of life to which they had attained". Telepathy could not provide precognition.

What of the unconscious? Certainly, Lombroso admits, some psychic phenomena find their explanation "in that singular state of the brain in which latent energies are set in motion of which we have no consciousness and which develop a marvellous power". He quotes a whole galaxy of creative geniuses—from St. Paul to Nietzsche, from Berlioz to Dostoievsky to describe this process. But the *unconscious*, he pointed out, is not equivalent to the *non-existent*. While the subconscious powers may bring to the surface ideas and facts that had been forgotten—they cannot do the same for facts which the individual had never learned. He gave some striking examples of this difference:

> ...If one end of a thread is tied to a woman's finger and the other end to a ring that dangles in the centre of an empty

goblet, her age can be known, even though she is unwilling to tell it, because the ring will tinkle as many times as she has consciously lived years. This is very true; but the woman knows the number of years. Hence one part of the enigma is cleared up. But when the spirit speaks Chinese to a European who is ignorant of the language, but understands it while in trance, there is no use in talking of the unconscious, because in this case even the unconscious has to work upon acquired cognitions.

...And so we may say of cryptomnesia (or unconscious memory). Under certain circumstances, e.g., when I am at a great altitude, say six or seven thousand feet, I remember Italian, Latin, and even Greek verses which had been forgotten for years. But I know very well that I read them in early youth. Similarly, during certain dreams in nights when I am afflicted with conditions showing intestinal poisonings, disagreeable moments of years previous are reproduced with precision, and with particulars so minute and exact that I could not possibly recall them when awake. Yet I observe that they are always fragmentary and incomplete recollections and depend more on the condition of the sentiments than on the intelligence.

Fiercely, almost defiantly, Lombroso continued to eliminate —at least to his own satisfaction—all the "normal", materialistic explanations of the occult phenomena which were considered genuine. He thought that mediumistic phenomena were so numerous and so well-proved that even their biology and psychology could be constructed. In a way this was the attitude of Saul who had been struck by the lightning of revelation and as Paul on the road of Damascus had found what he accepted as the only truth.

Lombroso died rather suddenly and his main declaration of faith, the book *After Death—What?* was published posthumously. Whether one accepts his conclusions or not, whether one is sympathetic to his conversion or ascribes it to self-delusion and weakness, he certainly deserves a special place in the pantheon of the pioneers of the unseen.

RAPHAEL SCHERMANN

The Café Ritz in Vienna was a popular meeting place of
Bohemians and the upper middle-class. It never closed, dis-
pensing food and drink twenty-four hours a day.

In October 1921, about eleven o'clock in the evening, a
man of around forty, with a high forehead, strongly marked
eyebrows, a thin, straight nose and a clipped dark moustache,
was sitting with a group of friends in one of the booths at the
back of the café. He looked up and saw two men who entered
at the same time. One of them seemed to attract his special
attention. He turned to his friends and said:

"That man ... over there ... he's going to use a gun in this
place before the night is over ..."

The group around him did not smile or scoff at this strange
utterance. For the man in the Café Ritz was Raphael Schermann—one of the strangest and most efficient clairvoyants in
the world. Instead of ignoring or pooh-poohing his forecast,
they sent for the owner of the café. Herr Breitschwantz, the
proprietor, listened to Schermann, then invited him and his
party to descend to the bar in the basement where the two men
had already moved. There Schermann would be able to
watch the "subject" whom he suspected of such dangerous
and unorthodox behaviour. Herr Breitschwantz who made a
point of knowing all his regular guests, knew him quite well
and was highly sceptical about Schermann's prophecy—yet
at the same time he was also getting somewhat uneasy. A
scandal involving gunplay—that would hardly be good publicity. It had to be prevented at all costs.

About an hour later the wife of Schermann's "subject"
arrived at the Café Ritz. Herr Breitschwantz had told the
clairvoyant that the couple were separated though no divorce

proceedings had yet been started. The lady, a striking blonde, was accompanied by two men and another woman.

As soon as the husband whom Schermann watched closely, saw them enter, he jumped up and ran from the bar, vaulting the stairs in a desperate hurry.

"He's gone to fetch his gun," Schermann declared. "Tell his wife and her friends to leave at once—or there'll be a tragedy."

Breitschwantz carried out the clairvoyant's instructions promptly and faithfully. He explained the situation with the utmost tact; the four people paid their bill and left.

A few minutes later the husband who had rushed out so precipitately, returned. His right hand was hidden in his coat pocket. He was obviously looking for his wife and her companions—but they were, of course, gone. He sat down with the air of a man who realized that a final decision had been postponed, still tense and restless.

Schermann asked the café proprietor once again to intervene. He sent the agitated guest a message—telling him that he was interested in his handwriting as a graphologist. To his own friends, Schermann asserted firmly that the desperate husband's signature would show the shape of a—revolver.

Startled by the request, the man did not refuse. He signed his name on a piece of paper and sent it to Schermann's table with Herr Breitschwantz. And Schermann was proved triumphantly right—though he had never met the man before. The signature's initial letter, a capital "S" was clearly shaped like a gun.

Herr Breitschwantz then introduced the graphologist to the unhappy husband. They sat down in a corner—and this time Schermann asked for another signature—written in ink. Once again the shape of the revolver was clearly marked.

For a couple of hours the two men talked. It was quite obvious that "S." was on the verge of a complete breakdown, driven by almost insane jealousy. Schermann got the wife's telephone number from him, called her and persuaded her to come back to the café. Husband and wife were reconciled. The "psychographologist", the pioneer of an entirely new branch of parapsychology, saved a couple of lives. Not for the first, nor for the last time, in his amazing career.

Raphael Schermann was born in Cracow which was then part of the Austrian province of Galicia, the southwestern portion of dismembered Poland. He was still a child when he began to collect envelopes while his contemporaries concentrated on coloured pencils, marbles, stamps or butterflies. He used to play with these envelopes in his nursery and tell himself stories about their writers. Later he compared handwritings with the people to whom they belonged. One day at school he discovered that the script of a hunchback boy showed certain flourishes which he could not detect in the writing of any of his other schoolmates. He succeeded—though not without a good deal of trouble and a remarkable persistence for such a young boy—getting samples of the writing of several hunchbacks—and found that they all had certain characteristics, identical with those shown by his misshapen classmate. He was barely twelve when he started an album, asking all his acquaintances and friends, children and adults, to write a few words in it so that he could find the parallels between their hand and their physical appearance. Still later, he began to study the psychological side of the problem, the physiognomy of handwriting. Gradually he realized that whatever a human being experienced was somehow mirrored in his writing, leaving its mark like a seal impressing itself on wax. He found that the handwriting of many people could be read like the open book of their past and future.

Early in this century Schermann spent some time in the United States. In New York a distinguished graphologist proposed to go into partnership with him—but Schermann preferred to return to Cracow. About 1910 he settled in Vienna. He had a fairly commonplace job—he worked for several insurance companies as a claims inspector. But he was anything but an ordinary investigator. At first he demonstrated his analytical, prophetic and "reconstructive" powers only in private circles. But gradually his reputation grew. He was not only consulted by the police but was appointed as an official handwriting expert by the Vienna Central Law Court.

However, this was only a small part of his work. Above all, he was deeply concerned with helping troubled, unhappy people —without any financial reward and often enough, quite anonymously.

During the early part of the first world war he served with distinction in the Austrian army but was badly wounded and, after a painful spell in hospital, was invalided out of the forces. It was in 1916 that my father, Cornelius Tabori, met him for the first time. As a criminologist and writer, he was specially interested in Schermann's gifts. Recently I came upon the notes he made about their first encounters; they are dated April 16, 1916:

"It is now almost a year since the most distinguished medical men, psychologists and criminologists have taken up publicly the case of Herr Schermann. They seek an explanation of his strange talents, to find a classification and evaluation of what must be called his genius. Today he is once again the centre of admiration, doubt and curiosity and through him a most interesting and still developing science, graphology, has come to the forefront.

"Herr Schermann uses handwriting *as a springboard* for his new and unique experiments which often touch on psychometry and other occult disciplines. He calls himself a graphologist—or, sometimes, a psycho-graphologist. In his experiments he always operates at the farthest limits of this art and provides most valuable data for its understanding. I have spent now several weeks in his company, having obtained two months' leave from my work as war correspondent in Transylvania and Serbia—a kind of convalescence leave for I have had several bouts of illness.

"I showed Schermann an envelope addressed by a lady he certainly did not know. He glanced at it briefly and then set to work. He described in minute detail the lady's appearance, her figure, the colour of her hair, her features and—suddenly it seemed as if she came to life in front of me—he imitated her manner of talking, her inflection, her turns of speech, using exactly the same gestures as she would use. He appeared to know everything about her character, did not neglect a single peculiarity; he quoted long-forgotten actions and utterances, disclosed secret motives, explained the inexplicable.

"He told me her life story; as if he had suddenly become part of her very existence, he described with uncanny exactitude and certainty her milieu: people, objects and events. When he reached the more important happenings, the highlights, so to speak, he more or less *acted* and lived them. He used dialogues which I remembered well; they were reproduced in the same words, the same pauses and gestures. I have never experienced the like of it in all my life.

"Next I showed him an unopened letter. From the handwriting on the envelope he told me that the writer was demanding money and using threats to obtain it. I opened the letter and read it: every single detail was correct. Next we put ten different envelopes on the table, each written by a different person. Without the slightest hesitation, Herr Schermann pointed out which of them were connected—the handwritings of husband and wife, mother and daughter; he described their relationships, their histories, their features, forecast their futures. In three cases out of ten these forecasts proved already true—though only a week has passed..."

Graphology of course, is far from being a new science. Suetonius, in his *Life of the Caesars*, described a peculiarity of the Emperor Augustus. He never divided words at the end of a line but would put the letters to be carried over under the last word and draw a circle around them. There are many references to handwriting in classical literature but it was only in 1622 that Camillo Baldo published his *Trattato come da una lettera missiva si cognoscano la natura e qualità delle scrittore*—an essay about the manner in which the nature and qualities of a person can be learned from a letter. The Bolognese author is generally accepted as the founding father of graphology though the name itself was coined by the French Abbé Michon in 1871. Goethe and Leibnitz were fascinated by the subject. Crépieux-Jamin defined it as "a science of observation". The others who developed and explored this subject—Grohmann, Henze, Moreau, Hocquart, Delestre, Fladrin, Langenbruch, Lombroso and Klages were perhaps the most outstanding—all agreed that the personality, the character, the physical and mental qualities of the individual are invariably manifested in the handwriting. A vast literature has grown up around the subject with theories and classifications, methods of analysis and even computerized filing systems and today, of course, criminologists and courts of law have equally accepted the handwriting expert as representing an orthodox, established science.

But Raphael Schermann was far more than such an expert, a theoretical graphologist who could provide reliable answers to orthodox questions. He combined something unique with his analytical knowledge—telepathy, clairvoyance, second sight, precognition. All these are rather vague names for what was in him a very personal talent; something that science has described and registered but for which it could not offer any explanation within the existing laws of nature or the canons of psychology.

A few weeks after my father ended his first series of experiments with Schermann, a grisly discovery was made in a derelict house at Cinkota, a rather shabby suburb of Budapest, the Hungarian capital. Seven hermetically sealed tin cylinders or barrels were each found to contain a somewhat shrivelled but otherwise well-preserved nude female body. After some concentrated and hectic enquiries the police established the identity of the victims. All of them were domestic servants, all had been lured to their deaths by small ads in which a "gentleman of independent means" sought a "life-partner". Their savings wheedled out of them, their few pitiful possessions pawned, they ended their lives in the cellar of a plumber's workshop. The only clue to the murderer was a postcard which he wrote to one of his intended victims—a few hasty lines which the Budapest police, totally baffled by now, submitted to Schermann.

The psycho-graphologist was particularly excited by this specimen and provided a long analysis. Among other details, he declared that the murderer received the first impulse for his crimes from his frequent visits to prostitutes.

"It was clear to him," Schermann continued, "that his own

humble position in life was insufficient to satisfy his passions and subconscious urges. He must have felt deeply unhappy and even at a very young age he must have devoted much of his time and energies to his sex life. He needed variety and almost daily orgasms. Driven by his strong sensuality, he soon learned the art of seducing women of all types quickly and easily. I am sure that he must have been reading a good many crime stories—especially those dealing with the mass-killers of women. He must be a good-looking man with insinuating manners who had little trouble in making acquaintances; whenever he began a new affair, he tried to liquidate the earlier ones. It must have happened at this stage that he decided to get rid of a clinging, insistent female by killing her. He found it unexpectedly easy to carry out his plan, no one suspected him, the woman's disappearance remained unnoticed—after which he was determined to use the same methods with any female who threatened to become a burden. He must have got rid of his own wife in the same way—of whom, I understand, no trace has ever been found since the entry at the registry office. He left his employment and set up on his own but his craft—whatever it was—was only intended as a cover, a front that enabled him to follow his murderous activities with greater convenience and security..."

Schermann was certain that the Hungarian Landru acted alone, that he had no accomplices though he may have involved others to strengthen his cover. "...His handwriting shows great self-control and even self-censorship; he is always on guard and has never shown his true self, except perhaps in the final moments before he finished off his victims. This self-control and self-censorship had become such an ingrained habit that he used it even in the most insignificant details; it is shown in his habit of painstakingly crossing the t's and dotting the i's, correcting an incomplete letter even when such correction would be hardly necessary..."

Schermann pointed to certain rounded, coneshaped letters which indicated the murderer's jovial, amiable front he put on to attract his victims. Some of the flourishes indicated to considerable acting talent; but his writing was a clear sign that his friendly, informal manner was only pretence.

"Inside him a terrible struggle continued permanently and in many places there is a strong decline, descent of the words. His total reserve is most rigorous; the letters 'a', 'g' and 'd' are completely closed, without the slightest opening on top. The way he crosses his 't's' shows that he is jealously guarding his privacy, admits to his home or workshop only his very few intimates—or those whom he has chosen to destroy. It is quite possible that he lived near a cemetery or was in some relationship with a gravedigger . . . An extremely cunning man, he preferred older women because he assumed that they had more money, more time to save a nest-egg. His fiery sensuality served to kindle a responsive flame in some middle-aged spinster or long-neglected widow. His courtship naturally flattered them. And while they did not give him the sexual pleasure he sought, he could always find that with other, younger, prettier females. It is an interesting fact that whenever he uses the letter 'z' (the lower case one) it is always 'crippled'—especially in female names. I assume that he must have hurt or strained his right hand when he crammed the bodies into those tin barrels. Such a sprain can last quite a long time and as he could not get help in this grisly occupation, his condition must have grown steadily worse and he could only follow a certain rhythm in writing. Thus his method of disposing of his victims is mirrored in the letter 'z'. If he happened to spend some time in a hospital, it is probable that he exchanged his own name card with that of a dying man and thus wiped out his identity... He was a born impostor. His sexual appetite was insatiable. I think he was most stimulated by redheads. The way his curved lines merge into a hard, straight line show a rock-hard resolution and energy ... I believe he is still alive and uses a different script, imitating the handwriting of the person whose name he has taken. But there are certain characteristics of his handwriting which he is quite unable to disguise. If there is some other handwriting material available—some registration form or other document he had to fill out, he could still be traced. Unfortunately the immense publicity given to the case excludes the possibility of any trap being set successfully. Maybe he has left something behind in the hospital where I am sure he has spent some time. He is a murderer but not a pervert. His sexual orientation is strictly heterosexual if on the border of satyriasis..."

The murderer of Cinkota, though identified as a plumber called Béla Kiss, was never found. However, his circumstances, his character, his activities were all fully established—and they fitted Schermann's theories perfectly. Kiss had been called to the colours immediately upon the outbreak of the 1914-18 war and was taken prisoner in the initial Russian offensive that invaded, though only temporarily, the land south of the Carpathians. For many years there were rumours of Kiss serving in the Foreign Legion, heading an important section of the Russian Cheka—but nothing was ever established definitely. The chances are that he died in a Serbian prisoner of war camp, having taken a different name.

But Schermann's clairvoyant deductions were fully justified by the statements of those who had known Kiss and by two or three of his would-be victims who had escaped by some accident or miracle.

An Austrian diplomat showed Schermann his handwriting. By turning it upside down, the psycho-graphologist discovered a pointing index finger in it, clearly outlined. He told the diplomat (whom he had never met before) that he must be interested in palmistry and chiromancy, a zealous student of the subject. The diplomat immediately admitted the truth of this. In the same way, in another handwriting Schermann discovered the signs of a—sniffing nose and deduced correctly that its owner had a hyper-sensitive sense of smell. In Count Zeppelin's signature he clearly traced the shape of the famous dirigibles named after their inventor. In still another script he found the shape of legal paragraphs—whereupon it was disclosed that the writer had broken certain provisions of criminal law, had become involved in a sensational trial and suffered a disastrous interruption of his career. In the writing of an unmarried mother Schermann discerned clearly the details of infanticide including the knotted clothes line and the child's head. Still another handwriting told him that the writer was planning a sea-voyage—he had, quite unconsciously, drawn the shape of a boat, including its smoking chimney, all within the address: 'Wien II' (Vienna). A man had disappeared, leaving a farewell letter in which he announced his intention of committing suicide. After a brief glimpse at his writing, Schermann announced that the missing man had simply absconded with the proceeds of a robbery; he had also grown a huge, waxed moustache. There were other indications in the writing—and on the basis of Schermann's analysis the fugitive was arrested in Marseilles. His moustache was exactly of the shape the psycho-graphologist had described!

A Prague family was constantly pestered and hoaxed by anonymous telephone calls. For instance, Count B., an old friend of the house, left a message that he would visit them in the evening. The family made elaborate preparations, other guests were invited—but the Count did not put in an appearance. Later he declared that he had not sent any message and had been actually out of town. On another occasion the Baroness C. invited the family to her box at the opera. They duly arrived for the performance—only to find that the lady had already disposed of the places in her box and knew nothing of the invitation. Schermann, asked to help, provided himself with samples of the handwriting of the family's various friends both male and female. One of them clearly showed—the outline of a telephone receiver. The hoaxer—a bitter, resentful old maid—was trapped and the nuisance ceased.

"Where *our* graphology ends, Schermann's begins," said a handwriting expert. And certainly, some of his analyses showed an eerie talent of penetrating the most secret recesses of the human mind. More than that—a definite prophetic, clairvoyant ability.

In December 1919 Schermann visited Budapest and delivered a lecture about *The Secrets of Handwriting*. The editor of one of the Hungarian dailies showed him a letter, written in 1916 by a man who was then a prisoner-of-war in Russia. The signature was hidden from the analyst.

Schermann stared for about three or four minutes at the letter, then dictated the following analysis:

"Born of a poor, simple family. Brooded a long time as to what career to follow, what road to choose. Did not find the right one. Became involved in some community from which he could not free himself. His life was bitter, he had little pleasure during the years. When he saw others, less talented, succeeding better than he did, he became embittered and this bitterness developed gradually into a universal hate of mankind. His parents and relatives noticed this and tried to steer him in a different direction—but all in vain. Slowly he sank deeper and deeper and was no longer master of his decisions. He mixed with a clique; his main concern was not to be considered weak. He was completely submerged by the influence of this group, became one of its leaders and yet was afraid of it..."

When Schermann reached this stage in his analysis, he was no longer looking at the handwriting. He stared into space and spoke as if in a trance:

"Capable of any inhuman, horrible action—but he is not the executor, he makes others perform it. He is the voice of those who surround him, yes, he is almost their medium. In his later years he is going to play an important short-lived role. And this role will be closely connected with the characteristics I have described. This can become his doom. If he is lucky and manages to find good people, maybe he will do good—but he inclines more and more to those in whom baseness and cruelty predominate. In this setting the low instincts will awaken in him, too; he will be even more ruthless than the others. And when the beast awakens in him, he will commit the most outrageous acts. He clings greedily to life. He is not one of those who desire death. Therefore he will do everything to save his life. But finally he will die a violent death. He will either commit suicide or he will be killed. I am inclined to think that he will die by his own hand..."

The handwriting was that of Tibor Szamuely, the "Marat of

the Hungarian Soviet Republic", leader of the Communist terrorists who tortured and murdered hundreds of innocent people. In August 1919 when the Béla Kun regime fell, he was the only one refused political asylum by neighbouring Austria —whereupon he committed suicide.

In September 1922, the editor of a German newspaper asked Max Hayek, Schermann's biographer and most enthusiastic supporter, to submit two letters, both written by women, to the graphologist. "As you know," the editor wrote, "Schermann has already looked at my own writing some months ago. At that time he foretold that I would marry a brunette— though all my girl-friends were blondes and I did not like dark-haired women. That's why I was unwilling to believe anything he said. But now I *did* meet a brunette. She is only twenty-one; I met her recently. This should be enough for you and Schermann to know."

Hayek presented the two specimens to Schermann three days later and took down his analysis:

"This lady met your friend by accident and both of them are grateful to fate because they very quickly found a spiritual and intellectual affinity. He has almost begun a new life; his often depressed mood was lightened by her and these days he feels so young as he hasn't for years. She is like a melody for him, a phrase of music constantly singing in his mind. Both of them feel as if they were caught in the net of some magic—so that it is almost uncanny and, strangely enough, they often regret that they had ever met. Their happiness is so intense that the thought of losing it spells disaster for both of them. This is no ordinary, purely physical love but a spiritual union, binding them tightly— and unless it is broken by outside circumstances they are hardly likely to free themselves from it. Both must be extremely careful because the people around them will try to destroy their great happiness and joy out of sheer jealousy. She feels as if she had woken from a nightmare, she is happy and does not want to emerge from her happy daze. She has **given him so much strength that he works with redoubled** zeal, everything he touches is successful and he is going on to still greater triumphs in the future. They must hold back from any rash steps in order to discover whether this supernatural force linking them is lasting or not and whether any untoward incidents could break their relationship. Only then can they proceed to solve problems which are already in the air today..."

Hayek sent on the analysis and a few days later the editor wrote to him:

"Schermann's achievement is again fabulous—at least as far as I am concerned. I have only known the young lady for a few weeks and therefore do not dare to pass judgment. But I think Schermann is right about her, too. Especially interesting is his remark that some people would try to destroy our relationship out of sheer jealousy. This is amazing—at the same moment when I read his analysis, I was informed about an anonymous letter sent to the young lady in an attempt to denounce me as a heartless philanderer!"

Schermann was also able to supply medical diagnoses on the basis of handwriting. Since Dr. Albert Erlenmeyer published his book about the physiology and pathology of handwriting in 1879, many scientists had examined the relationship between graphology and disease, among them Dr. Wilhelm Preyer, Professor Charcot and Dr. Duparchy-Jeannex. Schermann often traced, with signal success "the graphic curve of psychological and physical life" in the samples of writing. He was, of course, not a physician himself but succeeded in saving lives, warning about future illnesses, advising on treatment by referring people to a qualified medical practitioner.

One of his strangest cases concerned a Viennese police inspector. One day a young girl visited him and showed the handwriting of her fiancé. Schermann glanced at it and said: "He is not going to marry you. There's someone who influences him and is against you."

"He has a daughter born from his first marriage...She doesn't like me."

"Bring me a sample of her writing!"

When this was provided, Schermann was startled: "But

she's only a child—yet she has tremendous willpower! She's certainly your enemy."

Next day the police inspector called on Schermann; his fiancée had told him everything. Schermann examined *his* handwriting and was struck by the strange hooks in his "g's" and "e's" which looked like holes in a tapestry or woven fabric. He asked:

"Did you ever have stomach trouble?"

The inspector said, no, he had an unusually good digestion, he could eat anything.

"My dear friend," Schermann told him, "get married and don't have meals outside your home—or you'll have a serious illness—something to do with your wonderful stomach!"

In July 1920 there was a bad outbreak of dysentery in the canteen of Vienna Police Headquarters—food had been spoiled and caused a serious epidemic. Schermann received a call from a hospital. The inspector, yielding to his young daughter's pleas, had broken off his engagement and had continued to take his meals at the canteen. He was mortally ill. Paralysed down his right side, unable to speak, he had scrawled SCHER in huge letters on a piece of paper. After a while the nurses discovered what he meant. He wanted to see the graphologist—the man who had foretold his fate. He hoped that Schermann could save him. And Schermann did his best to comfort him though he knew that he was past help. A few days later the inspector was dead.

One of the most fantastic talents of Raphael Schermann was what he called "reconstruction". He was able to "reconstruct" a man's handwriting after a single meeting—without ever having seen an actual sample—or, even more extraordinary, from a photograph of the person. Several striking examples of this strange ability were reproduced in Max Hayek's book. Admiral E. H. Seymour, Lord Jellicoe, the Austrian writer Dr. Rudolf Lothar, the famous playwright Arthur Schnitzler were some of his "subjects". And while Schermann's "reconstructions" were by no means complete duplications of the original handwriting, the *basic characteristics* were always present, reproduced with uncanny fidelity.

All this would have been little more than an interesting series of experiments, a playful proof of Schermann's clairvoyant talents. But he was also able to turn it to practical account. One of his most interesting cases was a burglary. He was asked by the insurance company for which he acted as consultant to investigate the matter. The police had found no clues—and yet large quantities of luxury goods had been stolen from one of the best-known Viennese department stores. Schermann sensed that some employee or other must be involved. He visited the place, inspected discreetly the staff— and his suspicions centred on one of the assistants. He "saw" the man's handwriting, "reconstructing" it in his mind. Then he told the owner of the store to ask the young man to write a few words. The proprietor called the assistant into his office. The young man only put two words on paper: *"I have…"* when Schermann, watching him, became convinced that *this was the thief and that he would confess his crime.* He signalled to the head of the firm who declared immediately: "You are the thief!"

The young man jumped to his feet, protested violently, threatened to sue his accusers for slander and rushed towards the door. Schermann barred his way. "You'd better stay. I know you're guilty—and your handwriting told me that you were ready to confess!"

The two men stared at each other. The shop assistant tried to defy Schermann's quiet, searching look—but failed. Suddenly he collapsed, his resistance crumbling. He made a full confession.

"I see from your handwriting," Schermann told him, "that you're not completely depraved, that you can still be saved. You were corrupted by others, dragged into this ugly business. I'll put in a good word for you."

The proprietor of the department store decided not to prosecute. The loss was partly made good. But *not* by the insurance company. The policy, as Schermann pointed out with a smile, excluded any thefts by the staff. And so the owner had to be content, at least to some extent, with the confession and reform of a black sheep.

In July 1922 my father again recorded a striking Schermann case in his diary—this time the prevention of a crime.

"In recent years Schermann has been consulted more and more often by the police," he wrote, "and helped them in various complicated criminal investigations. Sometimes he succeeded in cases where all police methods had been used in vain. In all these exploits of his he is only concerned with saving human lives from destruction. Anyone who has strayed from the path of legality, who is threatened by social or physical disaster, can count on his help.

"On June 28th, the Vienna Banking Union (Wiener Bankverein), one of the biggest banks of Austria, received the following letter:

Vienna, June 27th, 1922

To the Vienna Bankverein.

I have the pleasure to inform you that on 23 June 1922 Kr. 100,000,000—one hundred million crowns—have been placed to my credit at your bank; but as my drawing account is with the Anglobank, Vienna I., Strauchgasse, I would ask you to transfer this sum after deduction of your costs, stamp duties and charges to my account:

Hermann Zagg, Anglobank, Central Branch

as soon as possible. As a fruit and vegetable wholesaler, I have considerable cash payments to make. My address is: Vienna VI, 8 Kapistrangasse IV.

Yours faithfully

Hermann Zagg.

"The letter was passed in the bank through the usual channels and reached the book-keeping department. There it was established that on June 23rd one hundred million crowns had been duly deposited to the credit of Herr Hermann Zagg. There was nothing to prevent the transfer of this money to the Anglobank as requested.

"But Herr Zagg was not to obtain this huge sum (about £80,000 at the rate of the June 1922 exchange) so easily. Through the negligence of a junior clerk who had to deal with the matter, the transfer was slightly delayed. Herr Zagg's letter remained on this clerk's desk for a day or two and when he came to deal with it, it was necessary for him to check once more the credit balance.

"The manager explained to me how such a payment was credited. At the teller's window the payment was entered in a so-called copy-book. The original of every page went to the book-keepers, the carbon copy remained in the teller's book. In this case the original page of June 23rd showed as the final item Herr Zagg's hundred millions. But the junior clerk, wanting to avoid the necessity of asking for the original (which would have led to the discovery of his negligence and the delay caused by it) consulted the *carbon* copy. To his considerable surprise he found no credit entered for Herr Zagg. Of course, he could not keep this information to himself. When the original ledger was consulted, it was established that someone in the book-keeping department had entered the hundred millions as Herr Zagg's credit balance; someone who obviously intended to profit by the forgery. But no such entry could be made on the carbon copy as the ledger remained with the teller.

"At first glance it seemed that a false entry had been made by a young female book-keeper. Whoever had made the entry had tried to imitate her handwriting and had succeeded pretty well. Thus suspicion first fell upon her. A clerk was dispatched to the address which the mysterious Zagg had given; he found that no one of that name lived there. It was now evident that the would-be crook must have an accomplice within the bank; someone who had made the false entry and was in a position to remove any letters or notices that would have unmasked the intended trickery.

"The police investigation was unsuccessful and Schermann was called in. His first task was to analyse the original, handwritten letter of Herr 'Zagg'. Schermann declared:

"'This is the handwriting of a fat, very tall man. He has a sedentary occupation which demands great concentration and leads to eye-strain. He probably spends a good deal of time bending over his work. It is not mental work but one involving precision and accuracy. He may be a watchmaker or a goldsmith.'

"This appeared to point to the fact that the writer of the letter did not work inside the bank. But the book-keeping entries must have been made by an employee. More than fifty of the bank clerks had their handwritings carefully analysed. Of one of them—it belonged to a man called L.B. —Schermann said: 'This is the man who made the entries. He is an artist of handwriting who can imitate the script of others with amazing fidelity. In this case he copied the writing of your girl book-keeper with complete success. He studied her writing for a long time. He is a dedicated criminal. He thought up the whole scheme himself and then looked for an outside accomplice who was to write the letter signed by 'Zagg'. I see how he tried to persuade him to write the letter. I believe his accomplice is a goldsmith whom he dazzles with promises to provide him with much gold for his work. I know that it will be very difficult to make him confess though he knows by now that his trickery has been discovered. Give me another specimen of his handwriting— make him write a few lines *today*.'

"This was done; and Schermann, looking at the new sample, added: 'He already knows that he is going to be unmasked. He told his parents yesterday that he had planned and executed the crime—and asked them to forgive him if he got into trouble. His father and mother are ill. The mother declared that if her son were sent to prison, she would commit suicide. The father would also be unlikely to survive the disgrace. In spite of this, the son has no intention to confess; he will insist on his innocence up to the very last moment. He is a scoundrel with a vicious character. Yet—for his parents' sake you ought to let him go. If you promise that, in case he confesses, you won't go to the police, I'll get him to admit his guilt.'

"As the bank had not actually lost any money, the promise was given after some hesitation. Schermann called the young clerk into his office. Everything happened as the psycho-graphologist foretold. The young man denied his guilt firmly. When Schermann asked him to write a few lines, he produced this:

Wiener Bank Verein
Organizations-Bureau
I had nothing to do with the hundred million crowns.

Vienna, July 11, 1922.

"These few lines betrayed his plans. Though his Christian name was *Ludwig,* he started his signature with 'Loui(s)', crossing out hastily this French form of the same name and replacing it with 'Ludwig'. Schermann thereupon told him that he had an accomplice who was a watchmaker and goldsmith and that he had discussed with him the plan to escape to Paris and live there under an assumed French name—Louis, instead of Ludwig.

"At this statement the would-be swindler collapsed. He gave the name of his accomplice—who turned out to be a goldsmith, weighing eighteen stone! Not only his profession but his physical appearance had also been correctly described by Schermann. The young clerk also spoke about his family and related his talk on the previous day with his ailing parents who had begged him to confess everything as they could not survive the disgrace of his arrest. This conversation, which Schermann had earlier put down on paper, was almost identical in every word with the young man's confession.

"As the bank had escaped any loss, the young man was simply dismissed but no charges were made against him. Later he wrote to Schermann:

" '. . . I am sending you these lines to give you my solemn promise and word of honour to behave in the future at all times correctly and honestly. I want to express my deepest thanks for saving me and guiding me on to the right path after my first attempted crime. God bless you for what you have done for me and my family.

In eternal gratitude,
L.B.' "

A good many psychologists and scientists experimented with Schermann. Dr. Oskar Fischer, a professor of psychology at Prague University was one of the first among them. In March 1918 he lectured about these experiments—which covered several years—in front of a gathering of German physicians in Bohemia.

"The first important fact about Schermann's work," Professor Fischer said, "is that it embraces both graphology and what we call telepathy. It must be stated that even Schermann's graphological achievements go far beyond the known limits of this science. He does not study the samples closely; a brief glance at the specimen is sufficient for him—and sometimes he prefers to turn the handwriting upside down. As a long series of tests has shown, he is also able to describe the writer's current mood; he could even establish, if necessary, whether he (or she) is hungry or well-fed. I repeatedly found that a few simple lines were sufficient for him to deliver a striking character-sketch of the writer. He is also able to do this when his eyes are bandaged and he can only use his sense of touch to trace the writing. He had equal success when samples were given to him in sealed envelopes. After touching the envelope, he was also able to reproduce—or, if you like, reconstruct—the unseen handwriting with often amazing fidelity. The experiments also covered telepathic tests. Several people, including myself, evoked in their minds a certain person in Schermann's presence. Schermann was able to describe these persons, often providing a fantastically faithful character-sketch and was able to imitate their handwriting, again with amazing closeness to the original. The circumstance that Schermann gave graphological analyses while looking at the samples, that he was able to do this by just touching the sealed sample or the visible sample with bandaged eyes, his talent of 'reconstructing' someone's handwriting—all this was examined and checked systematically. While Schermann's character-analyses were so striking that I was convinced about the impossibility of any coincidence or accident, it must be admitted that his character and personality descriptions (at least for those not intimately acquainted with the subjects) did not provide a sufficiently objective series of proof of an outstanding or extra-sensory talent. If Schermann's talent was based on a regular physiological function, it was necessary to establish that his descriptions and imitations or reconstructions should be identical whether he was simply looking at the handwriting, touching it while his eyes were bandaged or producing his analyses through the experimenter's invocation of the same person purely in his mind. In order, therefore, to discover whether the three different methods produced a coherent, complimentary result, I used a whole series of people whom I knew well, who had a clearly-marked character, well-differentiated. Both the character analysis which Schermann produced and the 'reconstructions' of the various handwritings were in every way correct—sometimes the originals were imitated with almost photographic fidelity. The series of experiments involved about two hundred different cases. Out of these over 71% were absolutely correct; about 8% proved failures and the remaining 21% could be described as indecisive. This statistical ratio established the regular, systematic nature of Schermann's gift and excludes any possibility of conscious or unconscious fraud..."

In a Vienna lecture a couple of years later Professor Fischer spoke at some length about what he called "psychic transference"—the term with which he described Schermann's extraordinary talents. Other specialists also conducted experiments with him—including the Viennese professor Moritz Benedikt, the Zurich physician Dr. Paul Cattani and the Vienna psychoanalyst, Dr. Wilhelm Stekel. Their opinions agreed completely with the views of Professor Fischer.

In 1923 Schermann was invited to the United States for some experiments and a series of lectures. On his way he stopped for a few days in London. WIZARD COMES TO ENGLAND, a daily paper headed its article and continued:

"One of the most interesting Viennese of whom little is known in the Anglo-Saxon countries will shortly arrive in our midst. In Austria people call him the 'modern wizard', 'the man with the X-ray eyes', 'the man who reads your soul', 'the seer who knows your past, present and future...'

"By profession he is nothing more romantic than an expert in insurance adjustments; his fame is due to his skill in graphology, or the law of personality based on handwriting analyses. His talent has been discussed by hundreds of newspapers and his lectures in Vienna, Budapest, Prague and Zurich have created a considerable stir.

"He has been tested by scientists of unchallenged standing; the late Professor Benedikt, the famous alienist of Vienna University, among them.

"Schermann, by glancing at a few lines of calligraphy, may say that the writer is a former naval officer who limps on the left leg and spends his leisure time in playing chess. And so it is.

"Last May Schermann met a London manufacturer, one Mr. Gestetner, then on business in Vienna. Looking at his handwriting, Schermann said that Mr. Gestetner was planning to undertake a journey by air. The manufacturer admitted that he meant to return to London by plane, also that he had frequently undertaken such trips before.

"Schermann warned him not to use the plane this time as he saw an impending disaster. Mr. Gestetner did not travel by air. Disaster did overtake the passenger plane and seven people lost their lives.

"Once Schermann detected the writer of an anonymous note containing a threat by deducing that the man's livelihood was breeding dogs.

"In another case the unknown mischief-maker was revealed as a woman with very thick ankles who wore particularly and unfashionably long dresses to hide this defect.

"Schermann once prevented the suicide of a young woman who called on him for advice and from whose handwriting he deduced not only her plan of self-destruction but also that she carried a gun in her handbag.

"Protesting that he is no clairvoyant or fortune-teller, the 'Wizard' asserts that a person's whole being is marked by tendencies that govern actions and that these are visibly expressed in the handwriting. Writing, he says, is a seismographic chart of a personality—the hand registers the most delicate vibrations of the mind..."

In London Schermann was shown a photographic copy of a signature which had been preserved for two centuries in the British Museum; it was thought to be the only known speci-

men of Shakespeare's handwriting. Schermann, according to
the newspaper reports, gave an exact description of his character and appearance (without knowing, of course, that the
handwriting was Shakespeare's)—a description that seemed to
fit perfectly what little fact was known of the Stratford genius.
When someone asked him where the writer of those lines was
now, Schermann replied: "Under ground."

The London paper acclaimed this "analysis" but at least
one Vienna daily struck a somewhat sour note:

"There is no authentic portrait of Shakespeare. Therefore
Schermann's statements are, to say the least, questionable—for
there is no way of checking them." (Obviously the Austrian
journalist did not know that there are two likenesses of Shakespeare generally regarded as authentic—the bust by Gerard
Johnson in Stratford and the frontispiece to the folio of 1625,
engraved by Martin Droeshout—though Droeshout "is unlikely to have had personal knowledge of the poet".)

After his short London stay Schermann went on to New
York where he was received with considerable interest. He
stayed at the Waldorf Astoria and as the news of his arrival
spread, he was literally besieged by people wanting to consult
him. He delivered several public lectures. The *Evening World*
arranged for him a visit to New York Police Headquarters
where he spent a day with Police Chief Richard Enright, his
deputy and the chief of the detectives. One of the cases they
discussed was the famous murder mystery involving James
Elwell, the well-known sportsman who had a celebrated stable
of horses. Enright showed Schermann samples of Elwell's
writing—and the psycho-graphologist described in some detail
how the murder was committed. Elwell was almost as fond of
women as of horses and though no definite clues had been
found, it was assumed that one of them had killed him, out of
jealousy or in revenge for some wrong. Among others, Schermann was shown a letter signed "Marjorie" which the police
assumed was written by one of Elwell's mistresses.

"Have you traced her?" asked Schermann.

"No. Not yet. We haven't been able to identify her."

"No wonder," the graphologist said. "The writer of this
letter is not a woman but a man."

The New York police were startled by his statement and began a new investigation. Three months after Schermann's visit they discovered that the woman who was seen calling on Elwell shortly before he was found dead, was a transvestite, a man dressed in female clothes. They tracked him down and found that he had committed suicide in a Florida hotel about eighteen months after the murder.

A number of American psychologists and neurologists tested Schermann's powers—among them Dr. Dana, a former President of the A.M.A., Drs. Hunt, Kennedy and Crampton—all of whom gave him glowing testimonials. "I am convinced," Dr. Dana said, "that there is something extraordinary about this man. I don't know whether to call his talent telepathy or clairvoyance; but in any case, he 'sees' something that cannot be explained by normal perception. He looks at the handwriting of a person and is then able to visualize both physical and mental characteristics."

When Schermann returned from the States, he was persuaded to try an entirely new career—that of a film star. Rudo films of Vienna produced two silent pictures with him in the lead, supported by casts of professional actors, among them the charming Austrian star Erika Glässner. The screenplays were based on Schermann's most interesting actual cases, suitably dramatized and the Austrian critics, at least, were highly complimentary about the result, pointing out that the films represented a new, original combination of documentary and drama. But this was just a brief episode in Schermann's career; he felt somewhat uneasy about exploiting his gifts commercially though he liked acclaim and appreciation and did not shun publicity.

In 1926 I met Schermann myself in Vienna. He was still working as consultant for a group of insurance companies but at the same time he spent more and more time on psychological experiments—for which he always refused to be paid. I was present at a series of such tests which were conducted (characteristically enough for Vienna) in a quiet corner of the famous Café Imperial. Professor Hans Thirring of Vienna University, the noted psychical researcher, had been persuaded for the first time to test Schermann's powers. Thirring was rather reserved and sceptical. He handed Schermann a few letters and said, a little sarcastically:

"Well, maestro, let's hear what you can tell me about these."

Schermann examined the material but I saw him stealing now and then a glance at Thirring. The professor was frowning; obviously there were some things he did not like—though now and then he nodded approvingly.

"This man's a dreamer," Schermann said about one of the letters.

"Possibly," Dr. Thirring agreed. "I don't know."

Of another, Schermann said that he was a cardiac case.

"That's not impossible," Thirring replied non-committally.

Schermann must have sensed that the professor was dissatisfied with results he was unable to check satisfactorily. So the psycho-graphologist suggested that they should try a few telepathic experiments where control could be more decisive. Thirring agreed.

Later he told me that he concentrated his thoughts (while keeping his face completely expressionless) on a friend of his who was living in Prague and whom no one among those present knew.

Schermann stared at the marble-topped table for about twenty seconds, then he said: "I've got him. An energetic man —in spite of his advanced age he sticks firmly to his views..."

Thirring kept silent; afterwards he confided to me that he was rather startled by this strikingly correct characterization but considered it just a strange coincidence.

"He's worked hard all his life," Schermann continued, "and always hated idleness. His financial position would permit him to retire—but he won't hear of it. He wants to take part in everything, he demands the right to speak out about every question. A man of noble ideas who has always tried to help his associates. He's never saved money. He's not a pushing, overbearing character yet can be seen everywhere ...He is very fond of his children—and spent lavishly on their education..."

"What is his physical appearance?" Thirring asked.

"He's of medium height, rather stocky."

"His general character?"

"He's not easy to deal with . . . Most people do not understand him—but in any case, he's not a very tractable person."

"His health?"

"Though he's old, he's in excellent condition."

"Is he religious?"

"He's both religious and superstitious."

"Is he wealthy?"

"He isn't rich—he's lived well and gave generously to others, especially his children."

Thirring was visibly shaken by this; privately he admitted to me that the description of his friend whom he had not named or identified in any way, was perfect.

Next day we met again. Thirring had prepared seven sealed envelopes. The first contained a visiting card on which one of his friends had written a few lines. The second held a letter whose writer Schermann had already analysed on the basis of a brief sample. Thirring had added his own signature to it. The third contained an Austrian banknote. The fourth had a piece of cardboard on which the professor had deposited his inked fingerprints. In the fifth there was a postcard; in the sixth an empty slip of paper on which Thirring had marked three crosses with his thumbnail; finally, the seventh was empty—though it had contained a letter addressed to the professor which he had removed that afternoon. The envelopes were shuffled and handed to Schermann in a random sequence as Thirring wanted to exclude any possibility of telepathy this time.

About half-a-dozen people, including myself, were present at the test.

"There are only a few lines here," Schermann said about envelope Number One. "Whoever wrote it was in a bad mood. A kind-hearted person but without much pleasure in life. Generous but no spendthrift."

(This, as Thirring declared later, was largely correct.)

"Is it a man or a woman?" he asked.

"I think, a woman."

(Schermann was mistaken; it was a man.)

"Is the person in good or bad health?"

"I feel there's some eye trouble..."

(Indeed, the writer's left eye was weak and he squinted a little.)

The second envelope made Schermann somewhat embarrassed—and he became visibly excited.

"A strong character," he said finally. "Serious, with a considerable lust for life—though he has not much cause for happiness. Had a strict upbringing; his self-discipline is considerable. An honest, grateful soul—but very often losing faith. I feel that the letter inside the envelope has a melancholy tone..."

(Though Thirring had no idea which envelope the graphologist was holding in his hand, he guessed it at once—for the analysis agreed completely with the one Schermann had given earlier of the same person.)

"How long is the letter?"

"Two closely written pages."

(This was correct.)

Thirring now told Schermann that the envelope contained something in addition to the letter.

"I was just about to ask you," the graphologist said quickly. "You must have seen that something irritated me..."

Thirring asked him whether he could name the writer of the letter?

"Put down ten names," suggested Schermann, "including the writer's."

Thirring moved to another table and wrote out ten different names. After a short interval, Schermann picked out unerringly the right name.

Now came the third envelope. Schermann said: "This is some kind of hocus-pocus. A small piece of paper full of writing and drawings."

"What sort of drawings?"

"I couldn't tell you. The writing is so small that it can only be read with a magnifying glass. There is also some printed image or picture on the paper..."

(Though Schermann did not explicitly name the banknote, he gave a reasonably close description of it.)

About the fourth envelope he said: "I do not feel anything.

I believe it's an empty piece of paper." (Here he had failed; this was the sheet with the fingerprints.) The graphologist now complained of exhaustion—so we agreed to a pause; but after half an hour he was ready to resume the tests.

Touching the fifth envelope, he said: "An excitable man, a disorderly, restless soul. He's a big eater and drinks a lot. Indifferent health. Not very sympathetic. Talks in a loud, rasping voice." (The characterization, as Thirring admitted, was perfect. The letter was written by a retired colonel who always talked as if he were shouting commands at his regiment.)

Of the sixth envelope, Schermann merely said: "This contains an idea."

"Can you add anything else?"

"No ... perhaps if I could touch the paper ..."

Thirring took the slip of paper from the envelope. Schermann turned away his head and passed his fingertips over its surface. He stopped (he could not see the paper) at the three crosses marked with a thumbnail.

"There is something here ... some pattern ... but it symbolizes an idea ... Something that demands respect. I feel that one has to doff one's hat when seeing it ..."

Here Julius Sachs, the editor of a Viennese paper, an old friend of Schermann, interjected humorously (of course, he knew nothing about the crosses): "What do you do if you don't wear a hat?"

"You kneel," replied Schermann.

This was certainly an extraordinary achievement. Professor Thirring told me that he would have never believed it if someone else had told him about it. When *he* made the marks, he was thinking of the x-es illiterates use for their signature—not of the symbol of Christianity. Therefore even telepathy was eliminated here.

Of the seventh envelope Schermann declared without the slightest hesitation that it was empty—as, indeed, it was.

A few days later it was my turn to test Schermann's ability. I showed him four handwritten words, without a signature.

"This is a strong, determined character," the psychograph-

ologist began. "He was very nervous or excited when he wrote
this for his conceptions were opposed by everybody else. He
hopes that the situation might improve at the last moment.
But he mustn't expect too much—that's what I am saying—
and he loses the enthusiasm for further activity. The grave
obstacles that are beyond his control depress him."

"What is his occupation?"

"He has beyond doubt a leading position. His profession
or, let us say, his avocation, is determined by his birth. Everything is given to him in his cradle..."

His lips twitched, he frowned and he said: "It's a bit
difficult... this is not an original manuscript..."

He was right—it was a photo copy, with the lines softer,
less clearly defined.

"He is no longer young," continued Schermann after a
brief pause, "but very well preserved if no athlete. That is, he
was—for he is no longer alive. I see violence, death, they are
after his life..."

I interrupted him:

"You are wrong—he died a natural death."

"Wait a moment!" Schermann interrupted, a little testily.
"I said I see violence and death. But I did not say that the
attempted assassination is successful. He dies much later. A
few years ago, only... I see a knife, menacing him. It penetrates his shoulder. But something hard weakens the blow,
something glittering deflects it..."

"Do you see blood?"

"No, no. I see the glitter, it's copper or gold or something
similar, which prevents the killing... Now the would-be
assassin is thrown to the ground..."

The few words I had shown him had been written by the
Emperor Francis Joseph. History has recorded that there
had been two attempts on the Emperor's life: János Libényi
tried to kill him on February 18, 1853 and Wilhelm Oberdank
on December 22, 1882. Nothing was known, however, at the
time about the second attack; the details were only published
several years *after* I saw Schermann, having been locked up
in the secret archives of the Viennese Police. The Emperor,
not wanting to alarm Empress Elizabeth, had given strict

orders that nothing should be published and the whole episode was kept secret from his wife who had been ill at the time.
Oberdank wanted to smuggle several bombs to Trieste in
order to blow up Francis Joseph but he was arrested on the
frontier. The newspapers were not allowed to publish the fact
that Oberdank had a number of accomplices, as three decades
later Princip in Sarajevo in the successful assassination of
Francis Ferdinand. One of these accomplices actually tried to
stab Francis Joseph with a dagger. The Emperor wore the
full dress uniform of an admiral, with gold epaulettes—"the
hard, glittering" something saved his life. Schermann could
not know anything of this—neither did I, until the secret
archives were published in the early thirties.

I continued with my questions:

"What else do you see?"

"A harsh destiny! Bad luck, misfortune...perhaps even a
more tragic word is applicable here. Almost everything around
him is destroyed, ruined. In spite of all the glitter, a wretched
existence. His family life, too, is far from serene, becomes
more and more tragic. The children—it all goes badly with
them...One of them dies so young. His life becomes more and
more sombre..."

"Let us try to widen the circle...Can you say something
about his wife?"

"A good woman. She must have been a rare beauty. Her
head is striking...her hairdo. Interesting and impressive.
Attractive. Fate leads her far away. I see her travel. She is
extraordinarily restless. Takes ship to all the distant climes,
northwards, too, but more to the south. Her whole life is
most unhappy."

"Could you tell me, why?"

"She has no real home. It is her only good fortune that at
least she can afford to travel...I see a terrible destiny. All is
due to the position of her husband. Nothing but misfortune.
Her heart is breaking—she goes south to forget, she commis-
sions a temple or monument. But she cannot stay there. Her
mood darkens more and more...During her travel, on some
shore, an attack...she is stabbed...dies. That is how her
aimless wandering ends."

Schermann's face was twitching, his voice was hoarse:

"Also secret horrors... The children marry against the wish of the parents. In their lives, too, I see tragedies..."

The test I had devised concentrated on the past, did not involve any forecasts. But it was easy to control how perfectly Schermann reconstructed the events, the tragedies of the House of Hapsburg from the four words Francis Joseph had written in 1892. He invoked the Achilleion which Empress Elizabeth erected on the island of Corfu in memory of her son, Crown Prince Rudolph. And he gave a strikingly apt description of the assassination of Elizabeth by the Italian anarchist Luigi Luccheni in the summer of 1898, on the shore of Lac Léman, at Territet. He also indicated Elizabeth's special hairdo, her search for a home away from the stiff and uncomfortable Hofburg—all the details which provided striking proof for his clairvoyant talent.

I showed him two words of another letter. Schermann studied it for a few seconds, then he said:

"I feel that this is the handwriting of a man who has to decide over destinies. He has to guide important actions. His hand is not quite free. If he had been able to carry out his plans in every way, if frustrating, hostile elements had not intervened, he would have succeeded even in the most difficult, the impossible undertakings. But so, I feel, his cause ended in failure. He could not steer it to a happy end. He is convinced of the rightness of his plans but they were ruined by others. Many are jealous of him. His own followers, instead of helping him, smoothly and tenaciously, place obstacles in his way... A man of genius and a great lover of liberty. In spite of his comparatively weak constitution and his age he is unusually persistent and flexible. As for the preparation of plans and general foresight, he is a most extraordinary individual."

I showed him now the last letter of the signature and the flourish underneath.

The psycho-graphologist looked at the elliptical, swinging line and said slowly:

"In recent days he was thinking that his life would be saved

by some means of water transport . . . but his signature began
to develop much earlier in this form . . ."

I told him now that the handwriting was that of Lajos
Kossuth, the Hungarian national hero who reached England
by ship after the great freedom fight of 1848/49 was crushed
by Russian intervention.

"I am thinking more of a rowboat than a ship . . ." Schermann interposed.

I checked later and I found that Kossuth crossed the Danube
at Orsova in a rowboat to escape from Austrian revenge
and it was several months later that the British Government
sent a man-o'-war to Constantinople to fetch him and his
immediate supporters. Earlier his signature had been different; it was slowly that this flourish developed, which was the
stylized representation of a boat. And still later, in his long
exile in Turin, Italy, it gradually disappeared.

After this meeting there were others—experiments with a
number of different signatures and handwritings of other
famous people which my father and myself conducted with the
psycho-graphologist. They were equally successful and, in
some cases, almost incredibly, uncannily accurate.

I lost touch with Raphael Schermann in the early thirties
though there were occasional newspaper reports about his
cases and especially about his work with the Viennese police.
Nor was I able when I first decided to compose this pen-
portrait to discover his whereabouts—whether he was still
alive or not.

The answer to these questions was given to me, unexpectedly, during a visit to New York, early in 1962. Alexander
Incze, a distinguished Hungarian editor, stage producer and
impressario, had left his native country in 1938 and settled in
America.

"One man I very much wanted to bring with me," Mr.
Incze told me, "was Raphael Schermann. I was sure that he
would be an unqualified success in the States. But he refused.
He said that he was too old to leave Europe and settle in a new
world; that he planned to retire—he was financially indepen-

dent—and continue his work in psycho-graphology only as a hobby."

"Where did he retire then?" I asked.

"To his home-town, Cracow. And there he was killed during the Nazi occupation of Poland."

The man who had foretold the future of countless people, who had advised thousands as to their plans and the dangers to avoid was, by an ironic, cruel twist of fate, unable to foresee his own destiny. His death was a stupid waste of a great talent and the tragic end of an important pioneer in the exploration of the unseen.